English Idioms in Use

Advanced

60 units of vocabulary reference and practice

Self-study and classroom use

Felicity O'Dell
Michael McCarthy

CAMBRIDGE UNIVERSITY PRESS

CAMBRIDGE UNIVERSITY PRESS
Cambridge, New York, Melbourne, Madrid, Cape Town, Singapore,
São Paulo, Delhi, Dubai, Tokyo

Cambridge University Press
The Edinburgh Building, Cambridge CB2 8RU, UK

www.cambridge.org
Information on this title: www.cambridge.org/9780521744294

© Cambridge University Press 2010

This publication is in copyright. Subject to statutory exception
and to the provisions of relevant collective licensing agreements,
no reproduction of any part may take place without the written
permission of Cambridge University Press.

First published 2010

Printed in the United Kingdom at the University Press, Cambridge

A catalogue record for this publication is available from the British Library

ISBN 978-0-521-74429-4 Paperback

Cambridge University Press has no responsibility for the persistence or
accuracy of URLs for external or third-party internet websites referred to in
this publication, and does not guarantee that any content on such websites is,
or will remain, accurate or appropriate. Information regarding prices, travel
timetables and other factual information given in this work are correct at
the time of first printing but Cambridge University Press does not guarantee
the accuracy of such information thereafter.

Contents

Acknowledgements 3
Using this book 4

Learning about idioms

In this section the units deal with key aspects of what idioms are and how you can use them.
 1 What are idioms?
 2 When and how are idioms used?
 3 Using reference resources
 4 Common metaphors in idioms
 5 Using idioms accurately
 6 Playing with idioms
 7 Idioms from other varieties of English
 8 New idioms

Types of idiom

In this section the units deal with specific individual types of idiom.
 9 Similes
10 Binomials
11 Proverbs
12 Euphemisms
13 Clichés and fixed statements
14 Other languages

Idioms from the topic area of ...

In this section the units are organised around the aspect of life from which the idioms have originated.
15 Sailing
16 War and conflict
17 Transport
18 Animals
19 Parts of the body
20 Games and sport
21 Ancient myths and history
22 Shakespeare
23 Literature
24 Science and technology

Idioms to talk about ...

In this section the units are organised around the topic or functional area where they are most likely to be used.
25 Films, plays and books
26 Relationships – friends and family
27 People – character and behaviour
28 People – appearance
29 Crime and punishment
30 Work

31 Business news
32 Business meetings
33 Money
34 Society
35 Daily life
36 Positive feelings
37 Negative feelings
38 Problems

Idioms used in ...

This section focuses on some of the written contexts where idioms are frequently found.
39 Journalism
40 Advertising
41 Formal writing

Idioms used in conversation

This section focuses on ways in which idioms are typically used in spoken language.
42 Advising and warning
43 Telling stories
44 Responding to what people say
45 Agreeing and disagreeing
46 Expressing success and failure
47 Emphasising

Idioms using these keywords:

In this section each unit focuses on one keyword which has given rise to a particularly large number of English idioms.
48 Play and game
49 Half
50 Two
51 All
52 No
53 Hand
54 Heart
55 Life and live
56 Dead and death
57 Mind
58 Hard
59 Fall
60 Own

Key	126
List of phonemic symbols	161
Index	162

Acknowledgements

A book like this is far from being the product of its authors alone. First of all, we would like to thank the excellent editorial team at Cambridge University Press, especially Hazel Meek, Nick Robinson, Caroline Thiriau and Nóirín Burke. The combined experience and insight of this team provided invaluable guidance and support throughout the process of planning and writing this book. We also owe a huge debt of gratitude to the corpus and lexicography teams at Cambridge University Press. The book you see now is very largely based on the information gained from their ground-breaking work into language as it is actually used by both native speakers of English and by students.

We are grateful also to the following teachers and students whose comments on initial drafts of these materials have been of enormous help to us:

Garan Holcombe, UK

Manami Hitotsuyama, Japan

Maga Kijak, UK

Bo Chan (Chris) Kim, South Korea

Karolina Koryzna, Poland

Phuong Dzung Le, Vietnam

Piotr Plaskota, Poland

Eloy JM Romero-Munoz, Belgium

Justyna Szelwach, Poland

Hatsuki Takahashi, Japan

Last but not least, our domestic partners deserve thanks for their patience and loving support, with a special mention to Vlad, who sadly will not see the bound copies of a book that he helped with in so many different ways.

Produced by Kamae Design, Oxford

Illustrations by Laura Martinez, Sam Thompson, Theresa Tibbetts and Gary Wing.

Using this book

Why was this book written?

It was written to help you take your knowledge of idioms to a more advanced level. The ability to use idioms accurately and appropriately is an indicator that you have a truly advanced level of English, and so this book pays attention to the productive use of idioms as well as to the comprehension of their meaning. Many of you will have already worked with *English Idioms in Use Intermediate*, and this book builds on the work done there. However, it does not matter if you have gained your knowledge of idioms in a different way. We do not assume that you have used *English Idioms in Use Intermediate*, although we do present and practise different idioms from those that were presented in the lower-level book.

How were the idioms in this book selected?

The approximately 1000 idioms which are presented in this book were all selected from those identified as significant by the CANCODE corpus of spoken English, developed at the University of Nottingham in association with Cambridge University Press, and the Cambridge International Corpus of written and spoken English. The idioms selected are all also to be found in the *Cambridge Idioms Dictionary*, where you can find additional usage notes and examples. You can search this dictionary online by going to the following web site: http://dictionary.cambridge.org/

How is the book organised?

The book has 60 two-page units. The left-hand page explains the idioms that are presented in the unit. You will usually find an explanation of the meaning of the idiom, an example of it in use and, where appropriate, some comments on when and how it is used. The exercises on the right-hand page check that you have understood the information on the left-hand page and give you practice in using the material presented.

The units are organised into seven sections:

Learning about idioms (Units 1–8) gives important information relating to idioms in general, such as what they are, how to use them accurately and so on.

Types of idiom (Units 9–14) looks at some different types of idiom, dealing with such areas as *Similes, Euphemisms* and idioms from other languages.

Idioms from the topic area of ... (Units 15–24) focuses on idioms originating from different topic areas. For example, a great many idioms in English are based on sailing, a result of Britain's history as an island with a strong dependence on the sea. This section therefore opens with a unit dealing with idioms originating from the topic area of *Sailing*. Other units in this section deal with, for example, idioms based on *Parts of the body, Games and sport* and *Literature*. Many of us find it interesting to learn about the origins of idioms, and studying them in this way can also help to fix their meaning in your memory.

Idioms to talk about ... (Units 25–38) focuses on the topic areas where certain idioms are frequently used. For instance, there are units dealing with idioms used when talking about *Money*, about *Society* or about *Problems*.

Idioms used in ... (Units 39–41) looks at three types of writing where distinct types of idioms are used – *Journalism, Advertising* and *Formal writing*.

Idioms used in conversation (Units 42–47) presents idioms used in conversations from a functional point of view. For example, there are units dealing with *Telling stories, Agreeing and disagreeing* and *Emphasising*.

Idioms using these keywords (Units 48–60) groups idioms according to the keywords that they centre on. Unit 53, for instance, presents and practises idioms using the word *hand*, while Unit 59 focuses on idioms using the verb *fall*.

The book also contains a key and an index listing the idioms we deal with and indicating the units where they can be found.

How should I use this book?

We strongly recommend that you do the first two units in the book first – *What are idioms?* and *When and how are idioms used?* – as these give you basic information that underpins all the other units. After that, you may work on the units in any order that you prefer.

What else do I need in order to work with this book?

You need a notebook or file so that you can write down the idioms that you study in the book as well as any others that you come across elsewhere.

You also need to have access to a good dictionary. We strongly recommend the *Cambridge Idioms Dictionary*, as this gives you exactly the kind of information that you need to have about idioms. Your teacher, however, may also be able to recommend other dictionaries that you may find useful.

So all that remains is to say if you want to *stand out from the crowd* (Unit 40), start studying the idioms in this book. *There's no time like the present!* (Unit 40). We hope you'll find this an enjoyable and useful way to keep up and extend your knowledge of English idioms in use.

1 What are idioms?

A Formulaic language

Idioms are a type of formulaic language. Formulaic language consists of fixed expressions which you learn and understand as units rather than as individual words, for example:

type of formulaic language	examples
greetings and good wishes	Hi there! See you soon! Happy birthday!
prepositional phrases	at the moment, in a hurry, from time to time
sayings, proverbs and quotations	It's a small world! Don't put all your eggs in one basket. To be or not to be – that is the question.
compounds	car park, bus stop, home-made
phrasal verbs	take off, look after, turn down
collocations	blonde hair, deeply disappointed

B Idioms

Idioms are fixed combinations of words whose meaning is often difficult to guess from the meaning of each individual word.

For example, if I say 'I **put my foot in it** the other day at Linda's house – I asked her if she was going to marry Simon', what does it mean? If you do not know that **put your foot in it** means *say something accidentally which upsets or embarrasses someone*, it is difficult to know exactly what the sentence means. It has a non-literal or idiomatic meaning.

Idioms are constructed in different ways and this book gives you practice in a wide variety of types of idiom. Here are some examples:

Tim **took a shine to** [immediately liked] his teacher. (verb + object + preposition)
The band's number one hit was just **a flash in the pan** [something that happens only once] (idiomatic noun phrase)
Little Jimmy has been **as quiet as a mouse** [extremely quiet] all day. (simile. **See Unit 9 for more similes.**)
We arrived **safe and sound** [safely]. (binomial. **See Unit 10 for more binomials.**)

Idioms are often based on everyday things and ideas, for example, the human body:
Mark and Alistair **don't see eye to eye.** [don't agree with each other]

C How can I use idioms?

Many idioms are quite informal, so use them carefully. You will need to be able to understand a lot of idioms if you want to read English fiction, newspapers or magazines, or understand TV shows, films and songs. People also often use idioms for humour or to comment on themselves, other people and situations.

You will also sound more natural and fluent if you can use idioms in everyday conversation or informal writing. Be careful not to use too many, though!

> **ERROR WARNING**
> The words and word order of idioms are usually fixed, and we cannot change them in any way. For example, we cannot say *gave a shine to* or *sound and safe*.

Exercises

1.1 Read the beginning of this story and label the type of formulaic language used in the words in bold. Use the information in A to help you.

In 2009, I **set off** on a long journey. As I left my house, my neighbour shouted, '**Good luck!**' I didn't know **at that moment** that I would not see him again for three years. I **boarded** the **plane** at Heathrow, and soon it **took off** for Malaysia. When we **touched down** in Kuala Lumpur, I couldn't wait to **get off** the plane. I **took a bus** to the **city centre** and **spent the night** at a **youth hostel**. The first person I met was someone I had been **at school** with years ago. '**It's a small world!**' he said when he saw me.

1.2 Underline the seven idioms in the rest of the story you read in 1.1.

My friend suggested that we join forces. 'There's safety in numbers,' he said. 'Let's hit the road together.' I was in two minds whether to go with him but finally decided to say yes. We travelled together for six months and had a whale of a time. We spent money like there was no tomorrow, so I had to twist my dad's arm and persuade him to send me some more money so I could travel further.

1.3 Choose the correct answer.

1 His first novel was just a) a flash in a pan b) a flash of the pan c) a flash in the pan.
2 I think Philip has a) given a shine to b) taken a shine to c) got a shine to his new babysitter.
3 I hope you have a good trip and come home a) safely and soundly b) sound and safe c) safe and sound.
4 Oh dear! I think I've a) had a foot in it b) put my foot in it c) got my foot in it!
5 Kate is really noisy, but her best friend is a) as quiet as a cat b) as quiet as a mouse c) as quiet like a mouse.

1.4 Look at these newspaper headlines. Each one has an idiom based on a part of the human body. What do you think they mean? Choose the correct answer.

> UNIVERSITY **GOES CAP IN HAND** TO FINANCE MINISTER

1 A university a) apologises to the minister b) asks the minister for financial help c) awards the minister a great honour.

> AIRLINE **FOOTS THE BILL** FOR DELAYS AND CANCELLATIONS

2 An airline a) has refused to pay the costs b) sends the bill to someone else c) will pay the costs.

> RITA SORAZ IS **THE APPLE OF** HOLLYWOOD'S **EYE**

3 Rita Soraz is a) loved by everyone in Hollywood b) hated by everyone in Hollywood c) missed by everyone in Hollywood.

> GOVERNMENT IS **BURYING ITS HEAD IN THE SAND**, SAYS OPPOSITION LEADER

4 The government is a) refusing to face a difficult situation b) about to resign c) making unpopular plans.

2 When and how are idioms used?

A Idioms and change

Idioms frequently change in English. Although many idioms last for a long time, some disappear very quickly. Therefore, some idioms that were popular fifty years ago may sound very old-fashioned and odd today. For example, the idiom **as stiff / straight as a ramrod** [to sit or stand with a very straight and stiff back] is not frequently used nowadays. It is therefore important to be careful if you learn an idiom from, say, an older novel, as it may sound unnatural if you use it in your own speech or writing. In this book we focus only on up-to-date idioms which are still commonly used.

B What are idioms used for?

- For emphasis, e.g. The singer's second album **sank like a stone**. [failed completely]
- To agree with a previous speaker, e.g.
  A: Did you notice how Lisa started listening when you said her name?
  B: Yes, that certainly made her **prick** her **ears up**. [start listening carefully]
- To comment on people, e.g. Did you hear Tom has been invited for dinner with the prime minister? He's certainly **gone up in the world**! [gained a better social position – or more money – than before]
- To comment on a situation, e.g. The new finance minister wants to **knock** the economy **into shape**. [take action to get something into a good condition]
- To make an anecdote more interesting, e.g. It was just one disaster after another today, a sort of **domino effect**. [when something, usually bad, happens and causes a series of other things to happen]
- To catch the reader's eye. Idioms – particularly those with strong images – are often used in headlines, advertising slogans and the names of small businesses. The writer may play with the idiom or make a pun (a joke involving a play on words) in order to create a special effect, e.g. a *debt of dishonour* instead of the usual **debt of honour**. [a debt that you owe someone for moral rather than financial reasons]
- To indicate membership of a particular group, e.g. surfers **drop in on** someone, meaning to get on a wave another surfer is already on. This kind of group-specific idiom is outside the focus of this book.

C Where will you see or hear idioms?

You will see and hear idioms in all sorts of speaking and writing. They are particularly common in everyday conversation and in popular journalism. For example, they are often found in magazine horoscopes, e.g. You'll spend much of this week **licking your wounds** [trying to recover from a bad experience], or in problem pages, e.g. Do you think that my relationship has **run its course**? [come to a natural end] However, idioms are also used in more formal contexts, such as lectures, academic essays and business reports, e.g. It is hoped the regulations will **open the door to** better management. [let something new start] See Unit 41 for more idioms used in formal writing.

> **TIP** Look out for idioms being used in headlines and advertisements. Make a note of any interesting examples that you find.

Exercises

2.1 Are these sentences true or false? If the answer is false, say why.

1 Few idioms stay in frequent usage for a long time.
2 Your English may sound unnatural if you use certain idioms.
3 Idioms can be used for dramatic effect.
4 Idioms are frequently used to comment on people and situations.
5 Headline writers always use idioms in their correct form.
6 Idioms are only used in some types of speaking and writing.
7 Newspapers and magazines are a good place to find idioms in use.
8 Idioms are not used in academic writing.

2.2 Complete each idiom.

1 My essay is really not very good. Could you please help me knock it into ....
2 It's time you stopped .... your wounds and got back to your normal life.
3 Although the film cost a lot of money to make, it enjoyed no success at all; in fact, it sank like a ....
4 There was a kind of domino .... when Jill left the company. Others in her team decided to follow her example, and that then gave the idea to other employees too.
5 Ben and Sarah went out together for a long time, but the relationship eventually ran its .... – they're both happily married to other people now.
6 The children .... up their ears when they heard the word 'chocolate'.

2.3 Which idioms do these pictures make you think of?

1   2   3   4

2.4 Answer these questions.

1 Would *Going up in the world* be a better name for a mountain-climbing organisation or a furniture business?
2 Would *Knock yourself into shape* be a better slogan for dance classes or a boxing club?
3 Would *Let things run their course* be advising someone to act quickly or to be patient?
4 If a headline mentioned a *debt of honour*, would it be suggesting that the law or the person's conscience should be encouraging them to pay something back?
5 Would *This'll make you prick up your ears* be a better slogan for a hi-fi company or an earring business?

FOLLOW UP

This website lists the names of businesses that use puns: http://www.listology.com/content_show.cfm/content_id.21596/Jetsam. Go to the website and find three puns that you can explain.

3 Using reference resources

At advanced level, your aim will be not only to understand idioms, but also to use them accurately and appropriately. This book will help you achieve these aims. There are also other resources which you should use too.

A Dictionaries

To help you study idioms, you need a good learner's dictionary, ideally one which focuses on idioms. The *Cambridge Idioms Dictionary* gives you examples of how idioms are used, and also gives information on their use, e.g. whether they are used humorously, or informally, or in a more literary context. It also highlights the most important idioms to learn. You can access this dictionary online at http://dictionary.cambridge.org. The best learner's dictionaries are corpus-based, i.e. they focus on idioms that people actually use and give authentic examples of their use. *English Idioms in Use Advanced* and the *Cambridge Idioms Dictionary* are based on the *Cambridge International Corpus*, which is a collection of over one billion words of real spoken and written English. Here is an example of how idioms are presented in the *Cambridge Idioms Dictionary*:

> **like it or lump it** *informal*
> if you tell someone to like it or lump it, you mean they must accept a situation they do not like, because they cannot change it • *The fact remains, that's all we're going to pay him and he can like it or lump it.* • *Like it or lump it, romantic fiction is read regularly by thousands.*

B The Internet

You can use the Internet to find out more about the meanings and origins of idioms, and to see more examples of their use.

- Go to http://www.phrases.org.uk/ to discover the meanings and origins of many idioms. This site also provides examples of how the idioms are used, and you can even discuss the origins of other phrases not listed there.
- You can access the *British National Corpus* at http://www.natcorp.ox.ac.uk/ Type in an idiom and you will be given up to fifty authentic examples of its use.
- Use a search engine, e.g. http://www.google.co.uk/, to find further examples of idioms in use. Type in an idiom in double inverted commas (e.g. "like it or lump it") to get a list of sites including that idiom.

C Vocabulary notebooks

Always make good, detailed notes about idioms in your vocabulary notebook. Include an example of the idiom in context, as well as its meaning. Add any notes about its usage, e.g. *informal* or *literary*. Doing a quick drawing of an idiom may help you to learn it.

> Each time they asked him a question he was <u>like a deer caught in the headlights</u>.
> The speaker unfortunately looked <u>like a deer caught in the headlights</u> during most of the discussion.
> = looked very frightened, unable to move or think
> sometimes rabbit instead of deer

Exercises

3.1 Answer these questions. Use the information in A to help you.
1 What two things does a good idioms dictionary do, as well as explain the meaning of idioms?
2 How much language and what kind of language is in the *Cambridge International Corpus*?
3 What does the dictionary say about the usage of *like it or lump it*?

3.2 Use the *Cambridge Idioms Dictionary* (book or online) to match each idiom on the left with the label used in the dictionary on the right. Can you explain the meaning of the idioms?

1 get off your backside	informal
2 know no bounds	formal
3 the shit hits the fan	very informal
4 know sth inside out	old-fashioned
5 curl your lip	taboo
6 kith and kin	humorous
7 know your place	literary

3.3 Complete each sentence with an idiom from 3.2. You may need to change the form of the verb.
1 Henry will help you deal with these forms. He .... the system ....
2 There is a growing interest in genealogy, as people increasingly want to discover all they can about their ....
3 Joey can be so lazy. I wish he'd ....
4 Don't worry. I'll behave properly when I meet your boss. I .... !
5 If Greg finds out what you've done, ...
6 Don't you dare .... at me, young lady!
7 The old woman's kindness to us all ....

3.4 Search for "like it or lump it" in each of the three sites in B on the opposite page. What information does each site give you?

3.5 Underline the eight idioms in this newspaper article. What do you think each idiom means? Use a dictionary to help you.

SPORTS MINISTER HOPPING MAD

John Hamilton has made a name for himself by running a tight ship at the Ministry of Sport. So it was no surprise to his staff that he reportedly 'went spare' when he learnt what had been going on behind his back. Two of his leading advisors had been feathering their own nests with government money intended for young people's sports organisations. 'Such behaviour is quite beyond the pale,' said Hamilton, 'and the two people concerned have already been given the sack'.

FOLLOW UP Choose three idioms from 3.5. Use any of the websites in B to help you decide on a usage note, comment or drawing that would help you learn these idioms.

4 Common metaphors in idioms

A What is a metaphor?

Metaphors describe a person, object or situation by comparing it to something else with similar characteristics. They are often used in poetry and literature. In Shakespeare's *Romeo and Juliet*, for example, Romeo says 'Juliet is my sun,' suggesting that she is the most important force in his life, bringing him light and warmth.

Many idioms are based on metaphors. However, idioms are expressions that are used so frequently and are so fixed in the language that people often do not think about the metaphors behind them. The metaphors used in idioms are therefore much less original and thought-provoking than those used in literary contexts. People say, for example, 'The new president **was / took centre stage** at the meeting' [was the most important or noticeable thing or person], without thinking of the original image of a theatre.

B Work = war

The language of idioms seems to suggest that English speakers see work and business life as a kind of war, with many work and business idioms based on images connected with war and fighting. For example, companies **launch** marketing **campaigns** and they may **join forces with** each other. Business people might say that a situation **is a minefield** [is potentially dangerous] or that a company **is a casualty of** a difficult economic situation [was badly affected by it]. A manager may **pull rank** on his employees [use the power his position gives him to make them do something] and he may have to **get / take the flak** for a problem [receive strong criticism]. An employee may **be given** or **get his marching orders** [lose his job]. See Unit 16 for more idioms based on war and conflict.

C Understanding = seeing

Idioms often equate seeing with understanding. For example, we talk about **seeing sense** or **seeing reason** [becoming sensible / reasonable] or **seeing the point** [understanding the importance of something]. Similarly, if someone **sees the joke**, they understand it. To **see the light** can mean to suddenly understand something.

D Some other metaphors

Emotion = colour
Red, for example, can suggest anger, e.g. My brother **saw red** when I broke his MP3 player. Black is often associated with unpleasant feelings: if you get **a black mark** for something, it means people think you have done something bad and they will remember it in future.

Life = a journey
If someone **is at a crossroads**, they are at a stage in life when they have to make an important decision. If you say that you **are going / getting nowhere**, you mean you are making no progress. If you say something is taking you into **uncharted territory / waters**, you mean it is taking you into unknown areas of experience.

Life = a gamble
If you **have something up your sleeve**, you have a secret plan or idea (someone playing cards for money may hide a card up their sleeve). If you **bluff your way** into or out of a situation, you get yourself there by deception in the same way that a gambler may bluff (pretend to be in a weaker or stronger position than is really the case).

TIP Noticing the metaphors underlying many idioms will help you understand and learn them. Look out for other common concepts such as time = money.

Exercises

4.1 Answer these questions. Use the information in A to help you.
1 How do metaphors describe people, objects and situations?
2 In what kind of writing are metaphors frequently used?
3 How are the metaphors used in literary contexts different from those used in idioms?
4 Why do you think it can sometimes be useful for you to be aware of the origins of idioms?

4.2 Which idioms do these pictures make you think of?

1

2

3

4

4.3 Complete each idiom.
1 Tax legislation can be a .... for new businesses; there are so many rules to follow.
2 Our company is planning to .... a new marketing campaign in April.
3 Shouting at his manager got Jim a black .... at work.
4 I'm sure your boss will .... sense eventually and agree to your plan.
5 At first I didn't see the .... of going to university or college, but then I saw the .... and realised studying would give me more choices for the future.
6 If she doesn't offer to write the report, I'll .... rank on her and tell her to do it.
7 Noor is .... a crossroads in her life now that she has finished her medical degree. She has to decide what she is going to specialise in.
8 George doesn't know much about the job, but I'm sure he'll be able to .... his way through the interview.

4.4 Replace the underlined part of each sentence with an idiom.
1 Everyone else was laughing, but Katie couldn't <u>understand what was funny</u>.
2 Jean <u>is making no progress</u> with her research.
3 BritTel is going to <u>work together with</u> SatCom to lobby the government.
4 The teacher <u>was furious</u> when Matt refused to do his homework.
5 The errors in the report really weren't Ned's fault, but he <u>was blamed for</u> them.
6 Tina is hoping her father will eventually <u>become more reasonable</u> and let her drive the family car.
7 Unfortunately, my brother's transport business was <u>very seriously affected by</u> the rise in fuel prices.
8 As the president of a major company, Gary is used to <u>being the focus of attention</u>.

5 Using idioms accurately

All the examples in this unit come from the *Cambridge Learner Corpus*. This is a collection of over 95,000 exam scripts by students from over 190 countries taking Cambridge ESOL exams. The errors in this unit were actually made by learners in advanced-level exams, including CAE, Proficiency and IELTS (level 6+).

A major difficulty with idioms is that they are fixed expressions which cannot be changed – except when you are deliberately playing with the language. It is therefore very important to use idioms accurately. **See Unit 6 for more information on playing with idioms.**

A Getting the key words right

You say that rising unemployment figures are just **the tip of the iceberg** [a small part of a much bigger problem], NOT the ~~top~~ of the iceberg.

You say that the state is responsible for its citizens' welfare **from the cradle to the grave** [from birth to death], NOT from the cradle to the ~~coffin~~.

If you want to talk about people that you do not know or that you do not think are important, you can say **every Tom, Dick and / or Harry** could do that job, NOT every ~~Tom and Jerry~~!

If you pay for something yourself, you pay for it **out of your own pocket**, NOT out of your own ~~wallet~~.

If someone is in a bad mood, you can say they are **like a bear with a sore head**, NOT like a bear with a sore ~~throat~~.

When you remember the past nostalgically, you talk about **the good old days**, NOT the good old ~~time~~.

To say that someone or something will not exist for much longer, you can say their **days are numbered**, NOT their days are ~~counted~~.

To talk about limiting someone's freedom, you can use the idiom **to clip someone's wings**, NOT to ~~cut~~ someone's wings.

B Getting the details right

Using idioms accurately also means getting even the little words exactly right.

You must not add articles where they are not needed: someone has a **spirit of adventure** [enthusiasm for adventurous activities], NOT spirit of ~~an~~ adventure. You must not leave out articles either: fashion can be described as **up-to-the-minute** [new], NOT ~~up to minute~~.

Take care with prepositions too: someone can **be at a loss for words** [not know what to say], NOT at a loss ~~of~~ words.

Make sure that you use singular and plural forms correctly too: you talk about a couple **tying the knot** [getting married (informal)], NOT ~~tying the knots~~.

Word order is very important too: you can be **sick and tired of** something [angry and bored], NOT ~~tired and sick~~ of it.

> **ERROR WARNING**
>
> Translating idioms word for word can cause problems. For example, we **make a mountain out of a molehill** [make a small difficulty seem like a serious problem], NOT ~~make an elephant out of a mouse~~. Always check in a good dictionary before translating an idiom from your own language.

Exercises

5.1 Which idioms do these pictures make you think of?

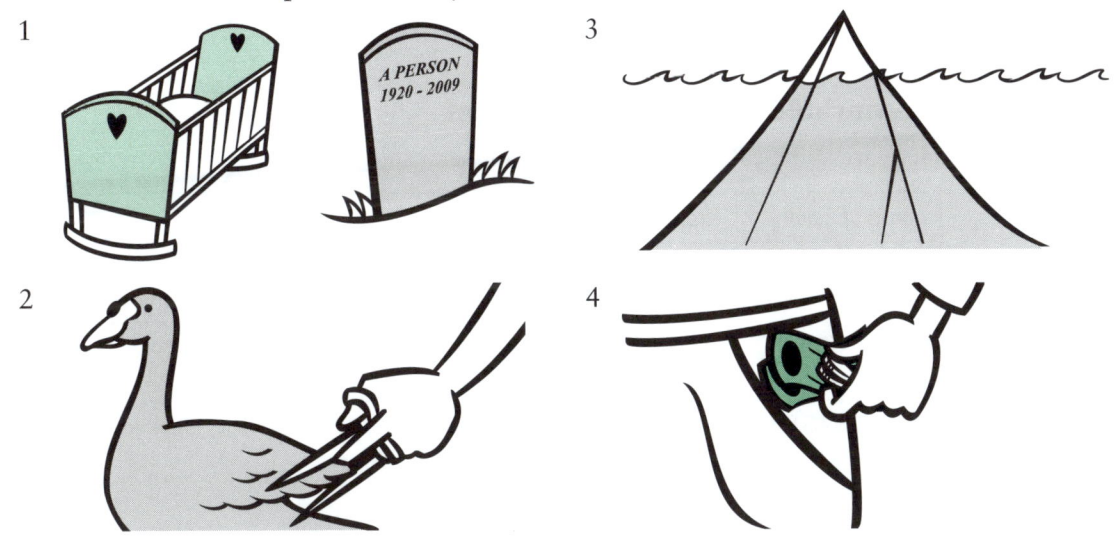

5.2 Are the idioms in these sentences used correctly? If not, correct them.

1 My sister is always buying up-to-minute gadgets.
2 I'm sick and tired of listening to him complaining all the time.
3 My granddad's always talking about good old days.
4 They've been engaged for six months but haven't made any plans about when they're going to tie the knots.
5 Jane was at a loss for words when her son told her he had quit his new job.
6 Engineering isn't the kind of job that every Tom, Dick or Henry could do.

5.3 Complete each idiom.

1 Don't make such a .... out of a molehill.
2 Everyone uses mobile phones now, so the days of the phone box on every street corner are ....
3 My son's got a real .... of adventure. He's going travelling around the world for a year.
4 We won free train tickets to Paris in the competition, but we had to pay for the hotel out of our own ....
5 Frank keeps shouting at everyone today. I don't know why he's behaving like a .... with a sore head.

5.4 Here are some errors made with idioms by candidates in advanced-level exams. Can you correct them? Looking up the word in brackets in a good idioms dictionary should help you find the correct idiom.

1 You'll pass your driving test if you really want to – <u>where there's a will, there's a power</u>. [WILL]
2 I get bored if I always do the same things at the weekend – <u>change is a spice of life</u>. [VARIETY]
3 Shh! Be quiet! There's no need to talk <u>at the top of your head</u>. [TOP]
4 He never saves any money. He spends whatever he has. <u>Easy coming easy going</u> is his motto. [EASY]
5 I was so upset when I failed the exam. I <u>wept my eyes out of my head</u>. [CRY]
6 She's a total optimist – she always manages to <u>look the good part</u>. [LOOK]

6 Playing with idioms

People often play with idioms for humorous effect or to make something more memorable. This wordplay is particularly common in journalism and advertising. See Unit 40 for more examples of idioms used in advertising.

A Memorable names for businesses

Here are some catchy names of hairdressers' salons.

name of salon	explanation
FRINGE BENEFITS	**Fringe benefits** are something extra you get because of your job in addition to your pay, e.g. a company car. A *fringe* is the hair that hangs down over your forehead.
BLOWN AWAY	If you **are blown away by** something (e.g. a performance or a piece of music), it amazes you because it is so good. A hairdresser *blows* hair dry with a hair dryer.
WAVELENGTHS	If two people **are on the same wavelength**, they think in the same way. People often have, or want, *waves* in their hair.

B News headlines

News headlines often play with idioms in some way, to attract people to read the article.

headline	explanation
DELIVERY DELAYS **PART AND PARCEL** OF POST OFFICE PROBLEMS Recent delays in the postal service are symptoms of wider problems, a government report claims.	a necessary part of an event or experience which cannot be avoided. (The Post Office delivers letters and *parcels*.)
FIREWORKS FUND **BURNING A HOLE IN THE POCKET OF** CITY COUNCIL The city council today voted to spend £100,000 on a massive public fireworks display.	If you have money burning a hole in your pocket, you want to spend it as soon as possible. (Fireworks *burn*, and if one burnt in your pocket, it would make a *hole*!)
OPTICIANS FAIL TO **SEE EYE TO EYE** The National Association of British Opticians (NABO) today disagreed about a new set of standards for the industry.	If two people do not see eye to eye, they disagree with each other. (Opticians care for people's *eyes* and help them see better.)
THEATRE MANAGERS FINALLY **GET THEIR ACT TOGETHER** The managers of the Cleo Theatre have come up with a rescue package to save the theatre.	organise themselves so that they do things efficiently (informal). (Actors *act* in a theatre, and performers have an *act* which they perform.)
AGRICULTURAL REFORM POLICY – FARMERS **SIT ON THE FENCE** The Farmers' Union has stated that it remains neutral over the latest plans for reform.	delay making a decision when they have to choose between two different options in a dispute. (Farms often have *fences* which separate the fields.)
CHESS COMPUTER BEATEN BY HUMAN – DESIGNERS **ARE BACK TO SQUARE ONE** Software engineers now have to rethink the design of the *Redray* software that failed to work as planned.	have to work on a plan from the beginning again because a previous attempt failed and the progress made was wasted. (A chess board has 64 *squares* on it.)

16 *English Idioms in Use Advanced*

Exercises

6.1 Look at A. Which idioms do these pictures make you think of?

1   2   3

6.2 These sentences all use idioms from the opposite page. Why are they humorous? Use a dictionary to find both the idiomatic and literal meanings of the expressions if necessary.

1 I was offered a job at a hairdresser's salon but the fringe benefits weren't very good, so I turned it down.
2 Both John and Margaret work as newsreaders for the local radio station, so I'm not surprised they're always on the same wavelength.
3 The audience were blown away by Tom's solo in the wind instrument competition.
4 Walking a lot and carrying heavy bags is part and parcel of working as a postman.
5 The two film stars have got their act together and resolved their marital problems.

6.3 Complete each idiom.

1 The money was burning .... my pocket.
2 Her two brothers don't see .... and haven't spoken to each other for over a year.
3 Learning how to manage your finances is part .... of becoming an adult.
4 It's time you got .... and found a job!
5 The president refused to make a decision and was accused of sitting ....
6 My computer crashed, so I'm back to .... with my assignment.

6.4 Match the idioms on the left with the companies or organisations on the right.

1 BACK TO SQUARE ONE   a delivery firm
2 GETTING OUR ACT TOGETHER   a gardening company
3 PART AND PARCEL   a company that makes board games
4 SITTING ON THE FENCE   a local drama club

> **FOLLOW UP**
> What products, organisations or services do you think these idioms from other units in this book could be used to advertise?
> *fighting fit* (Unit 47)
> *two left feet* (Unit 50)
> *it never rains but it pours* (Unit 11)

7 Idioms from other varieties of English

In this book we focus mainly on idioms which are widely understood throughout the English-speaking world. However, there are many other idioms which are typical of specific English-speaking countries. The idioms in this unit from Scotland and the US are included mainly for interest, but you may hear them if you visit, or watch a film from, one of these countries.

A Idioms from Scotland

My brother's really messy. His bedroom **has been stirred with a stick**. [is very untidy]
The old woman who lives next door is **tuned to the moon**. [eccentric]
Another new pair of shoes! That's Caroline **over the back**! [that's typical of Caroline]

B Idioms from the US

Many US idioms originate from baseball. For example, if you do something **right off the bat**, you do it immediately; and if you **throw someone a curveball**, you surprise them with something difficult or unpleasant to deal with. If someone **is batting a thousand**, they are doing something extremely well, better than they had hoped. If someone **drops the ball**, they do something stupid or careless.

Other examples of US idioms:
He's trying to **catch some z's** /ziːs/. [sleep (informal)]
The store **is fresh out of** tomatoes. [has just finished or sold all its supply]
His advice **isn't worth a dime**. [has little or no value]

C Regional variation

There are sometimes slightly different forms of idioms in US and British English. Here are some examples:

British English idiom	US English idiom	meaning
the icing on the cake	the frosting on the cake	something that makes a good thing even better
fight like cat and dog	fight like cats and dogs	argue violently all the time
donkey work	grunt work	hard, boring work
take the biscuit	take the cake	used informally to describe something the speaker finds very annoying
weep buckets	cry buckets	cry a lot (informal)
hard cash	cold cash	money in the form of cash or notes, not a cheque or credit card
like the cat that got the cream	like the cat that ate the canary	very pleased with oneself (informal, usually collocates with 'look', 'grin' or 'smile')

> **TIP** Idioms that are used mainly in one specific country will often not be easily understood by native English speakers from other parts of the world. You may not see or hear them outside the countries they originate from, so it's safer to use the idioms in this unit when you are in the appropriate country.

Exercises

7.1 Look at A. Answer these questions.

1 What would you need to do to a room if a Scottish friend complained that it had been stirred with stick?
2 Would you feel pleased if a Scottish friend said that you're tuned to the moon?
3 If a Scottish friend says, 'My brother did something silly? That's him over the back!' does your friend think her brother is often silly or rarely silly?

7.2 Complete each US idiom.

1 I'm exhausted after such a difficult day at work. I'm going to try to .... some z's before I have to go out again this evening.
2 I'm afraid we're .... out of milk. Try next door – maybe they have some.
3 Will was doing well at college until he had some problems with his girlfriend and .... the ball.
4 Wayne is very efficient – he always deals with jobs right off the ....
5 Her ring may look expensive, but it isn't .... a dime.
6 Karen's batting a .... at the moment – she's making a great success of her new job.
7 The speaker found it hard to answer the questions. He clearly wasn't expecting the audience to .... him so many curveballs.

7.3 Is each speaker more likely to be from the US or from Britain?

1 You have to pay the deposit for hiring the boat in cold cash.
2 Rhiannon and her sister have always fought like cat and dog.
3 It was such a sad film – I wept buckets.
4 There's a lot of grunt work to be done before we can open the new restaurant.
5 Having such perfect weather on holiday was the frosting on the cake.
6 Having to stay late at work on a holiday weekend really took the biscuit.
7 What's happened? You look like the cat that got the cream.

7.4 Rewrite the sentences in 7.3. If the speaker used US idioms, change them to the equivalent British idiom and vice versa.

7.5 Which idioms do these pictures make you think of?

1   2   3

FOLLOW UP Find out more about a variety of English that interests you at http://www.world-english.org/accent.htm. The site includes recordings so you can listen to the speech of people from different regions too.

8 New idioms

A Where do new idioms come from?

As units 15–24 show, many English idioms have very deep roots in history and culture. They have their origins in traditional skills, such as sailing (Unit 15), and in such things as ancient myths (Unit 21), literature (Unit 23) and war (Unit 16).

However, new idioms evolve all the time from TV, advertising, politics and business. These idioms often quickly become expressions understood and used by many people in their everyday lives. Some of these idioms will be popular for a few years but then get forgotten; others may last. In this unit we look at some examples of common, but relatively new, idioms.

B Some new idioms

example	meaning
Is Madonna still **the first lady of** pop?	the expert, or the best (by analogy with how the wife of a US president is referred to as *The First Lady*)
This programme looks at one couple's experience of living next to neighbours **from hell**.	People frequently refer to difficult people or unpopular things as being the … from hell, e.g. the neighbours from hell or the airport from hell.
That young politician was in the news every day for weeks, but now he seems to have **fallen off the radar**.	been forgotten
Jane is a wonderful nurse. She'll always **go the extra mile** for her patients.	make an extra big effort or do things that are more than is strictly necessary
The website www.cheapholidays.org **does exactly what it says on the tin**.	does exactly what it claims to do
Finding out what really happened is **like nailing jelly to a wall**.	difficult to understand or describe because it is not clear or focused enough
I'm cool with that.	I'm happy with a suggestion
It **doesn't float my boat**!	I don't agree with what you like or are interested in. (Also **Whatever floats your boat!**)
I'm fed up with him **big time** / He's into judo **big time**.	extremely

C New conversational fixed expressions

If you do not want to discuss anything further, you can say 'That's it! **End of (story)!**'

If you think that someone is telling you about very personal things that you do not want to hear about, you can stop them by saying '**Too much information!**'

If a friend starts talking about a subject you do not want to discuss, you could respond '**Don't even go there!**'

Exercises

8.1 Look at B. Are the idioms in these sentences used correctly? If not, correct them.

1 You have to be prepared to go the further mile if you want to get promoted.
2 Whatever happened to that pop star you used to like so much? He seems to have completely fallen off the radar now.
3 This shampoo is great – it does exactly what it writes on the tin.
4 I'd never share an apartment with her – she'd be the flatmate of hell.
5 Stella McCartney is often called the first lady of fashion.

8.2 Complete the dialogue with idioms from B and C. Use one word per space.

Jo: Hi, Meg. Great to see you again. Where's Kate?
Meg: She just texted. She's not coming. Apparently she's really sick and has been throwing up all night.
Jo: (1) .... ! I don't want to know! What shall we do then?
Meg: I really want to go that new photography exhibition.
Jo: Mmm, (2) ....
.... ! I know you're into art (3) ....,
but I'm not. How about the cinema instead?
Meg: Yeah, (4) ....
.... Is Matt coming too?
Jo: (5) .... !
We broke up.
Meg: Really? What happened?
Jo: I don't want to talk about it. We're finished. (6) ....!

8.3 Which idioms do these pictures make you think of?

1

2

3

4

8.4 Do these sentences make sense? Explain why / why not.

1 It could be fun to live next door to the neighbours from hell.
2 Tilly's father was happy about her plans to marry, but her mother was cool with it.
3 Rani loves that painter's work, but it doesn't float my boat.
4 Getting him to say what he thinks is like nailing jelly to a wall – he's always honest and open.

English Idioms in Use Advanced 21

9 Similes

A What are similes?

Similes are expressions which compare two things; they always include the words *as* or *like*. You can use similes to make your spoken and written English more colourful and your comparisons more powerful. For example:

My brother's **as thin as a rake**. [extremely thin]
The baby's skin is **as smooth as silk**. [extremely smooth]
Pilar is **as bright as a button**. [extremely clever]
I made so many mistakes! My boss must think I'm **as thick as two short planks**! [extremely unintelligent (offensive/humorous if used about yourself)]
I slept really well, so I feel **as fresh as a daisy** this morning. [extremely fresh and full of energy]
George **ran like the wind** to get the message to Paula before she left. [ran extremely fast]
I don't want to go in the car with Lizzie. She **drives like a maniac**! [drives fast and badly]
My new sweater **fits like a glove**. I'm so pleased with it. [fits extremely well]
The two men were in the next room, but I could hear every word they said **as clear as crystal**. [very clearly]
Ben claimed to be **as poor as a church mouse**, but we knew he was rich. [very poor]
As Judy walked in, the house was **as silent as the grave**. [totally silent]

You should learn similes as whole phrases, because it is usually not possible to change the individual words (e.g. we do not say as thin as a stick or as thin as a pole). Where it is possible to change the individual words, the meaning of the simile often changes, for example:
I needed a drink of water. My mouth was **as dry as a bone**. [extremely dry / thirsty]
His lecture was **as dry as dust** and everyone was bored. [extremely boring]

B Everyday similes

The similes in these emails are often used in everyday conversation and informal writing.

Hi Jacek,

It's so obvious you like Anna! You went **as red as a beetroot** when Stefan was talking about her, so it must be true! And you **were all over her like a rash** at the party last week too. Ask her out!
Hiroshi

Hi Freya,

Have you noticed how Chiara and Rita are **as thick as thieves** lately? Rita said she needed some help and **as quick as a flash** Chiara volunteered – you know, **as keen as mustard**. And just think, they used to hate each other and were always **fighting like cat and dog** over the most stupid things. Any idea what's happened? Anyway, speak later.
Fatima

Hello Manami,

I'll be late for the restaurant tonight – having a bad day at work. I've been **working like a dog** but the boss just came in with **a face like thunder** and said I'd made a mess of some sales figures. I've tried to argue with him, but he's **as stubborn as a mule** and you can never convince him that he's wrong.

Time to change my job! Mariusz

TIP Be careful how you use similes. They have strong meanings and are often used in a humorous or sarcastic way, e.g. *My teacher's explanations are **as clear as mud*** [not clear at all].

Exercises

9.1 Look at A. Match the beginning of each sentence with its ending. Then complete the sentence with *as* or *like*.

1 My new dress fits .... a maniac.
2 You'll need to run .... silk.
3 She's as thin .... a button.
4 Sandra always looks as fresh .... a bone.
5 He drove off .... a rake.
6 Her mouth felt as dry .... a glove.
7 Their son is as bright .... the wind to catch the train.
8 Her hair felt as smooth .... a daisy.

9.2 Choose the correct word to complete each simile.

1 That book was so boring. It was as dry as [a bone / dust].
2 I can't believe I didn't know the answer. I feel as thick as [two short planks / thieves].
3 You explained it so well – it's a difficult concept, but it's as clear as [crystal / mud] now.
4 I wonder what they're plotting – they look as thick as [two short planks / thieves].
5 After working in that airless room my mouth feels as dry as [a bone / dust].
6 I can't understand what he's trying to say – it's as clear as [crystal / mud].

9.3 Replace the underlined part of each sentence with a simile.

1 Tom and Rosa have been arguing all the time recently.
2 Amy blushed and looked very embarrassed when Lasse commented on her new dress.
3 When our teacher asks the class a difficult question, Hatsuki usually answers without a moment's hesitation.
4 It was early Sunday morning and the house was strangely silent.
5 Emma was behaving towards Jakob in a very affectionate way at the barbecue last week.
6 All her sisters are extremely poor.
7 Caterina felt full of energy after her shower.
8 The students in my class are great – hardworking, punctual and very enthusiastic.

9.4 Agree with what A says. Complete each response with a simile from the opposite page.

1 A: He looked really angry.
   B: Yes, he had ....

2 A: It's impossible to get him to change his mind.
   B: Yes, he's ....

3 A: He drove off very quickly, didn't he?
   B: Yes, he was driving ....

4 A: You've been very busy at work, haven't you?
   B: Yes, I've been ....

5 A: You can always rely on Suzie to organise the school concert.
   B: Yes, she's ....

10 Binomials

A What are binomials?

Binomials are a type of idiom in which two words are joined by a conjunction (linking word), usually *and*. The order of the two words is fixed. For example, we always say **black and white**, NOT ~~white and black~~: *Managing climate change isn't a **black and white** issue.* [separate and clear]

The words can be

- synonyms (words which mean the same): *Sara's work is always very **neat and tidy**.*
- opposites: *If you go for cheaper speakers, the sound quality may be a bit **hit and miss**.* [sometimes good, sometimes bad (informal)]
- the same word: *They finished the race **neck and neck**.* [equal]
- rhyming: *Tables in the canteen take a lot of **wear and tear**.* [damage through everyday use]
- alliterative: *After the match the players' legs were **black and blue**.* [very bruised]
- joined by words other than *and*: *The traffic was **bumper to bumper** all the way to the coast.* [very heavy] ***Little by little**, Vera gained the horse's confidence.* [gradually] *The house must be worth a quarter of a million, **give or take** a few thousand.* [plus or minus (informal)]

Trinomials are a similar type of idiom, in which three words are joined, e.g. *I've looked **here, there and everywhere** for my glasses but can't find them.* [everywhere]

B Other examples

example	meaning
Let's toss a coin to see who starts. You call: **heads or tails**?	heads is the side of a British coin with the monarch's head on it; tails is the other side
We're **at sixes and sevens** at work this week.	in a state of confusion (informal)
Hannah had flu last week, but she's **out and about** again now.	active, doing her usual activities (informal)
Although the twins look the same, when you talk to them you realise they're like **chalk and cheese**.	totally different (informal)
It's great to leave the **hustle and bustle** of the city at the weekend.	crowds and noise
I can't do up these tiny buttons – I'm **all fingers and thumbs** today.	am awkward with my hands, unable to do what I want to do (informal)
The money for the charity appeal came in **in dribs and drabs**, but we reached our target in the end.	small amounts at a time (informal)
It took a lot of **blood, sweat and tears** to get the business going.	hard work
I've asked you **time after time** not to do that.	many times (usually suggests irritation)
Her interest in painting **waxed and waned** over the years.	fluctuated (The literal meaning of *wax* and *wane* relates to the moon's changes in size.)
She really doesn't enjoy living in the countryside. She's a city person, **through and through**.	completely, typical (used about people)
We had a great holiday and explored **every nook and cranny** of the island.	every small place

Exercises

10.1 Look at A. Combine the words in the box to form ten binomials or trinomials. For each, you will need to add *and* or another joining word.

black	neck	little	bumper	everywhere	give	cranny	here	hit	little
bumper	miss	neat	blue	neck	nook	take	tear	there	tidy	wear

10.2 Complete each dialogue with an idiom.

1 A: Was the traffic bad on the way here?
  B: Yes, it was .... the whole way.
2 A: Did you get everything you needed today?
  B: Yes, but I had to go .... to find it all.
3 A: This sofa is only six months old, but it looks really old.
  B: Well, it gets a lot of ....
4 A: We're making very slow progress with this project.
  B: But we're getting there ....
5 A: Have you found your watch yet?
  B: No, I've searched in every .... but I still can't find it!
6 A: What's Galya's flat like?
  B: Well, you know how organised she is! It's very ....
7 A: Which horse won the race?
  B: Two of them finished ....
8 A: Were there a lot of people at the party?
  B: About a hundred, ... a few.

10.3 Which binomials do these pictures make you think of? Complete the captions.

1 'The .... of market day.'

2 'He's a United supporter ....'

3 '........................ ?'

4 'Her two dogs are like ....'

10.4 Rewrite each sentence using the word in brackets.

1 People started to gradually enter the room. [DRIBS]
2 Jack's commitment to work went up and down throughout the year. [WAXED]
3 Have a few days' rest and you'll be fully recovered in no time. [ABOUT]
4 I've often told him not to leave his car unlocked. [TIME]
5 The work required a lot of effort but it was worth it. [BLOOD]
6 The whole team's been in a state of confusion since Kay resigned. [SEVENS]
7 I keep dropping things today – I'm so clumsy. (THUMBS)
8 My mum and I are completely different people, but we get on well. (CHALK)

11 Proverbs

Proverbs are short sentences which refer to something most people have experienced and which give advice or warnings. Like idioms, their form is fixed, and it is not always possible to guess the meaning from looking at the individual words in the proverb.

A Positive situations

In these conversations, the second speaker uses a proverb to repeat and sum up what the first speaker says.

A: We all want to solve this problem, and I'm sure we'll find a solution.
B: Yes. **Where there's a will there's a way.** [if we really want to achieve something, we can]

A: Well, we'll have to invest all of our savings and work really hard, and there's still a chance the project won't succeed.
B: I know, but **nothing ventured, nothing gained.** [you need to take risks to achieve something]

A: I was upset when I didn't get into university, but at least it leaves me free to go travelling.
B: Yeah. **Every cloud has a silver lining.** [there is something good in every bad situation]

A: My job is different every day. It's never boring.
B: Well, **variety is the spice of life**, isn't it? [change makes life interesting]

A: Ron found it impossible to get a new job, so he set up his own business instead.
B: Yes, well, **necessity is the mother of invention.** [if people really need to do something, they will find a way to do it]

B Negative situations

In these conversations, the second speaker uses a proverb to repeat and sum up what the first speaker says.

A: Marta told her new boyfriend that she was five years younger than she really is.
B: **All's fair in love and war!** [all behaviour is acceptable in extreme situations, especially in romantic situations and competitions]

A: What a day! My car broke down and my wallet has been stolen.
B: **It never rains but it pours.** [problems always happen together]

A: I wonder why Sylvia and Anthony have broken up.
B: Well, **it takes two to tango.** [two people are equally responsible]

C Other popular proverbs

I'm really impatient to finish decorating my flat, but **Rome wasn't built in a day!** [it takes a long time to do important things properly]

We should buy extra travel insurance for our skiing trip. **Better safe than sorry.** [it is best not to take risks, even if it seems boring or hard work]

I have to study hard and do a lot of exams to become an accountant, but **no pain no gain.** [there must be some suffering in order to succeed]

We don't have enough tickets for everybody, so it's a case of **first come, first served.** [the first to arrive will get something]

Exercises

11.1 Look at A. Match the beginning of each sentence with its ending.

1 Every cloud	mother of invention.
2 Nothing ventured,	there's a way.
3 Necessity is the	spice of life.
4 Where there's a will,	nothing gained.
5 Variety is the	has a silver lining.

11.2 Look at B. Write a suitable response to each remark with a proverb.

1 A friend tells you that Jim and Fiona are getting divorced because they've both been having affairs.
2 Someone tells you about three bad things that happened to them all on the same day.
3 Someone tells you about a small lie they told in order to meet somebody that they really like.
4 A friend tells you that they missed the train they wanted to get, but the next train was cheaper and faster.
5 A friend tells you that they are frustrated that it is taking a long time to set up their own business.
6 A friend tells you that they are determined to save up enough money to go travelling, but they don't know how to do this.

11.3 Correct the mistakes in these proverbs.

1 We had no tent, so we made a shelter out of branches and leaves to protect ourselves from the storm. It was a case of need is the mother of invention.
2 I'm doing three jobs at the moment to pay for my studies. Still, they say that change is the spice of life!
3 I went to the gym every day for three months and felt so much fitter. It was very hard work but nothing pained, nothing gained.
4 I decided that bungee jumping was too dangerous and didn't go with my friends – better to be safe than dead.
5 We've got ten laptops at half-price. But hurry – it's first come, first serve.
6 Three big bills at the same time? It never pours but it rains!

11.4 Complete each proverb.

1 When we got there they had given away all the free CDs – it was a case of first .... , first ....
2 Take your time and don't be impatient; Rome wasn't .... in .... !
3 It's a shame you missed your flight, but at least we can spend more time together. They do say every .... has .... silver ....
4 All my problems seem to come at the same time. It's true what they say: it never .... it pours!
5 It's going to be a lot of hard work, but nothing .... , nothing ....
6 They are both in the wrong. It takes .... to ....

12 Euphemisms

A What are euphemisms and when do we use them?

Euphemisms are a type of idiom used to avoid saying words which may offend or be considered unpleasant. They are useful to learn, as they will help you communicate using language which is appropriate for the situation you are in.

Euphemisms are used:

- to talk about subjects which may upset or offend, such as death.
  It was obvious he was **not long for this world**, but he never lost his sense of humour. [going to die soon]
- to avoid using direct words for body functions.
  I'm just going to **spend a penny**. [use the toilet (UK public toilets used to charge a penny.)]
- for humorous effect when telling anecdotes.
  My boss was **effing and blinding** because he had lost a confidential report. [swearing (some common English swear words begin with f or b) (informal)]
  How embarrassing! The door opened and my neighbour saw me **in my birthday suit / in the altogether**! [naked]
- by the media or political institutions to tone down unpleasant situations.
  Many soldiers have **made the supreme / ultimate sacrifice** for their country. [died]
  He died in a **friendly fire** incident. [killed by his own side, not by the enemy]

B Other euphemisms

euphemism	example	meaning
four-letter words	The play may offend some people, as it's full of **four-letter words**.	swear words (Many of these have four letters in English.)
pardon my French	He's such a bloody idiot, **pardon my French**.	apologies for swearing (humorous)
powder my nose	I'm just going to **powder my nose**.	use the toilet
answer the call of nature	Go behind a tree if you need to **answer the call of nature**.	urinate (more direct)
a bit on the side	Did you know she had **a bit on the side**?	sexual partner in addition to the person's usual partner
play the field	He said he's too young to stop **playing the field** and settle down.	having many romantic or sexual relationships without committing to one partner
have a bun in the oven	Guess what! I've got **a bun in the oven**!	I'm pregnant (humorous)
my number was up	I saw the car heading straight for me and I thought **my number was up**.	I was about to die (informal)
breathe my last	'This is where I was born and where I will **breathe my last**,' said the old woman.	die
be six feet under	We'll all **be six feet under** by the time you finish writing your novel!	be dead (informal)

Exercises

12.1 Which idioms do these pictures make you think of?

1 2 3

12.2 Correct the mistakes in these euphemisms.

1 The poet breathed his latest on 20 January 1891.
2 Older dogs need to be let out more often to answer the cry of nature.
3 He'd only been married for a year before he found himself a bit on the edge.
4 For one dreadful moment I thought my number was over.
5 I hate my daughter's taste in music – it's full of five-letter words.
6 The old lady asked where she could go to powder her chin.
7 Did you know Marta had a cake in the oven?
8 Don't be such a bloody fool, pardon my German.

12.3 Complete each euphemism.

1 I could hear him effing and .... as he was fixing the car.
2 We are here today to honour those airmen who have made the ultimate
....
3 Laura will be back in a minute. She's just gone to .... a penny.
4 This problem won't be solved until we're all six feet .... !
5 'I'm afraid that your father may not be .... for this world,' said the doctor.
6 The nearest toilet is on the right, if you'd like to powder your ....

12.4 Rewrite each sentence using a euphemism from the opposite page. There may be more than one possible answer.

1 She's pregnant. ....
2 He's naked. ....
3 I'm just going to the toilet. ....
4 The old man knew he would soon die. ....
5 He has lots of girlfriends. ....
6 He's always swearing. ....
7 Excuse me for swearing! ....
8 We must reduce the number of times we accidentally fire on our own men.
....

12.5 The underlined euphemisms below are not on the opposite page. What do you think they mean? Use a dictionary to help you.

1 The doctors have just told him he's got <u>the big C</u>.
2 I think you're <u>being economical with the truth</u>.
3 The cat was so badly injured that we had to have it <u>put to sleep</u>.
4 Why didn't you tell me your sister was <u>eating for two</u>?
5 Shall we pause the meeting for <u>a comfort break</u> now?

13 Clichés and fixed statements

A Clichés

A cliché is a comment that is often used in certain common, everyday situations. It is a comment that most people are familiar with and is therefore not original. Clichés are often used in everyday conversation and they are also frequently played with in advertising slogans and newspaper headlines.

There are plenty more fish in the sea / pebbles on the beach. [There are plenty more people or possibilities. Often used to cheer up someone who has found one person or opportunity unsuccessful.]

Look on the bright side. [Try to see something good in a bad situation. This is usually followed by an explanation of what the bright side might be, e.g. you probably wouldn't have enjoyed the job if you'd got it.]

It's easy to be wise after the event or **Hindsight is a wonderful thing.** [When you know what happens next, it's easy to say what you or others should have done.]

It's not over until the fat lady sings. [You cannot be sure what will happen until the very end of something, often a sports event. The expression refers to a long opera which ends with a female singing the final song.]

Enough is as good as a feast. [You shouldn't have more of something than you need, e.g. food.]

Ignorance is bliss. [You may be happier sometimes when you do not know all the facts about a situation.]

You can lead a horse to water (but you can't make him drink). [You can give someone the opportunity to do something, but you cannot force them to do it. The second part of the idiom (but you can't make him drink) is often not actually said.]

Truth will out! [The truth will always become known.]

B Fixed statements

You can often hear and use these fixed statements in everyday conversation.

fixed statement	meaning
Get your skates on! (informal)	Hurry up!
I'll believe it when I see it.	I'm doubtful that it will happen.
Mum's the word. (informal)	I promise not to tell a secret.
Good riddance! (informal)	I'm happy something or someone has gone.
Take it easy!	Calm down! Relax!
Fair's fair. (informal)	Their behaviour is reasonable.
So far, so good.	Things are going well up to this point.
Give me a break! (informal)	Stop criticising me!

> ⚠ **ERROR WARNING** It is best not to use clichés in formal writing or when you want to express an original or complex idea.

Exercises

13.1 Look at A. Answer these questions.

1 Who do we say has to sing before we can be confident something has finished?
2 What do we say is as good as a feast?
3 What side do we say you have to look on if you are trying to be optimistic?
4 What do we say there are plenty more of on the beach?
5 What do we say that ignorance is?
6 When do we say that it is easy to be wise?
7 Which animal do we say you can lead to water but not make drink?
8 What do we say there are plenty more of in the sea?
9 What do we say will happen with truth?

13.2 Complete each dialogue with an idiom from the opposite page.

1 A: You won't tell anyone what I told you, will you?
   B: No, I promise. ....
2 A: You're always late. It's just not good enough.
   B: That's not fair. .... ! It's only the third time this week.
3 A: Sheena says she'll have finished her dissertation by Friday.
   B: Hmm. ....
4 A: .... ! We need to leave in five minutes.
   B: Don't worry – I'm nearly ready.
5 A: I'm not sorry Boris is leaving our office. Are you?
   B: Not at all. .... !
6 A: I'm never going to get this finished in time.
   B: .... ! Don't panic. I'll help you, if you like.
7 A: Sonia's made a bit of a mess of this work, hasn't she?
   B: Just .... It's only her second day here.
8 A: How are you enjoying your new job?
   B: .... But it's early days yet.
9 A: Why do you think Vic changed his mind at the last moment?
   B: I don't know. It's a complex situation. I suspect ....
10 A: Who do you think was behind the plot to bring down the government?
   B: I don't know, but I'm sure we'll find out. ....

13.3 Correct the mistakes in these idioms.

1 Let me a break!
2 There are plenty more sharks in the sea.
3 So long, so good.
4 It's not over until the fat lady dies.
5 Truth will escape.
6 Dad's the word.

> **FOLLOW UP**
> Go to http://www.clichesite.com and look up these clichés by searching on the underlined word in each. Any *friend* of yours is a friend of mine. *Beauty* is only skin deep. *Money* is the root of all evil. What does each cliché mean? Write a short dialogue illustrating it in use.

14 Other languages

As you probably know, English includes many words from other languages. The idiomatic expressions in this unit all come from Latin or French.

A Latin

idiom	example	meaning
ad hoc /æd'hɒk/	He was paid on an **ad hoc** basis.	not planned but arranged or done when needed
ad infinitum /ˌædɪnfɪ'naɪtəm/	Their list of demands seemed to go on **ad infinitum**.	without end, forever
compos mentis /ˌkɒmpɒs'mentɪs/	My grandfather is nearly 100 but he is perfectly **compos mentis**.	in control of his actions, mentally healthy
de facto /deɪ'fæktəʊ/	Jorge is the **de facto** head of the organisation.	existing but not officially agreed (formal)
non sequitur /nɒn'sekwɪtə/	Keiko's response seemed like a complete **non sequitur** to me.	a statement which does not seem to be connected with what was said before
status quo /ˌsteɪtəs'kwəʊ/	The Conservatives favoured maintaining the **status quo**, while the Liberals hoped for change.	the present situation

B French

A: Are you familiar with our health and safety procedures?
B: No, I'm not really **au fait** /əʊ'feɪ/ with them yet. [fully knowledgeable about]

A: I hate people who talk loudly on their mobile phones on trains.
B: I agree. They're my absolute **bête noire** /bet'nwɑː/. [what the speaker hates most]

A: It's always beautiful weather when you have to study for exams.
B: I know. It's always the way. **C'est la vie** /seɪ.læ'viː/! [you say this when something happens that you do not like but which you have to accept]

A: Only the very best students are accepted on this course.
B: I know. They really are the **crème de la crème** /krem.də.lɑː'krem/. [very best]

A: I wish he'd consulted with us first about changing the computer systems.
B: Yes, he just presented us with **a fait accompli** /fet.əkɒm'pliː/. [a decision that has been made or a completed action that cannot be changed]

A: I think she should make more effort to control her children.
B: Yes, she has quite a **laissez-faire** /ˌleɪseɪ'feə/ approach, doesn't she? [desire not to control]

A: The older generation criticising young people! There's nothing new about that.
B: Yes, **plus ça change** /pluː sæ' ʃɒnʒ/! [times change, but some things stay the same.]

Exercises

14.1 Look at A. Complete each sentence with a Latin expression.

1 We don't receive many complaints, so we just deal with them on an .... basis.
2 The .... government will remain in power until the election results are finalised.
3 This sentence in your essay is a .... – it's not logically connected to your previous point.
4 I could go on .... about the advantages of moving to the countryside.
5 Whenever a new person takes over as manager, they disturb the .... , at least to some extent.
6 His lawyer claims he wasn't fully .... when he admitted he was guilty.

14.2 Replace the underlined part of each sentence with an expression from the opposite page.

1 There were no opportunities for discussion; the reform was presented as a <u>decision which had already been made</u>.
2 All players must be <u>confident that they know</u> the rules of the game.
3 I can't come out tonight because I have to work late. Oh well, <u>it can't be helped</u>.
4 Of course I love being a movie star, but I must say that awards ceremonies are <u>what I most detest</u>.
5 So Dan has been arguing with his boss again. <u>Things don't change</u>!
6 A lot of the parents are not very happy about the new headmaster's <u>liberal</u> attitude to behaviour.

14.3 Are these sentences true or false? If the answer is false, say why.

1 A laissez-faire approach is strict and intolerant.
2 A de facto leader is the officially recognised leader of an organisation.
3 The crème de la crème of applicants are the best applicants for the job.
4 It is good to include non sequiturs in your writing.
5 A bête noire is something that you do not like.
6 If you are compos mentis, you are not responsible for your actions.
7 A fait accompli can easily and quickly be changed.
8 If someone talks about something ad infinitum, they talk about it for a long time.

FOLLOW UP Match the following literal translations to idioms on the opposite page: *cream of the cream, it does not follow, a done deed*. What is the connection between the translation and the way the idiom is used in English?

15 Sailing

As Britain is an island nation, with the sea playing a major role in the country's history and its economy, it is not surprising that the language has developed many idioms from sailing.

A Talking about a business

Read this magazine article about a couple who bought a hotel.

> When we took over the hotel five years ago, the business was **on the rocks**[1]. The economy was doing badly and people **were giving** luxury hotels like ours **a wide berth**[2]. The previous owners had decided to **cut and run**[3], but we loved the place and were sure we could make a go of it. We **battened down the hatches**[4] by cutting costs as much as possible and did all we could to **run a tight ship**[5]. Holidays and any other luxuries for our own family **went by the board**[6] for two years. However, we managed to **weather the storm**[7] and are now **making good headway**[8]. We have lots of major bookings **in the offing**[9] and are confident of making excellent profits this year.

[1] in serious difficulty
[2] avoiding (*berth* is an old sailing term meaning the distance a ship should leave between itself and a potential danger such as rocks)
[3] avoid a difficult situation by leaving suddenly (the image comes from cutting mooring ropes in order to make a quick departure)
[4] got ready for a difficult situation by preparing in every way possible (the image comes from closing the ship's doors securely when a storm is likely)
[5] control a business or organisation firmly and effectively
[6] were abandoned (the image comes from something being thrown overboard into the sea)
[7] survive difficult times
[8] making good progress
[9] likely to happen soon (*offing* was a term used to refer to the part of the sea on the horizon)

B More sailing idioms

idiom	example	explanation
be taken aback	We **were taken aback** when Ben announced his resignation.	were very surprised (If a boat is taken aback, it is suddenly attacked from behind.)
leave high and dry	Many holidaymakers were **left high and dry** when the tour company collapsed.	put in a difficult situation which they could not improve (The image is of a boat stuck on a sandbank and unable to move.)
take the wind out of someone's sails	Sally was keen to become an actor, but her teacher's criticism of her performance **took the wind out of her sails**.	made her feel less confident, by saying or doing something unexpected (If there is no wind in a boat's sails, then it is unable to move.)
in the wake of sb / sth *or* in sb's / sth's wake	Thousands of people lost their jobs **in the wake of** the recession. The consultant strode through the hospital, several students **in his wake**.	following closely behind (The wake is the trail of foam left by a boat as it moves.)
all hands on deck	We'll need **all hands on deck** if we're going to be ready for the party on time.	everyone must help (A *hand* is a sailing term for a sailor and *deck* is the area you walk on outside on a boat.)
any port in a storm	I really don't like staying there, but I had no choice but to accept Jan's offer. **Any port in a storm**, I'm afraid!	You must accept any help you're offered when you're in a difficult situation. (When there is a storm at sea a boat has to go to the nearest port.)

34 English Idioms in Use Advanced

Exercises

15.1 Look at A. Choose the correct answer.

1 Are you more likely to cut and run if a) things are going badly or b) things are going well?
2 Would you give a wide berth to a) something that attracts you or b) something that you do not want to approach?
3 If a politician is said to have weathered the storm, has he a) got through some problems or b) created some problems?
4 Would you batten down the hatches if you are a) expecting problems or b) expecting a relaxed period?
5 Is your daily exercise regime more likely to go by the board if a) you have some extra time or b) you are very busy?
6 If you were making good headway with your language studies, would you be a) pleased or b) upset?
7 If an event is in the offing, has it a) already happened or b) is it still in the future?
8 If a boss likes to run a tight ship, is he/she a) strict or b) relaxed?
9 If you had a business which was on the rocks would you be a) pleased or b) worried?

15.2 Complete each idiom.

1 I'd like all hands on .... for the next few hours, please.
2 The bad reviews of his first CD took the .... out of the singer's sails.
3 He wrote an interesting article about European politics .... the wake of the war.
4 I was quite .... aback to hear that Maura had handed in her notice.
5 Alex went home early, leaving me .... and dry at the party with no one else to talk to.
6 Unfortunately, our plans to go on holiday this summer have had to go by the .... , as we're moving house.
7 I didn't want to sleep on my aunt's sofa for two weeks, but any port in a .... , as they say.
8 Despite the financial problems, I am confident that the company will succeed in .... the storm.

15.3 Match the beginning of each sentence with its ending.

1 There's trouble ahead, so we'd better batten down the   offing.
2 It's a long journey, but we're making good   wake.
3 The business is doing so badly that I'm tempted to cut and   hatches.
4 There are some interesting plans for new projects in the   sails.
5 The film star left the room with a group of journalists in her run.
6 It's about time someone took the wind out of Marco's   headway.

15.4 Rewrite the underlined part of each sentence using the word in brackets.

1 I try to avoid the city centre on Saturdays if I possibly can. (BERTH)
2 Jaime's mother was very surprised by his decision to leave school. (ABACK)
3 Amy's plans to buy a new car were abandoned when she lost her job. (BOARD)
4 Their relationship has been in serious difficulty for some months. (ROCKS)
5 Asim controls the business in a firm and efficient way. (SHIP)
6 The cost of home insurance has risen as a result of last summer's floods. (WAKE)
7 We were in a difficult situation when the babysitter didn't turn up. (HIGH)
8 I know it's been hard for you, but I'm sure you'll get through the bad times. (STORM)

16 War and conflict

A Idioms based on war

Many idioms come from the topic of war. They are used to refer to actions and events that are seen as similar to battles, conflicts or struggles.

In these newspaper cuttings, the first sentence explains the idiom in the headline.

EMOTIONAL CALL TO ARMS INSPIRES A GENERATION
President Forga's recent challenge to young people to show solidarity and vote in the next election has won widespread support.

SALES TAX – PM BEATS A RETREAT
After widespread negative reaction to his suggestion yesterday that sales tax should be raised, the prime minister today said there were 'no immediate plans for an increase'.

MORE BAD NEWS FOR SHELL-SHOCKED INVESTORS
Investors, who are already suffering from the financial crisis, are feeling nervous today as Southern Bank prepares to announce unexpectedly high losses.

MINISTER DROPS AN ECONOMIC BOMBSHELL
The shock announcement by Ms Hanaria that the country is in a deep economic crisis, and that the currency must be devalued, stunned city economists today.

SCHOOL CLOSURES – PARENTS ON THE WARPATH
'Parents are very angry and have decided to take action immediately,' said a spokesperson. Demonstrations are planned for all major cities.

TEACHERS COME OUT FIGHTING
The head of the teachers' union said today that teachers would not accept a drop in salary and would oppose the decision to the very end.

B Idioms connected with firearms

I think you **shot yourself in the foot** by leaving your old job before getting a new one. [unintentionally did or said something foolish which made your situation worse]

When I suggested raising the membership fee, Sergio **shot me down in flames**. [immediately criticised my idea and refused to accept it]

I think we should **hang fire** before making any rash decisions about redundancies. [delay making a decision]

C Idioms connected with violent events, armies, conflict and struggle

Now that I have a PhD, I've at least got **a fighting chance** of getting a teaching job in a university. [a small but real possibility]

Winning the cup in 1998 was just **a flash in the pan** – they haven't won a match since then! [something that happened only once and was not repeated]

Our new IT manager had a **baptism of fire** on her first day at work – all the computers crashed! [very difficult first experience of something]

As she left the studio, Dana Freen had to **run the gauntlet** of reporters asking her about her controversial new film. [face a lot of people who were criticising or attacking her]

Sometimes it's a real **battle of wills** between me and my dog – he wants to go one way across the park and I want to go another! [conflict between two different, strong desires or intentions]

After college, I **joined the ranks of** the unemployed for a year before I got my first job. [became (unemployed)]

Zetec **stole a march on** its rivals by launching its new car model six months earlier than expected. [got an advantage by acting before their rivals did]

Exercises

16.1 Look at A. Complete each idiom.

Teachers are on the (1) .... after the education minister yesterday dropped his (2) .... about government plans to reduce teachers' pay and increase their working hours. Teaching unions have issued a call to (3) .... , and (4) ....-shocked teachers have instantly agreed to oppose the plans, with strike action if necessary. 'All our members have come out (5) .... and we are confident that the government will be forced to (6) .... a retreat,' said union leader Chris Banks at a press conference this afternoon.

16.2 Match words from each box to form six idioms.

| shoot down in | baptism | a flash in | of fire | the pan | of wills | flames |
| a battle | run | hang | fire | the gauntlet | | |

16.3 Complete each dialogue with an idiom from 16.2. You may need to change the form of the verb.

1. A: I think it would be better to postpone making a decision for a bit.
   B: Yes, let's .... until the situation is clearer.
2. A: Well, your first day at work was certainly full of drama.
   B: Yes, it was a real ....
3. A: Has he written any other books?
   B: No, I think the first one was just ....
4. A: Would you like to be a celebrity?
   B: No, I'd hate to have to .... of the paparazzi whenever I left the house.
5. A: He's very critical, isn't he, your boss?
   B: Yes, all my ideas usually get ....
6. A: Why do parents and teenagers always seem to clash?
   B: Well, you often have .... , especially between sons and fathers.

16.4 Correct the ten mistakes with idioms in this paragraph.

When Ali graduated, he decided he didn't want to meet the ranks of commuters struggling to work every day. He wanted to set up his own online gift-ordering business so that he could work from home. He knew it was a risk but felt he would have at least a fighting opportunity of success. Initially, he and a college friend planned to start the business together. Ali had the idea and Igor, his friend, had the money to invest in the company. But then just weeks before the launch, Igor dropped a bomb: he said he no longer wanted to be part of Ali's plans. Despite Ali's attempts to persuade him to wait fire on his decision, Igor said he was no longer prepared to take the risk and was going to hit a retreat before it was too late. However, two weeks later Igor took a march on Ali by launching his own online gift-ordering company. Ali was gun-shocked by this betrayal, but he soon came out battling. He took Igor's behaviour as a call to weapons and has persuaded a bank to lend him the money he needs. Ali's introduction to the business world has certainly been a beginning of fire, but I'm sure he will be really successful.

> **FOLLOW UP**
> Use a search engine to search for these words, or search for them on the British National Corpus (http://www.natcorp.ox.ac.uk/): *warpath, shell-shocked, bombshell, gauntlet*. Write down an example sentence where each word is used in an idiom.

17 Transport

As transport is such an everyday experience for many people, it is unsurprisingly a rich source of idioms.

A Trains

Karl was full of enthusiasm when he started his university course. He worked extremely hard at first but, after a couple of years, he **ran out of steam**[1] and lost interest in his studies. He spent much more time going to parties and staying out all night than studying, and his tutor worried that he had **gone off the rails**[2]. But then Karl fell in love with a student in his department. Now, six months **down the line**[3], he is **back on track**[4] towards gaining an excellent degree and fulfilling his dreams.

[1] lost energy or interest
[2] started behaving in an unacceptable way
[3] later
[4] again on the way to achieving something

B Cars

We use **at / behind the wheel** to mean 'be the driver' (NB in this expression *wheel* refers to the steering wheel): I saw their car this morning but couldn't make out who was **at the wheel**.

We talk about someone being **in the driving seat** to mean that they are in control of the situation: Although the general manager is officially in charge, everyone knows his deputy is really **in the driving seat**.

We talk about **life in the fast lane** to mean a life that is active, exciting and dangerous. **Life in the slow lane** is correspondingly lacking in excitement and danger: I've had enough of **life in the fast lane**, so I'm giving up my executive sales job and moving to the countryside.

Doing a U-turn means changing direction, and it is used idiomatically when talking about politics: Initially the minister was against increasing road tax, but he has now **done a U-turn** and is defending the plan.

If we **go / move / step up a gear**, we start to work or play more effectively or quickly than before: After half-time the team **stepped up a gear** and managed to score three goals.

C Planes

idiom	example	meaning
be flying high	The company had some initial problems but now it **is flying high**.	is very successful
fly by the seat of your pants	We had no business experience before opening the shop, so we were really **flying by the seat of our pants** at first.	doing something difficult without much experience or ability (informal)
do something on autopilot	I've written so many references now that I can more or less **do it on autopilot**.	doing something without thinking (informal)
take a nosedive	Share prices **took a nosedive** last week.	went down suddenly and fast
be on a collision course	The two countries **are on a collision course**, and it seems that nothing can be done to prevent serious trouble.	behaving in such a way that is likely to cause a major disagreement or fight
come to a standstill	Production has **come to a standstill** because of the strike.	stopped

Exercises

17.1 Which idioms do these pictures make you think of?

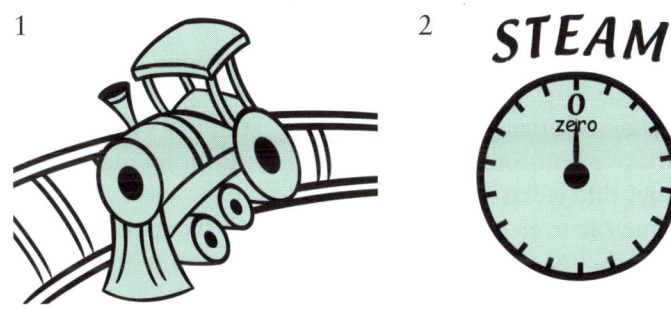

1 go ....
2 run ....
3 do ....

17.2 Complete each dialogue with an idiom.

1 Tim: Edward's moving to New York. He said he needs more excitement in his life.
   Ruth: Yes, I think he's tired of ....
2 Rob: The government have changed their mind completely on the new vehicle tax!
   Pierre: Yes, they've ....
3 Mona: Their son has started getting into trouble with the police.
   Ken: Yes, he seems to have ....
4 Rajiv: They were so enthusiastic when they started the new conservation scheme, but now it all seems to have slowed down.
   Nick: Yes, the whole project seems to have ....
5 Ursula: We need to start doing things more effectively and quickly.
   Ray: Yes, we definitely need to ....
6 Freda: Did you see who was driving when the accident happened?
   Krishnan: No, I couldn't see who was ....

17.3 Match the beginning of each sentence with its ending.

1 I'm glad to say that things are now back   driving seat any more.
2 We don't know what could happen a year down   a collision course.
3 Things are out of control. Nobody seems to be in the   the line.
4 Profits of internet-based companies have taken   a complete standstill.
5 I think the employers and the unions are on   on track.
6 Nothing's happening. Things have come to   a nosedive recently.

17.4 Choose the correct answer.

1 If a business is flying high, it is a) failing   b) just starting up   c) doing well and is profitable.
2 If you do something on autopilot, you do it a) without thinking   b) using a computer   c) deliberately.
3 If someone is back on track, they are a) being punished for bad behaviour   b) behaving in a less responsible way   c) behaving responsibly again.
4 If you are flying by the seat of your pants, you are doing something a) without much ability or experience   b) without thinking about it   c) which is very exciting.

> **FOLLOW UP**
> Find the meanings of these idioms in a dictionary and make a note of them in your notebook under the heading 'Transport idioms'. Note down the definition, an example sentence and any other useful information, such as whether it is formal or informal, etc.: *drive someone round the bend, a back-seat driver, step on it, put the brakes on, give / get the green light*.

18 Animals

A Cats and dogs

A: Trevor and Sue are so arrogant.
B: Yes, they think they're **the cat's whiskers**. [better than everyone else]
A: Do you think he'll get the job?
B: With no qualifications or experience? He **hasn't** got **a cat in hell's chance**! [no chance at all]
A: It's not fair that we have exams immediately after the school holidays!
B: I know, **it's a dog's life**! [life is hard and unpleasant]
A: I know I don't need the car over the weekend, but I don't want you to use it either.
B: Don't be such a **dog in the manger**! [you're keeping it only so that I can't have it, not because you really want it yourself]

B Farm animals

idiom	example	meaning
flog a dead horse	You're **flogging a dead horse** trying to persuade Kim to move house again.	wasting time trying to do something that won't succeed (usually used in continuous tenses)
(straight) from the horse's mouth	Guess what? Juan is going to work in Moscow! I got it **straight from the horse's mouth**!	from the person concerned
until the cows come home	You can argue **until the cows come home** but I'll never agree.	for a very long time
sort (out) the sheep from the goats	Setting the class such a difficult exercise will certainly **sort the sheep from the goats**.	find the people or things of high quality from a group of mixed quality
might as well be hung for a sheep as a lamb	You're already late, so just take all day off. You **might as well be hung for a sheep as a lamb**!	might as well do something more serious as you are going to be punished anyway

C Wild animals

In these conversations, the second speaker uses an idiom to repeat and sum up what the first speaker says.

A: The president's just pretending to be upset about the situation, don't you think?
B: Yes, he's **shedding crocodile tears** to get popular support.
A: Thomas was really upset when his team let in an own goal.
B: Yes, he was **sick as a parrot**, wasn't he?
A: Ana's hoping that Carlos will stop gambling once they're married, but I doubt he will.
B: No, **a leopard can't change its spots**.
A: He complained his business was about to fail so often that no one believed him when it finally did.
B: Yes, he **cried wolf** once too often.
A: He looks kind and gentle but he's not like that at all.
B: You're right. He really is **a wolf in sheep's clothing**.
A: I'm sure everyone is thinking about the divorce, but no one ever mentions it.
B: That's right. It's certainly **the elephant in the room**.

Exercises

18.1 Look at A. Complete each dialogue with an idiom.

1. A: She obviously thinks she looks really good in that new dress, doesn't she?
   B: Yes, she thinks ....
2. A: Things are pretty hard for you at the moment, I guess.
   B: Yes, it's .... !
3. A: Do you think you'll pass your driving test?
   B: No, I haven't got ....
4. A: Her husband is so selfish. he never shares anything, even if he doesn't want it.
   B: Yes, he has a real .... attitude.

18.2 Which idioms do these pictures make you think of?

18.3 Complete each idiom.

1. He's flogging a dead .... trying to revive that old idea.
2. He'll never stop causing trouble – a .... can't change its spots.
3. Luc will argue with you about that until the .... come home.
4. He was sick as a .... not to make the finals.
5. Let's stay out a bit longer. We might as well be hung for a .... as a ....

18.4 Replace the underlined part of each sentence with an idiom.

1. Don't <u>pretend there's an emergency</u> or no one will help when you really need it.
2. The minister <u>pretends to be upset</u> about homelessness, but does nothing about it.
3. I hate our neighbours' <u>selfish</u> attitude – they don't want the parking space but they won't let us have it.
4. We can discuss it <u>for a very long time</u>, but I won't change my mind.

FOLLOW UP Look up these animals in your dictionary: *snake*, *fish*, *rat*. Can you find an idiom using each of them?

19 Parts of the body

A The head and face

You should face up to your problems. Don't just **bury your head in the sand**[1].

My dad **has a good head for**[4] figures. He can do complicated sums in seconds.

There's more to this news story **than meets the eye**[6].

Let's **put our heads together**[8] and organise a surprise birthday party for Sam.

I think the success of his first film **has gone to his head**[10]. He thinks he's wonderful.

She won't apologise because she doesn't want to **lose face**[12].

Kate **is head and shoulders above**[2] her twin sister when it comes to passing exams.

I don't know why I didn't get the job. Perhaps **my face** just **didn't fit**[13].

It **was one in the eye for**[3] his critics when he won the tennis tournament.

I just **held / bit my tongue**[5] and said nothing.

As an English speaker, I find it difficult to **get my tongue round**[7] Scandinavian names.

After some **teething troubles**[9], our new wireless network is working well.

I like my economic history class. I've enjoyed **getting my teeth into**[11] a new subject.

In a **face-saving**[14] exercise, the minister agreed to meet the demands of the striking firefighters.

[1] refuse to think about unpleasant facts or problems because you do not want to deal with them [2] a lot better than [3] a disappointment for [4] is good at something; collocates strongly with business, figures or heights [5] stopped myself from saying something which I really wanted to say [6] it is more difficult to understand or involves more things than one thought [7] pronounce [8] plan something together [9] problems in the early stages of doing something new [10] made him think he's very important and made him a less pleasant person [11] becoming involved in something enthusiastically [12] lose the respect of others [13] my appearance or personality was not suitable for the job [14] done so that other people will continue to respect them

B Other body idioms

I would give my right arm for a job in the film industry. I've always loved the movies. [would very much like to have]

I don't want to **tread on your toes**, but would it be OK if I added a few paragraphs to your report? [do something that could upset someone by getting involved in something that is their responsibility]

The media tend to **point the finger at** the government for most of the current problems. [accuse of being responsible for]

He gave an awful speech. He made lots of jokes but nobody laughed. It **made my toes curl**. [made you feel extremely embarrassed or ashamed for someone else]

You have to read the newspapers daily if you want to **keep your finger on the pulse**. [stay up-to-date]

> **TIP** Draw pictures to help you remember the idioms, e.g. draw toes and write the 'toes curl' idiom in it.
>
> made my toes curl

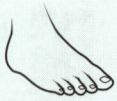

Exercises

19.1 Look at A. Correct the mistakes in these idioms.

1 I wonder what is really behind the president's decision. I'm sure there's more to it than meets the mind.
2 Melissa is head and hair above her brother when it comes to maths.
3 I'm sure we can think of a good present for Jim if we put our hearts together.
4 Kasia really loves getting her mouth into a new project.
5 You mustn't bury your feet in the sand – problems don't go away if you ignore them.
6 It was one in the nose for Liliana's brother when she passed her driving test first time – it had taken him five attempts.

19.2 Read these statements and answer the questions.

1 The government is anxious not to lose face and so is refusing to back down.
Is the government afraid of losing respect or money?
2 Danny finds it very hard to bite his tongue when his boss says something foolish.
Does Danny want to laugh or to speak?
3 The novelist said she always enjoyed getting her teeth into a new book.
Is the novelist talking about starting or finishing a new book?
4 Management has introduced some face-saving measures in the attempt to make the problems seem less serious.
Is management concerned about a loss of staff or a loss of respect?
5 Winning the prize has gone to Lucia's head.
Is Lucia nicer or less nice because of her success?

19.3 Match the statements on the left with a suitable response on the right.

1 Let's talk about planning the party.	Yes, there's more to it than meets the eye.
2 Bruno was upset when he lost the race to his rival.	That's right, his face didn't fit.
3 Ahmed's been so arrogant since he won that competition.	Yes, he was afraid of losing face.
4 He didn't want people to think less of him.	Yes, it was one in the eye for him.
5 They never really liked him in his old job.	Yes, they're all pointing the finger at him.
6 It's a very complicated issue, I think.	Yes, let's put our heads together.
7 Everyone says that Ian's to blame.	Well, it's good to keep your finger on the pulse.
8 I read a newspaper every day.	Yes, it's really gone to his head.

19.4 Rewrite the underlined part of each sentence using the word in brackets.

1 I <u>wish I could</u> go to Japan with you! (ARM)
2 After some <u>initial small problems</u>, the business began to do well. (TEETHING)
3 I find it very hard to <u>pronounce</u> some Welsh place names. (TONGUE)
4 I don't know why they're <u>accusing</u> me – I'm not guilty. [FINGER]
5 I'm not very good at maths, but my brother <u>understands all about</u> figures. (HEAD)
6 I hope I'm not <u>interfering</u>, but could I suggest you try a different approach? (TOES)
7 Paulo's speech at the wedding <u>was so embarrassing</u>! (TOES)
8 I don't see how you can <u>keep in touch with what's going on in the world</u> if you never watch TV or listen to the radio. [FINGER]

20 Games and sport

A Card games and board games

You'd think it was **monopoly money**, the amount he spent last week. [money that has no value and is used only in games]

I wanted the job in Paris, but I knew **the dice were loaded against** me because my French isn't very good. [I would be unlikely to succeed]

He drives so fast! You're **dicing with death** if you let him drive you. [taking a great risk]

The audience sat there **poker-faced** all through the play. [expressionless; this comes from the card game *poker*, where you must not let your face reveal whether you have good or bad cards]

Management found that the union **held all the cards** in the pay talks. [was in a strong position]

I **kept / played my cards close to my chest** in the interview. [didn't reveal my plans]

The politician **played his ace / trump card** by promising lower taxes for all on the day of the election. [used his advantage, especially one others did not know about]

B Ball games

Hi Daniel
Having a bad day at work. My boss has just increased my sales targets, again! It's so unfair. He just keeps **moving the goalposts**[1]. On top of that, my colleague Jen has just announced she's leaving, which has completely **knocked me for six**[2] because I really like working with her. Apparently she **got the red card**[3] from Jerry because she was late a few times, and she's decided to leave.
Anyway, fancy going to see a film tonight?
Craig

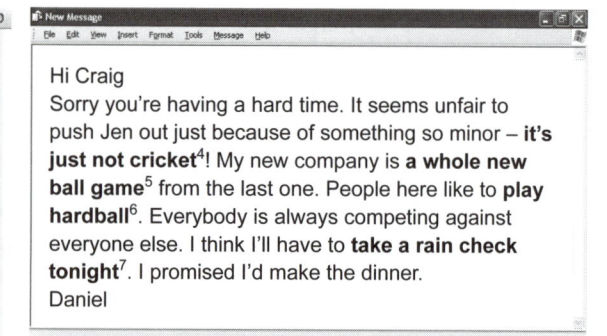

Hi Craig
Sorry you're having a hard time. It seems unfair to push Jen out just because of something so minor – **it's just not cricket**[4]! My new company is **a whole new ball game**[5] from the last one. People here like to **play hardball**[6]. Everybody is always competing against everyone else. I think I'll have to **take a rain check tonight**[7]. I promised I'd make the dinner.
Daniel

[1] changing the rules in a situation in a way that is not fair [2] surprised and upset me [3] received official criticism for bad behaviour [4] not right or fair behaviour; usually used humorously [5] a completely different situation [6] be so determined to get what they want that they use unfair methods [7] something you say when you have to refuse someone's invitation to something that you would like to do at another time

C Boxing

idiom	example	explanation
not pull any punches	The coach did**n't pull any punches** when he told the team how badly they had played.	speak in an honest and direct way without trying to be tactful
be / feel punch-drunk	The trade fair was so noisy and busy that I **felt punch-drunk** by the end of the week.	was tired and confused (If a boxer is punch-drunk, they are dazed as a result of being hit on the head.)
below the belt	It was **below the belt** to mention his rival's marital problems to the journalist.	an unfair attack (In boxing, hitting someone below the belt is not allowed.)
throw in the sponge / towel	Kisho will never agree to **throw in the sponge**, even if he has lost any chance of winning the election.	In the past, throwing the sponge or towel into the ring meant admitting defeat.

Exercises

20.1 Look at A. Which idioms do these pictures make you think of?

1. play / keep ....
2. hold ....
3. m..................
4. the dice ....
5. dicing ....
6. play ....

20.2 Rewrite the underlined part of each sentence using an idiom from 20.1.
1. I felt I was <u>taking a huge risk</u> riding at high speed on the back of his motorbike.
2. I <u>didn't tell anyone about my plans</u> and didn't mention that I was going to resign soon.
3. He's so rich. He spends money as if it were <u>toy money</u>.
4. The barrister <u>used an advantage none of us knew about</u> and revealed the final piece of evidence.
5. I wanted a job in politics, but felt <u>I was unlikely to succeed</u> as I had no personal contacts in the political world.
6. Masa is so much more qualified and experienced than I am. He <u>has all the advantages</u> if we both apply for the same job.

20.3 Read these statements and answer the questions.
a. Joseph just sat there with a blank expression on his face.
b. I think Ivana was unfair when she mentioned to her boss that Kim had once been in prison.
c. Jung said he was too busy to come with us this time, so we went without him.
d. The news obviously surprised and upset Gina a lot.
1. Who said something that was below the belt? ....
2. Who took a rain check? ....
3. Who was knocked for six by something? ....
4. Who was poker-faced? ....

20.4 Complete each idiom.
1. Jin's in a very powerful position; he .... all the ....
2. The teacher has .... the .... so many times that none of the students knows what the rules are any more.
3. Simon is very direct with people; he never .... any ....
4. What? The headteacher changed the holiday from a whole day to a half day! Poor kids! It's just not .... , is it?
5. The two presidential candidates have played .... recently and have made quite personal attacks on each other.
6. Advertising on TV is not the same as it was 20 years ago; it's a whole .... now.
7. Everyone felt .... after six hours of political debate.
8. At 10 pm on the night of the election, the president threw .... and admitted he had lost.

English Idioms in Use Advanced 45

21 Ancient myths and history

A Greek mythology

Read these comments made by politicians:

I think this party has a great future, but corruption seems to be our **Achilles heel**.

In his latest speech criticising the prime minister's actions, the finance minister has opened a **Pandora's box** of political and legal problems.

Our leader has shown that she has **the Midas touch** when it comes to economic planning.

His appointment to leader has caused many problems within the party, with some members accusing him of being **a Trojan horse**, sent to destroy the party from within.

Another stock market crash is hanging over this government like **the sword of Damocles**.

person or place	explanation
Achilles /ə.kɪli:z/	Achilles' heel was the only place on his body that the hero could be wounded or killed. It was his one weak point.
Pandora	Pandora carried a box which held all the evils of the world. When she opened it, evil escaped into the world.
King Midas	Everything Midas touched turned into gold.
Troy	The Greeks sent a huge wooden horse into the city of Troy as a gift. Soldiers were hiding inside, who then attacked the city.
Damocles	During a banquet, Damocles saw a sword hanging by just one hair above his head, ready to fall and kill him.

B Other expressions related to ancient myths and history

In these conversations, the second speaker uses an idiom to repeat and sum up what the first speaker says.

A: The government needs to act now before it's too late!
B: I know. It's like they're **fiddling while Rome burns**.
A: We've won an important victory, but we must fight on.
B: Yes. We mustn't **rest on our laurels**.
A: I'll examine every word in every single document until I find the answer.
B: Yes – **leave no stone unturned**.
A: We knew it was going to end in disaster. It was so obvious!
B: I know – we all **saw the writing on the wall**.
A: The early days of our business were such fun, and we were so successful!
B: Yes, they really were **the halcyon days**.
A: I don't think we should react to their insults.
B: I agree. Let's just **turn the other cheek**.
A: We won our court case, but we've got no money left. It wasn't such a great victory after all!
B: No. I agree. It was more of **a Pyrrhic victory**.
A: So Marco accepted responsibility for the situation and resigned as director?
B: Yes, he decided to **fall on his sword**.
A: The last thing Gerard said to his boss when he left the job was that she was a fool!
B: Yes, that wasn't such a great **parting shot**, was it?
A: The dispute has got bigger and bigger – everyone's involved now.
B: Yes, it seems to have grown to **epic proportions**.

Exercises

21.1 Look at A. Which idioms do these pictures make you think of?

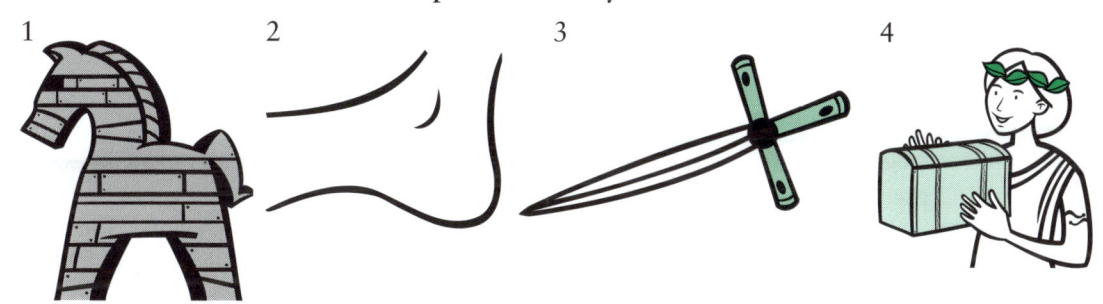

1   2   3   4

21.2 Complete each sentence with an idiom from 21.1.
1 New financial regulations are hanging over the banking industry like ……………………………………………………………… . Bankers are extremely worried.
2 One famous type of computer virus works like ……………………………………………………… . It attacks your computer from inside the system.
3 He's a good worker in many ways, but planning is his ……………………………………………………… . He's so disorganised.
4 She opened ……………………………………………………… when she started investigating corruption in the building industry.

21.3 Complete the crossword.

Across
1 the writing on the ………………………………
2 a ……………………………… victory
3 leave no stone ………………………………

Down
4 ……………………………… days
5 Don't ……………………………… on your laurels.
6 turn the other ………………………………

21.4 Correct the mistakes in these idioms.
1 Julia's leaving shot as she walked out of the room was to say that she never wanted to see any of us ever again.
2 The police left no stones unturned in trying to trace the missing child.
3 Piero fell into his sword and accepted full responsibility for the disaster.
4 She really has the Pandora touch – everything she does is hugely successful.
5 It was a task of epic size, but everyone tried their hardest to succeed.
6 We should continue to work hard and not sleep on our laurels.
7 If we are faced with a violent attack, we should just turn the other face and not react.
8 Doing nothing at this stage would be like singing while Rome burns.

> **FOLLOW UP** Use the Internet to find out where the idioms in B come from. You can use a search engine like Google or a specific site about idioms, e.g. www.phrases.org.uk

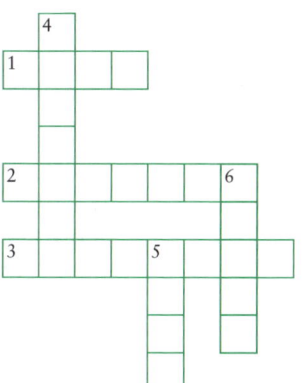

22 Shakespeare

Many common idioms actually come from the works of Shakespeare (1564–1616), the famous English poet and dramatist who wrote 38 plays, including *Romeo and Juliet* and *Hamlet*. Here are some idioms from Shakespeare's plays that are used in everyday English.

modern-day example	meaning	origin
Their relationship was ruined by **the green-eyed monster**.	jealousy	Iago: O, beware, my lord, of jealousy; It is the green-eyed monster which doth mock / The meat it feeds on. (*Othello*)
By criticising the company and the team's performance, the new manager succeeded in upsetting everyone **at one fell swoop**.	suddenly, at the same time	Macduff (on hearing that all his family have been killed): What, all my pretty chickens and their dam / At one fell swoop? (*Macbeth*)
My nephews came to stay at the weekend and have **eaten me out of house and home**.	eaten all the food there is in my house (informal)	Mistress Quickly: He hath eaten me out of house and home; he hath put all my substance into that fat belly of his. (*Henry IV Pt II*)
It was a terrifying film – it **made my hair stand on end**.	frightened me very much	Ghost: I could a tale unfold [which] would … make each particular hair to stand on end, like quills upon the fretful porpentine. (*Hamlet*)
Let me finish this email – I'll be with you **in the twinkling of an eye**.	in an instant	Launcelot: I'll take my leave of the Jew in the twinkling of an eye. (*The Merchant of Venice*)
The police were sent on **a wild-goose chase** looking for the money that the criminals had already spent.	a search that has no hope of success (informal)	Mercutio: If thy wits run the wild-goose chase, I have done. (*Romeo and Juliet*)
The TV presenter **laid it on with a trowel** when he was introducing that film star.	praised somebody or something excessively (informal)	Celia: Well said: that was laid on with a trowel. (*As You Like It*)
The film is a classic love story about **star-crossed lovers**.	people unlucky in love	Prologue: A pair of star-crossed lovers take their life. (*Romeo and Juliet*)
The prime minister **was hoist with his own petard** when the tax laws he had introduced led to his downfall.	caused problems for himself (by doing something that he thought would help him or that would hurt other people)	Hamlet: For 'tis the sport to have the enginer / Hoist with his own petard. (*Hamlet*)
Ted and Sylvia have broken up again! **The course of true love never did run smooth**.	There are always difficulties to face in romantic relationships.	Lysander: The course of true love never did run smooth. (*A Midsummer Night's Dream*)

Exercises

22.1 Replace the underlined part of each sentence with an idiom.

1 The film is about two <u>people unlucky in love</u> and their relationship.
2 Dom and his friends <u>managed to eat all the food I had in the house</u>.
3 Harry's driving <u>terrified me</u>, but we arrived safely.
4 He set off on <u>a hopeless quest</u> to find the buried treasure he'd read about.
5 Having criticised the previous government for their financial scandals, the new president was <u>caught in his own trap</u> when he was arrested for fraud.
6 Masha prepared a delicious meal <u>in what seemed like no time at all</u>.
7 <u>Jealousy</u> is responsible for many crimes of passion.
8 The reviewer didn't praise the play subtly – he <u>went on and on about how wonderful it was</u>.

22.2 Complete each idiom.

1 So, Helen's parents are trying to persuade her not to get married to Tom? Oh well, the course of .... love never did run .... !
2 This thriller is terrifying. It'll make your hair stand on ....
3 I need to go shopping. The kids have eaten us out of .... and home.
4 I'll just let the cat out, then I'll be with you in the twinkling of an ....
5 Let's try and write all our holiday postcards at one fell .... this morning.

22.3 Which idioms do these pictures make you think of?

1
2
3
4

22.4 Complete each sentence with an idiom from 22.3.

1 The bank robbers left the country after they had cleverly managed to send the police off on a ....
2 The ghost story David told made ....
3 Maya and Harry's relationship was destroyed by ....
4 Simply tell your daughter that you like her work. There's no need to ....

> **FOLLOW UP**
> 'Pound of flesh' and 'send someone packing' are two other idioms from Shakespeare. Look at this website and check their meanings. You could also make a note of any other Shakespearean idioms in common usage that you find there: http://www.phrases.org.uk/meanings/phrases-sayings-shakespeare.html

23 Literature

A Famous literary characters

example	explanation
My grandmother's attic was **an Aladdin's cave** of old paintings and other valuable objects.	In *The Arabian Nights*, Aladdin is imprisoned in a cave full of treasure.
All the cameras on our streets mean that **Big Brother** is watching us all the time.	Big Brother is the dictator who watches everybody all the time in George Orwell's novel *1984*.
When I was learning to play golf, Jack was my **Man Friday**. He advised me and even carried all my equipment. (You may also see **Girl** or **Person Friday**)	Man Friday is the servant on a desert island in Daniel Defoe's novel *Robinson Crusoe*.
Larry is a real **Jekyll and Hyde** character. One minute he's happy and friendly, the next minute he's aggressive and violent.	Jekyll and Hyde represent two opposite sides of Dr Jekyll's personality in R. L. Stevenson's novel *The Strange Case of Dr Jekyll and Mr Hyde*.
I'm single and still waiting for **Prince Charming** to appear on his white horse!	Prince Charming is the handsome prince in many fairy tales. The expression is often used humorously.

B Horoscopes

The idioms in these horoscopes all come from novels, plays, fairy tales and poems.

ARIES Someone asks you to take on a big responsibility, but be careful: it may become **an albatross around your neck**[1].

TAURUS You meet someone this week who you think will play an important role in your life. But be prepared to say goodbye; you may **be like ships that pass in the night**[2].

GEMINI You sometimes feel that your hopes and ambitions are just **castles in the air**[3]. But hold on to your dreams; one of them will soon come true.

CANCER You find yourself in **a Catch-22 situation**[4] with someone very close to you. One of you needs to be mature and act first, but who will it be?

LEO You have decided you need a new challenge. Why not **go the whole hog**[5]: sell your house, leave town and travel the world?

VIRGO Spending all your time studying has put you in **an ivory tower**[6]. Try to live life more in the real world, not just with your books.

LIBRA There may be a big argument with someone close to you. But don't worry: it will just be **a storm in a teacup**[7].

SCORPIO You don't like offending people, but sometimes you have **to call a spade a spade**[8]. Don't be afraid to say something that may hurt someone.

[1] a problem that it is difficult to be free of [2] people who come into your life and leave again after a short time [3] plans that have very little chance of happening [4] an impossible situation where you are prevented from doing one thing until you have done another thing, but you cannot do the other thing until you have done the first thing [5] do something as completely as possible [6] a situation where you are separated from the ordinary and unpleasant things that happen in life [7] a situation where people get very angry or worried about something that is not important [8] to tell the truth about something, even if it is not polite or pleasant

Exercises

23.1 Answer these questions. Use the information in A to help you.

1 Which servant helped Robinson Crusoe?
2 What was the surname of Dr Jekyll's evil persona?
3 Who do fairy-tale heroines fall in love with?
4 Which authoritarian figure do we say watches everything we do?
5 Who found himself in a cave full of treasure?

23.2 Complete each sentence with a literary character from 23.1.

1 My sister's getting married next week. I'm so happy she's found her ....
2 The internet service providers know exactly which websites we visit – .... is watching us all the time.
3 My life is totally chaotic. I need a .... to help me with everything.
4 The old cupboard was a(n) ....'s cave of valuable objects.
5 Roberto is a real Jekyll and .... character. You can never predict how he's going to behave.

23.3 Rewrite the underlined part of each sentence using the word in brackets.

1 Don't worry, it's just <u>one of those problems where everyone gets upset and then it's forgotten</u>. (STORM)
2 He wants to borrow a lot of money to go travelling, but paying it back could become <u>a problem that he can't escape from.</u> (NECK)
3 Why are you just getting a new fridge and cooker? Why not <u>do things completely</u> and get a new kitchen? (WHOLE)
4 He's always got some new money-making plan or scheme, but most of the time they're just <u>plans that will never happen</u>. (AIR)
5 I met him ten years ago and then saw him again last year. We seem to <u>be like people who enter and leave each other's lives after a short time</u>. (SHIPS)

23.4 Match the beginning of each sentence with its ending.

1 She's very direct and always calls	Catch-22 situation.
2 I found myself in a ridiculous	a storm in a teacup.
3 People say that academics live in	ivory towers.
4 There's nothing to worry about; it's just	a spade a spade.

23.5 Which idioms do these pictures make you think of?

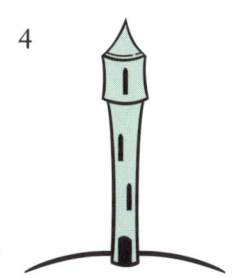

> **FOLLOW UP**
> Use the Internet to find out the literary origins of the idioms in B. The Phrase Finder at www.phrases.org.uk is a good place to start your research.

24 Science and technology

A Science and technology idioms in positive contexts

Some science- and technology-based idioms are used to evaluate things in a positive way. Read these magazine reviews and note the idioms.

> The *Soundboom 88* software suite is **at the cutting edge**[1] of audio technology, providing a complete home studio.

> This new web search engine is **the brainchild of**[3] Alex Wells, who originally developed the *Worldseek* software.

> **Hot off the press**[2], this online survey of consumer preferences is essential for anyone setting up a small business.

> With its modern design and functionality, the *Autoband* USB turntable **pushes** all **the right buttons**[4].

[1] at the most recent stage of development in a particular type of work or activity [2] has just been printed and contains the most recent information [3] a clever and original idea, plan or invention [4] does exactly what is necessary to get the result you want

B Science and technology idioms in negative contexts

Science- and technology-based idioms can also be used to evaluate things in a more negative way. Read this conversation about a problem at work and note the idioms.

Archie: We're **light years away from**[1] developing good software for our customer database. The hardware doesn't help either. The main computer **is on the blink**[2] and needs replacing.

Joanna: Well, we can replace the computer, but I thought the database was OK.

Archie: So did I, but Krishnan **threw a spanner in the works**[3] when he found some faults in its design.

Joanna: Well, we should be able to sort that out. I mean, **it's not rocket science**[4], is it? There must be software we can use. Trying to do it all ourselves may mean we're just **reinventing the wheel**[5].

Archie: Yes, but we want to do it properly. In some ways, the old system we had worked fine – you know what they say, '**If it ain't broke, don't fix it**[6]!'

Joanna: Well, if we don't fix things soon, the system will **go haywire**[7] and we won't be able to contact our customers. I think you should order a new computer and replace the software.

Archie: I'm not authorised to do that. I'm just **a** small **cog in the machine** here[8].

[1] it will be a very long time before [2] not working correctly [3] did something that prevented a plan from succeeding [4] used to say that something is not very difficult to do or to understand (humorous) [5] wasting time trying to create something that someone else has already created [6] said when you see that something works well, and there is no reason to try to change it [7] stop working normally and start working in a different and strange way (informal) [8] one part of a large organisation

C Other science- and technology-based idioms

The government has **set the wheels in motion**[1] for a complete reform of the tax system.
My new car is very economical. The old one was such a **gas guzzler**[2].
Government investment has **oiled the wheels**[3] of economic development in the poorer regions.

[1] done something which will cause a series of actions to start [2] car that uses a lot of fuel [3] made it easier for something to happen

Exercises

24.1
Look at A. Read these statements and answer the questions.

Rob: I got his new book the day it was published.
Matthew: My new MP3 player is great: it's easy to use, it looks good, and it was cheap.
Clara: This phone has features that no other phone has yet; it's amazing.
Julian: Apparently it was invented by a Russian scientist who worked on it for ten years.

Who is talking about ...	name
1 something that is at the cutting edge of technology?	
2 something that was hot off the press?	
3 something that pushes the right buttons?	
4 something that was the brainchild of someone?	

24.2
Rewrite the underlined part of each sentence using the word in brackets.

1 I try my best to do my job well, but sometimes I feel as if I'm just an unimportant person in a massive organisation. (MACHINE)
2 I don't want to do anything to prevent your plan from working, but I think you should apply for official permission first. (SPANNER)
3 I worry sometimes that we're just wasting time doing something someone has already done in our research. (WHEEL)
4 I'm afraid I couldn't print the document; our printer is not working properly. (BLINK)
5 There was a power failure and everything suddenly stopped working. (HAYWIRE)
6 She should be able to write a simple text message. I mean, it's not a difficult thing to do, is it? (SCIENCE)
7 I think we're a long time away from finding a cure for this terrible disease. (LIGHT)
8 Why change the system? If it works OK, we don't need to do anything! (BROKE)

24.3
Choose the correct answer.

1 If you oil the wheels of something, you a) make something happen very suddenly b) make it easier for something to happen c) stop something happening.
2 A gas guzzler is a) a type of cooker b) a person who drinks a lot c) a type of car.
3 If you set the wheels in motion for something, you a) cause it to start b) create complications for it c) cause it to stop.
4 If a machine is on the blink, it a) is working correctly b) is not working at all c) is working, but not correctly.

24.4
Here are some errors made with idioms by candidates in advanced-level exams. Can you correct them?

1 My school was new. We had all kinds of cutting-hedge technology.
2 Suddenly, everything went hayware and there was complete chaos.
3 She felt she was just a cog in the wheel and that no one ever noticed her.
4 The city council set the wheel to turn for the construction of the new park.

25 Films, plays and books

A Idioms from film and theatre reviews

The show had the audience **rolling in the aisles**[1].

The plot will **keep you on the edge of your seat**[4].

The finale **brought the house down**[2].

His dramatic performance **sent shivers down my spine**[5].

Helena Good **stole the show**[3] with a fantastic performance.

[1] laughing a lot [2] made the audience laugh or clap a lot; was extremely successful [3] got all the attention and praise at an event or performance [4] keep you excited and interested in what happens next [5] was very moving

B Talking about books

Ken: I read that novel that Laura recommended. I eventually managed to **wade through**[1] all 400 pages, but I didn't like it very much. It was really **heavy going**[2]. It's not what I would call **a page-turner**[3]!

Nina: Yeah. The critics in the Sunday papers certainly **did a hatchet job on**[4] it.

Ken: Well, it's pretty easy to **pick holes in**[5] the plot. I didn't think it was at all convincing.

Nina: Mind you, I could never write a short story, let alone a novel.

Ken: Yes, it's much easier to be **an armchair critic**[6], isn't it?

[1] finish reading something, but with difficulty [2] difficult to read or understand [3] a book that is so exciting that you have to read it quickly [4] criticised strongly and cruelly [5] find mistakes in; criticise 6 criticise, but without any personal expertise in what is being criticised (You can also say 'armchair traveller' and 'armchair gardener'.)

C An actor's career

Portia Cole had always dreamt of **having her name in lights**[1]. At school she was **a leading light**[2] of the drama club, and she spent all her free time **treading the boards**[3]. Portia's tendency to **play to the gallery**[4] meant she was quickly noticed when she started acting professionally. When she got the opportunity to take over the leading role in a popular new **crowd-puller**[5] in a major London theatre, she was **waiting in the wings**[6], ready and eager to **take centre stage**[7]. She was surprised to feel very nervous before her opening night. However, all her friends and relatives assured her that it would be **all right on the night**[8], and it was! The audience and the critics loved her, and her career was well and truly launched.

[1] being famous [2] an important member [3] acting on stage (in the theatre) [4] behave in a way to make people admire or support her; often slightly disapproving [5] something attracting a lot of attention and interest [6] ready to become important (this idiom is often used in non-theatrical contexts too, e.g. 'Investors are **waiting in the wings**, ready to act if the business is sold'.) [7] become the most important person in the play (this idiom is often used in non-theatrical contexts too, e.g. 'Education **took centre stage** in the new political manifesto'.) [8] without problems on the day of the actual performance

Exercises

25.1 Match the beginning of each sentence with its ending.

1 The critics didn't hesitate to pick
2 The hero's dying words sent
3 The comedian's jokes brought
4 It took me all of my holiday to wade
5 The singers were all great, but the young soprano stole
6 The play was so funny it had the audience rolling
7 The film was really exciting and kept us on the edge
8 The *Sunday News* critic hated the book and did a

shivers down my spine.
in the aisles.
hatchet job on it.
holes in the actor's performance.
of our seats.
through that novel.
the show.
the house down.

25.2 Which idioms do these pictures make you think of?

25.3 Complete each sentence. There may be more than one possible answer.

1 When a politician plays to the gallery, it is because they want people to .... them.
2 People say 'It'll be all right on the night' when they want to .... you.
3 The boards referred to in 'tread the boards' are those of a ....
4 .... people would be at a crowd-pulling show.
5 .... people do not usually enjoy taking centre stage.

25.4 Rewrite the underlined part of each sentence using the word in brackets.

1 Richard is an important person in the local tennis club. (LIGHT)
2 The teacher was very critical of my essay. (PICKED)
3 Don't worry about your presentation. It'll all go well, I'm sure. (NIGHT)
4 The dog got all the attention in the evening's performance. (STOLE)
5 She spent years acting in the theatre before getting a part in a TV soap. (BOARDS)
6 The new manager is good at saying things that make her popular. (GALLERY)
7 The book was very difficult to read. (HEAVY)
8 I can't believe that the *Sunday News* critic described such a boring novel as a book you just have to read quickly. (PAGE)

26 Relationships – friends and family

A Family relationships

Liz and Tricia are talking about their families. The idioms they use are fairly informal.

Liz: How quickly time passes! It seems like only yesterday that my son Jason was **a twinkle in his father's eye**[1], and now suddenly he's eighteen and about to **fly the nest**[2]. He's got a job in Spain, so he's moving there.

Tricia: Yes, my son Richard's the same. He's twenty-one, and he's **the spitting image of**[3] his dad now. He's just like him in character too – he's a real **chip off the old block**[4]! They're both so tall too – tall men seem to **run in the family**[5]. Richard's already left home – we only see him a couple of times a year.

Liz: Yes, it's sad when your **nearest and dearest**[6] move away. Our daughter lives in the US, and we hardly ever see her. It's hard not being able to visit **your own flesh and blood**[7] very often.

Tricia: Yes. But then, you know, our family always preferred being independent. We never **lived in each other's pockets**[8], so I suppose this is the result.

[1] was not even born (humorous) [2] leave home to live independently [3] looks very much like [4] similar in personality to one of his parents or an older family member [5] a lot of people in the family have that characteristic 6 your family (humorous) [7] relatives [8] did everything together

B Friends and other social contacts

Note the idioms in these horoscopes.

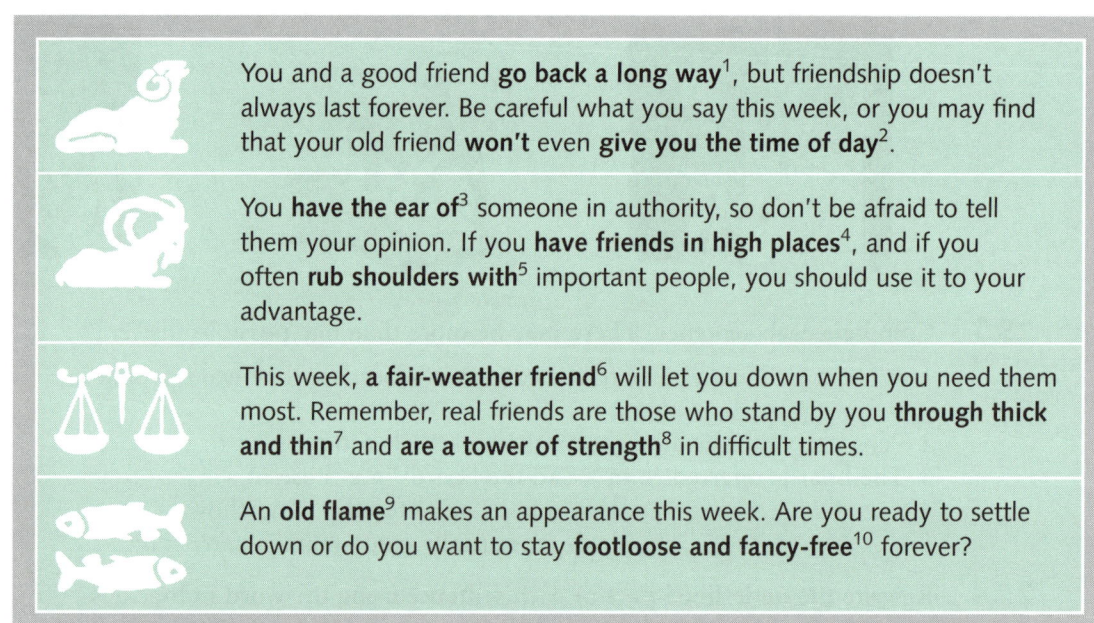

> You and a good friend **go back a long way**[1], but friendship doesn't always last forever. Be careful what you say this week, or you may find that your old friend **won't** even **give you the time of day**[2].

> You **have the ear of**[3] someone in authority, so don't be afraid to tell them your opinion. If you **have friends in high places**[4], and if you often **rub shoulders with**[5] important people, you should use it to your advantage.

> This week, **a fair-weather friend**[6] will let you down when you need them most. Remember, real friends are those who stand by you **through thick and thin**[7] and **are a tower of strength**[8] in difficult times.

> An **old flame**[9] makes an appearance this week. Are you ready to settle down or do you want to stay **footloose and fancy-free**[10] forever?

[1] have known each other a long time [2] will refuse to speak to you because they think they're better than you or they don't like you [3] the person is ready to listen to your views and ideas [4] know important and influential people [5] spend time with important or famous people [6] someone who is your friend only when things are going well for you [7] through good and bad situations [8] someone who supports you a lot in difficult situations. (You can also say 'pillar of strength'.) [9] someone you had a romantic relationship with in the past [10] free and without responsibilities to anyone

Exercises

26.1 Look at A. Match the beginning of each sentence with its ending.

1 They invited their nearest
2 We don't live in each other's
3 He has deserted his own flesh
4 Young Walter is the spitting
5 She was just a twinkle in her
6 When he turned 18, he flew
7 Harry is a real chip off
8 Kay and her mum are pretty. Good looks

father's eye three years ago!
the old block – he's just like his uncle Rex.
the nest and went to live in Australia.
and dearest to the wedding.
run in the family.
pockets, but we're a happy family.
and blood and gone to join the army.
image of his grandfather.

26.2 Complete each sentence with an idiom from 26.1.

1 Heather is the .... her mother – she looks just like her.
2 How could you harm your brother? He's your own .... and ....
3 She was born in 1986. In 1983, she was just a .... in ....
4 All her .... and .... gathered round her for a family photo on her 90th birthday.
5 I'd hate the sort of family where everybody lives ....
6 He's 42 and still living with his parents. Most people .... a lot earlier.
7 All of her sisters are really musical too. It must ....
8 Max is as generous as his dad. He's a ....

26.3 Read these statements and answer the questions.

Lidia: My so-called friend Sheila doesn't even give me the time of day any more.
Connor: My friend Lorna has been with me through thick and thin.
Ashley: I've got friends in high places, you know.
Chelsea: My best friend and I go back a long way.
Zenab: I've come to the conclusion that Ben is just a fair-weather friend.

1 Who has known someone for many years?	
2 Who has a friend who is only there when things are going well?	
3 Who has a friend who won't speak to her?	
4 Who has a friend who has given a lot of support in difficult times?	
5 Who knows powerful and influential people?	

26.4 Rewrite each sentence using an idiom from the opposite page.

1 If the boss listens to him and respects his ideas, we should let him represent us.
2 Joanna was incredibly supportive when I was going through a bad time.
3 Hilda has invited a former boyfriend of hers to the party on Saturday.
4 My friend Roger has stood by me through good times and bad times.
5 He was independent and had no responsibilities until he was 25; then he got married.
6 I've known Raisa a very long time.

27 People – character and behaviour

A Positive characteristics and behaviour

In this conversation, Lucy uses an idiom to repeat and sum up what Beth says.

Lucy: I'm trying to organise a quiz team. Who do you think I should ask?
Beth: Why not ask Jim? He knows a lot about all sorts of different things.
Lucy: You're right. He's **a mine of information**.
Beth: He can do all sorts of different things too. He's good at sport and he's set up his own software business, which is doing very well, I believe.
Lucy: That's right. He's **a man of many parts**[1].
Beth: Why don't you ask Matt as well? He's young, but he's so clever and really successful.
Lucy: Yes, he's **a whizz kid**, if ever there was one! Good idea!
Beth: His sister Sue is nice too, isn't she? Full of energy and enthusiasm.
Lucy: That's right. She's got plenty of **get-up and go**.
Beth: She'd be great in a quiz too. She's a trained chef; she's a qualified singing teacher, so she knows about music; and she's studying film at college.
Lucy: Yes, she **has plenty of strings to her bow**. Thanks, Beth. I'll ask them all!

[1] You can also say 'woman of many parts'.

B Negative characteristics and behaviour

idiom	example	meaning
a glutton for punishment	She's certainly **a glutton for punishment**. She's started doing a second degree, even though she's got a full-time job and two small children.	someone who likes working hard or doing things other people would find unpleasant (humorous)
highly strung	She's so **highly strung** that even a loud noise can make her jump.	very nervous and easily upset
act / play the fool	He'd be a nicer person if he didn't **play the fool** so much.	behave in a silly way, often to make people laugh
look out for number one	Trust Fred to take the last piece of cake. He always **looks out for number one**.	puts himself first, as he thinks he is the most important person (informal)
eat sb for breakfast	The lawyers are going to **eat** the accused man **for breakfast**.	speak angrily or critically to easily control or defeat someone
a love-rat	Movie star Jake King was exposed as **a love-rat** yesterday, when details of his affair with co-star Kelly Black emerged.	a man having a secret sexual relationship with someone not his wife or girlfriend. (informal, mainly used in popular journalism)
a wet blanket	Stop complaining about the weather. It's not that cold. Enjoy the picnic and stop being such **a wet blanket**.	someone who says or does something that stops others from enjoying themselves (informal)
a loose cannon	Our sales manager is **a loose cannon**. You never know what he'll say or do next.	someone who cannot be trusted because they act in an unpredictable way

Exercises

27.1 Look at A. Complete each idiom.

1 Let's hire Dan. He has a lot of get .... and go, and will really inspire the team.
2 He's a person with many skills and talents, a true man of many ....
3 The restaurant is popular with banking whizz .... , all talking loudly about the financial deals they're doing.
4 Schools often encourage their students to collect as many .... to their bow as possible.
5 Ask Aunt Fran to help with your geography project – she's a .... of information about different places.

27.2 Correct the mistakes in these idioms.

1 Concentrate on your homework and stop playing a fool!
2 I hope Joe doesn't come to the party – he's such a cold blanket.
3 I suppose that everyone ultimately has to look out for figure one.
4 Kate volunteers for all the jobs that no one else will do – she's a real glutton for work.
5 I always said she was a loose gun, so I'm not surprised she's causing trouble.
6 The newspapers are claiming that the prince is a love-snake.
7 Be extra kind and calm with Jarek – he's very tightly strung.
8 Everyone admires the young entrepreneur for his get-up and buy.

27.3 Which idioms do these pictures make you think of?

1
2
3
4

27.4 Replace the underlined part of each sentence with an idiom.

1 I'm really scared about meeting them. I'm sure they'll <u>be angry and criticise me</u>.
2 I don't want to be <u>miserable and spoil your fun</u>, but please can you turn the music down? It's too loud.
3 Some people say that to succeed in business, you need to <u>put your own interests first</u>.
4 There always seems to be a child in every class who <u>acts in a silly way</u> to make the other pupils laugh.
5 Martina would be easier to live with if she weren't so <u>nervous and easily upset</u>.
6 Some see him as <u>an unpredictable and untrustworty person</u>, but this is unfair.

28 People – appearance

A Talking about people's looks

Amy: That new sales manager is very **easy on the eye**[1], isn't he?
Kate: Yes, he's **drop-dead gorgeous**[2]!
Amy: It's nice to have some **eye candy**[3] at work.
Kate: It certainly makes a change. The last sales manager **wasn't much to look at**[4].
Amy: Didn't you think so? I thought he was quite good-looking. Oh well. **Beauty's in the eye of the beholder**[5], I suppose.
Kate: How very wise you are!
Amy: Well, I'm **not just a pretty face**[6]!

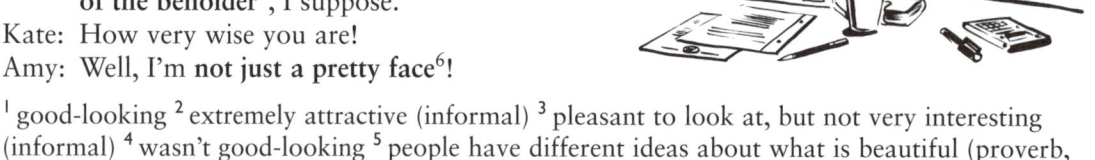

[1] good-looking [2] extremely attractive (informal) [3] pleasant to look at, but not very interesting (informal) [4] wasn't good-looking [5] people have different ideas about what is beautiful (proverb, *behold* is an old-fashioned word meaning *see*) [6] clever as well as attractive (humorous)

B Ways of dressing

idiom	example	meaning
done up / dressed up like a dog's dinner	She was **dressed up like a dog's dinner** at the reception, in a big hat, lots of make-up and ridiculous shoes.	wearing clothes which made her look silly when she had dressed for a formal occasion (informal)
done up / dressed up to the nines	I never normally wear smart clothes or much make-up, but it's fun to get **done up to the nines** occasionally.	wearing very stylish and fashionable clothes, often for a particular occasion (informal)
dressed to kill	Selina's **dressed to kill** today, isn't she! I wonder who she's trying to impress?	intentionally wearing clothes to attract attention and admiration
your glad rags	Come on, put **your glad rags** on. I'm going to take you out to dinner.	your best clothes (humorous)
mutton dressed as lamb	A miniskirt at her age? She looks like **mutton dressed as lamb**!	dressed in a way more suitable for a younger woman (*mutton* is meat from an older sheep, whereas *lamb* is meat from a young sheep) (informal, disapproving)
down-at-heel	Henry is very **down-at-heel** since his business collapsed.	wearing old clothes that are in bad condition because of not having enough money

C Other appearance idioms

I'm developing quite **a middle-age spread** – I must start doing more exercise. [fat around the waist that sometimes develops as you get older]

Timmy was a naughty little boy, but he always looked as if **butter wouldn't melt in his mouth**. [he could never do anything wrong]

If you're going for a job as a lawyer, you'd better **look the part** and wear a smart suit for the interview. [look suitable for a particular situation]

She's **the spitting image of** her grandmother. [looks exactly like]

Exercises

28.1 Look at A. Correct the mistakes in these idioms.

1 Her new boyfriend is really attractive, but he's so boring! He's just eye sweets.
2 Beauty is in the eye of the spectator.
3 Of course my idea's a good one! I'm not just a pretty head!
4 I've never met my brother's boss, but my brother says she's not much for looking at.
5 I love that film star. He's fall-dead gorgeous!
6 His new girlfriend is really pretty; she's very simple on the eye.

28.2 Which idiom is the odd one out? Choose a, b or c.

1 The woman was a) easy on the eye b) drop-dead gorgeous c) not just a pretty face.
2 Milly went out a) dressed to kill b) like mutton dressed as lamb c) done up to the nines.
3 The new teacher a) isn't much to look at b) is rather down-at-heel c) is easy on the eye.
4 My uncle a) is the spitting image of Ted b) has developed a serious middle-age spread c) has put his glad rags on.

28.3 Complete each idiom.

1 done up / dressed up like a dog's ....
2 your .... rags
3 look the ....
4 dressed to ....
5 .... dressed as lamb
6 not just a .... face

28.4 Complete each sentence with an idiom from 28.3.

1 We'll need to leave for the wedding soon. Hurry up and put .... on.
2 She's 50, but she dresses like a teenager. She looks like ....
3 If you want to get a good job in a bank, you'll have to stop dressing like a student and make an effort to ....
4 Even on an ordinary day at work, Gemma is .... in high heels and a smart suit. I wonder who she's trying to impress!
5 As well as being extremely good-looking, that actor is a very good businessman. He's .... !
6 The actress looked ridiculous at the film première – too much jewellery and a very short dress. She really was ....

28.5 Agree with what A says. Complete each dialogue with an idiom.

1 A: Karl has put on a lot of weight since he hit 50, hasn't he?
  B: Yes, he's getting a real ....
2 A: Paul looks just like George Clooney, doesn't he?
  B: Absolutely. He's ....
3 A: It's unlike Naomi to be so badly dressed, isn't it?
  B: That's right. She's never normally so ....
4 A: I don't like his new girlfriend. She's not even that good-looking.
  B: No, she's ....
5 A: You'd never believe that Billy could be so naughty, would you?
  B: No, he looks as if ....

29 Crime and punishment

A Crime

Carlos and Ayse are talking about a crime at work. Read the conversation and note the idioms. All the idioms they use are informal.

Carlos: I'd never have dreamt Russ **was on the fiddle**[1], would you?
Ayse: Well, no. I knew money was going missing, but I never thought it would be **an inside job**[2]. Russ seemed so honest, yet he **had his hand in the till**[3] all the time.
Carlos: Yeah, he **pulled the wool over everyone's eyes**[4].
Ayse: I can't believe he was **taking us all for a ride**[5]. He was so strict with us and yet he **was lining his own pockets**[6] the whole time!
Carlos: He sacked Jay when he was found selling things **under the counter**[7] last year.
Ayse: I know! And now Russ has **done a runner**[8].
Carlos: Well, I hope they catch up with him.

[1] was getting money in an illegal or dishonest way
[2] a crime committed by someone from within the organisation affected
[3] was stealing the business's money
[4] deceived everyone
[5] tricking us
[6] was making money for himself in a dishonest way
[7] secretly; illegally
[8] run away to avoid a difficult situation

Today we'd like you to tell us what you think about police and punishment in today's world. Is **the long arm of the law**[1] doing a good job?

They're too quick to **throw the book at**[2] people. Why should someone **do a stretch**[3] for a minor offence? **Doing time**[4] just makes people more likely to commit another crime when they're released.

The boys in blue[8] should recruit more reformed criminals. There's nothing more effective than a **poacher turned gamekeeper**[9]!

I think young offenders should always be **brought to book**[5]. **A short sharp shock**[6] would keep them **on the straight and narrow**[7] in future.

B Punishment

[1] the police (suggesting it has far-reaching powers)
[2] punish someone as severely as possible (informal)
[3] have a prison sentence (informal)
[4] spending time in prison (informal)
[5] be punished (usually used in the passive)
[6] a brief but severe punishment
[7] behaving in an honest, moral way
[8] the police (informal)
[9] someone whose job involves working against the kind of person they used to be

Exercises

29.1 Read these comments about people's attitudes to banks. Complete each idiom.

Interviewer: 'Do you think banks are honest and open?'

1 'No. There's too much secrecy and too many deals done under the .... They should be more open.'
2 'Well, I think there are a minority of bankers who are just .... own .... , which gives the banks a bad name.'
3 'They're OK on the whole. But occasionally you get major financial crime involving billions of pounds. And often it's an inside .... involving someone working in the bank. We all suffer then.'
4 'No, banks are on the .... all the time, defrauding us and pulling the .... over our .... about what's really going on.'
5 'Well, I think the banks are .... us all for a .... They never lose out – it's always the ordinary customers who suffer.'

29.2 Match each statement (1–9) with a suitable response (a–i).

1 I think teenagers who commit a crime should be sent to prison for a week and given a really hard time.
2 I see the police have been called in about the missing money at the tennis club.
3 People who throw litter in the street ought to be prosecuted.
4 Wow, the police charged Tony with every possible offence they could think of!
5 It didn't take long for the police to arrive, did it?
6 I heard that Donald was actually in prison years ago.
7 Apparently, Angela Smith was in prison when she was younger.
8 That famous computer hacker, Jin Soon, is apparently a reformed character.
9 It's amazing how that former burglar is helping the police investigate crime in the neigbourhood.

a Yes, they say she did time for attacking her husband's lover.
b Yes, it's a real case of poacher turned gamekeeper.
c Yes, I agree. They should be brought to book.
d Yes, someone told me he had done a stretch, but I don't know what for.
e Yes, the thieves won't be able to escape from the long arm of the law.
f Yes, a short sharp shock would do them good!
g No, the boys in blue were soon on the scene!
h Yes, they really threw the book at him, didn't they!
i Yes, he's back on the straight and narrow.

29.3 Are these sentences true or false? If the answer is false, say why.

1 If someone has their hand in the till, they are illegally taking money from a business.
2 If someone does a runner, they chase after a criminal.
3 An inside job is a crime committed by someone from within the organisation affected.
4 If someone does a stretch, they tell the police who committed a crime.

> **FOLLOW UP**
> Find a newspaper article relating to crime on the Internet. Either go to a newspaper site or use a search engine to look for 'crime stories in the news'. Try to find three or four idioms used in the article. Write them down in their context.

30 Work

A Describing people's work situation

Read these comments by people about work situations. Idioms marked * in this unit are particularly informal.

'Clare's babysitting job is such **a cushy number***. All she has to do is take the children to the beach and watch them play.' [a very easy job]

'Sylvia's really **at the top of the ladder** now. She finally has the success she deserves.' [in the highest position in an organisation]

'I took the job at Linderhoffs to **get a foot in the door**, even though it wasn't well paid.' [a job at a low level in an organisation, which you take because you want a better job in the same organisation in the future]

'I **slogged my guts out*** for years in the water company and never got a pay rise.' [worked very hard or used a lot of effort]

'Trevor doesn't do very much, even though he owns half the company. He's just **a sleeping partner**.' [a partner in a company who does not take an active part in its management, but often provides some of the money; you can also say 'silent partner']

'Erica has a good **track record** as a sales person. She deserves to be promoted.' [all the achievements or failures that someone or something has had in the past]

'Did Charlie get **a golden handshake** when he left the company?' [a large payment made to someone when they leave their job, either because their employer has asked them to leave, or as a reward for good service when they retire]

'She got a very generous **golden hello** when she started her first job after university.' [a large payment made to someone when they accept a new job]

B The world of work

These business news cuttings contain idioms used to talk about the world of work and business. Idioms describing work and business are often quite strong and colourful.

Roaflex is **doing a roaring trade**[1]* and has effectively **cornered the market**[2] in camping equipment. 'The company is **going great guns**[3]*. We've had a record year,' its president said today.

More travel agents will **go belly up**[4]* if the economic recession continues. Two major operators have already **gone to the wall**[5]: Worldex **went bust**[6]* in February, and Overglobe closed in April.

'The big international companies dominate the fast-food market and we're **shutting up shop**[7]*. We can't compete any more. I'm getting out of **the rat race**[8] and retiring to Spain,' said the owner of a small sandwich bar.

'I worked very hard and hoped I would get a promotion,' said Ms Kirby, 'but now I realise I've hit **a glass ceiling**[9] and won't go any further in this company.'

[1] selling a lot of goods very quickly [2] become so successful at selling a product that almost no one else sells it [3] doing something very successfully [4] fail [5] been destroyed financially [6] was forced to close because of financial problems [7] closing the business [8] a way of life in which people compete with each other for power and money [9] a point after which you cannot progress in your career (The idiom is mainly used to express the idea that women are unable to progress because the top jobs are only given to men in some companies.)

> **TIP** Always make a special note if an idiom is very informal, and be careful not to use informal idioms in formal situations.

Exercises

30.1 Which idioms do these pictures make you think of?

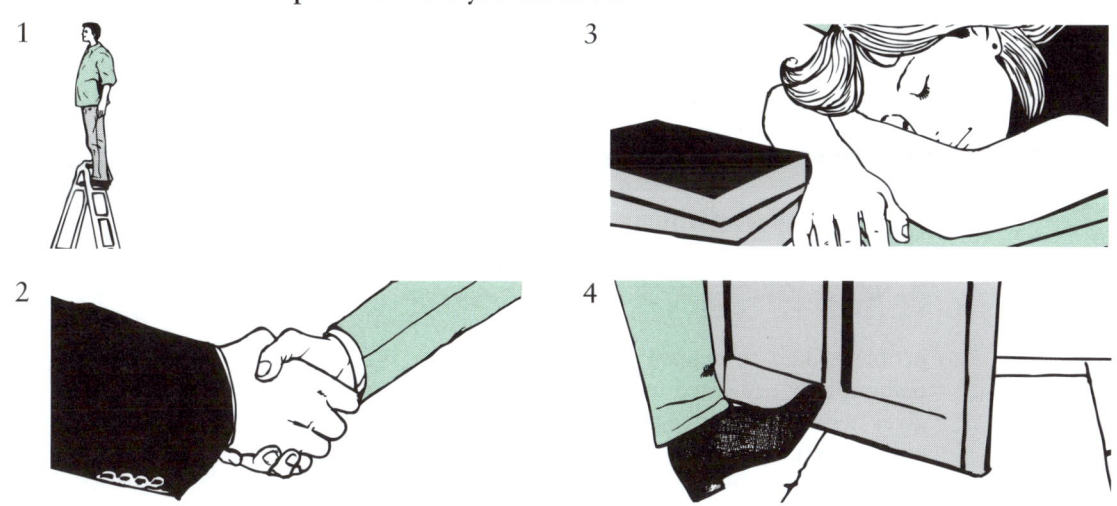

1
2
3
4

30.2 Complete each sentence with an idiom from 30.1.

1 She founded the company, but she's not very active in it now. She's just a ....
2 He desperately wanted to work in the film industry, so he got a job carrying camera equipment to get ....
3 When he retired, the company gave him a ....
4 It took him years to become chief executive, but he's .... now.

30.3 Do these sentences make sense? Explain why / why not.

1 She had a good track record, so they fired her.
2 It was a cushy number, so he had to work very hard indeed.
3 I slogged my guts out and was exhausted.
4 She changed jobs and got a golden hello from her new employer.
5 The shop was doing a roaring trade, so they had to close down.
6 Porterfax Ltd went belly up and employed 30 new staff.
7 Opticarm cornered the market in digital cameras and faced strong competition.
8 He went to live in the country because he was tired of the rat race.

30.4 Rewrite the underlined part of each sentence using the word in brackets.

1 Our new online business is <u>doing extremely well</u>. (GUNS)
2 Some airlines are in danger of <u>collapsing financially</u>. (WALL)
3 That new farmers' market seems to be <u>selling a lot of goods</u>. (ROAR)
4 Mr Olsen decided to <u>close his business</u> and retire to the coast. (SHOP)
5 Another insurance company <u>was forced to close down</u> last week. (BUST)
6 She realised she had hit a <u>point where she could go no higher</u> at work. (GLASS)

31 Business news

A Metaphors in business news

Metaphors (see Unit 4) are frequently used when journalists are writing about business. Notice how these headlines use metaphors from the weather, religion, horse riding, the natural world and the sea.

CLOUD ON THE HORIZON[1] FOR LOCAL FIRM

SMITH OPTS TO BE **BIG FISH IN SMALL POND**[4]

TIME TO STOP **WORSHIPPING AT THE ALTAR OF**[2] CONSUMERISM

AXCO **SADDLED WITH**[5] DEBT

BANK **THROWS** SMALL COMPANIES **A LIFELINE**[3]

[1] problem likely to happen in the future
[2] being totally dedicated to (You can also say 'worship at the shrine / temple of'.)
[3] gives help to someone in a very difficult situation
[4] an important person in a not very important organisation
[5] given a problem which will cause them a lot of difficulty

B Financial news

idiom	example	meaning
the bottom drops / falls out of the market	The bottom **has dropped / fallen out of the** housing **market**.	people have stopped buying something
a ballpark figure	What's **a ballpark figure** for replacing the office furniture?	an estimated price
shoot / soar sky-high	Oil prices **shot sky-high** last month.	rose dramatically
take a nosedive	The company's shares **took a nosedive** yesterday.	fell suddenly and quickly
receive a windfall	Investors will each **receive a windfall** of $10,000.	get some unexpected money
rein in spending	Many firms try to **rein in spending** during times of financial difficulty.	spend less
across the board	The impact of the reorganisation will be felt **across the board**.	by people at every level

C Management news

Following the company's disastrous performance, the CEO has announced that **heads will roll**. [people will be severely punished, often by losing their jobs]

The managing director of Lo-cost supermarkets has been put on **gardening leave** since being offered a new job with rival company Costless. [told not to come into work during their notice period, although they will receive payment for this period]

The EatWell restaurant chain **takes** luxury catering **to the next level**. [makes something even more special or dramatic]

The company's controversial sales manager has been warned that he will lose his job if he does not **fall into line**. [start to follow the rules]

The director said that she **is under no illusions** about how difficult it will be for the company to survive. [understands the truth]

Exercises

31.1 Look at A. Which idioms do these pictures make you think of?

1 2 3 4

31.2 Look at B. Answer these questions.
1 Which idiom is a horse riding metaphor?
2 Which two idioms are metaphors based on flying?
3 Which of the two flying metaphors relates to a bird and which to a plane?
4 Which idiom is based on a metaphor relating to fruit trees?
5 Which idiom is based on a sporting metaphor?
6 Which idiom is based on a metaphor relating to a breaking box?

31.3 Are the idioms in these sentences used correctly? If not, correct them.
1 The speaker said he was concerned about the way in which young people queue at the altar of instant gratification.
2 If people are given gardening leave, they are not allowed to come into work during their notice period.
3 Receiving a sizeable winddrop from one of our investments allowed us to extend our premises.
4 Changes in the company's structure will take place across the boards.
5 Jackson was underneath no illusions about how long it would take his business to get established.
6 Unfortunately, our profits took a nosedive last month.
7 It's time we considered how we can take our business to the next step.
8 The senior staff all went into line with the new CEO's demands.

31.4 Match the beginning of each sentence with its ending.

1 The latest crisis at work means that heads will   with debt.
2 I can't tell you the exact price, but I can give you a ballpark   in a small pond.
3 No one will want to take over a company so saddled   horizon.
4 As our profits have fallen, we'll have to rein   of the market.
5 Jake likes being a big fish   board.
6 There are fears that the bottom may fall out   roll.
7 For the first time in ages there are no clouds on the company's figure.
8 The plan is to implement substantial changes across the in spending.

> **FOLLOW UP**
> Look at the business news on an English-language business newspaper website, e.g. *The Financial Times*, www.ft.com. Make a note of any idioms that you find there.

32 Business meetings

A Features of business language

Business language can be lively but it is sometimes criticised for certain negative features. For example, it can be 'wordy', using more words than are necessary, for example, using **at this moment in time** (instead of 'now') or **on a weekly basis** (instead of 'weekly').

A second negative feature of business language is its use of clichés (certain phrases that are used so often in specific contexts that they lose their originality), for example, **have a window** (have some time available) or **touch base** (talk to each other).

A: Can we **touch base** next week?
B: Sure, I **have a window** on Monday afternoon between two and four.

Many of the idioms in this unit could also be considered clichés.

B Idioms in business meetings

I have two issues to **bring to the table** at our next meeting. [raise for discussion]

It's hard to know what do. We're **between a rock and a hard place**. [whichever decision we make, there is a problem]

The fact of the matter is that we are in a very difficult situation. [the truth is]

I think Hari is the ideal person for the job. He **ticks all the boxes**. [has all the characteristics we want]

The two managers used to be polite to each other; but now **the gloves are off**, and they make no attempt to hide their feelings. [they challenge each other in an unpleasant way (informal)]

We must work **24 / 7** [twenty four seven] to achieve our aims. [all the hours we can]

It's a **dog-eat-dog** world in our line of business. [situation where people will do anything to be successful, even if it is harmful to others]

C Idioms to talk about business ideas

idiom	example	meaning
at the cutting edge	We have to try to develop a product that is truly **at the cutting edge**.	the most up-to-date and advanced
blue-sky thinking	Management are going away for a weekend of **blue-sky thinking** about the company's future.	creative thinking
think outside the box	We hired Frank because of his ability to **think outside the box**.	think in an original and imaginative way
push the envelope	We don't want to lose our company's reputation for **pushing the envelope**.	innovating; going beyond normal boundaries
joined-up thinking	Unfortunately, there hasn't been enough **joined-up thinking** in our approach over the last year.	making appropriate connections
suck it and see	The idea might work, and it might not. We need to just **suck it and see**.	do something you have not done before to find out whether it is successful or not (informal)

Exercises

32.1 Read these comments and answer the questions.

1. "When do you next **have a window**, Sandra?"
   What does the speaker want to find out?

2. "We'll need to **touch base** soon."
   What is the speaker suggesting?

3. "Things are rather difficult **at this moment in time**."
   Why would some people not like this expression?

4. "We should have a meeting **on a weekly basis**."
   Does this sentence mean exactly the same as 'We should have a meeting every week'?

32.2 Which idioms do these pictures make you think of?

32.3 Complete each idiom.

1. I don't know what to advise. The only solution is to .... it and see.
2. The .... of the matter is that the company is now in a very difficult position.
3. We've tried all the obvious solutions. Now we'll have to try thinking outside the ....
4. The two managers have become serious rivals, and the gloves are ....
5. In the business world, it's a matter of dog eat ....
6. There is a need for more joined-.................................. thinking from our managers.
7. It's a very difficult situation. We're between a .... and a hard place.
8. Some of his ideas are very innovative; they really push the ....

32.4 Replace the underlined part of each sentence with an idiom.

1. Do you have any points that you would like <u>us to discuss</u> today?
2. We need to prove that our products are <u>the most up-to-date</u> if we are to stay competitive.
3. They've been working <u>all hours of the day and night</u> to complete the project.
4. <u>The truth is</u> that our previous advertising campaign was not as successful as we had hoped.
5. I have <u>some time when we could meet</u> on Thursday afternoon if that suits you.
6. They chose Mark for the job because he <u>had everything they were looking for</u>.

33 Money

A People's financial circumstances

Alex: If this business idea is as successful as we think it'll be, we'll **be quids in** for a change. [make a profit; *quid* is a colloquial word for a pound sterling (informal)]

Sam: Yes, we'll be **laughing all the way to the bank**. [making a lot of money easily]

Alex: And it will be so easy too – it really will be **money for old rope**. [money that is easily earned (informal)]

Lee: I'd love to get a job with a decent salary. I'm tired of **living on a shoestring**. [living on very little money]

Kumiko: Me too. It would be great **to be rolling in it**, wouldn't it? [to have lots of money (informal)]

Paula: Since my husband lost his job, **I'm the breadwinner** in my family. [person who earns the money the family needs]

Mary: Really? Well, I guess I **bring home the bacon** in my family too. [earn the money the family lives on (informal)]

Pat: Could you lend me twenty pounds?

Phil: Sorry, mate, I'm a bit **strapped for cash** at the moment. [not have enough money]

Dave: That singer's ex-wife – you know the one I mean – she **took him to the cleaner's** when they got divorced. He's ruined! [got as much money from him as she could]

Di: I know – she's so greedy, isn't she? She **would sell her own grandmother**. [would do anything to get money (informal)]

Laura: I can't believe you've bought a new car! We can't afford to **throw money down the drain**. [waste money]

Tim: It's OK. It was **going for a song** – I only paid a few hundred pounds. [being sold very cheaply]

B How people use money

Enter our **rags to riches**[1] competition!

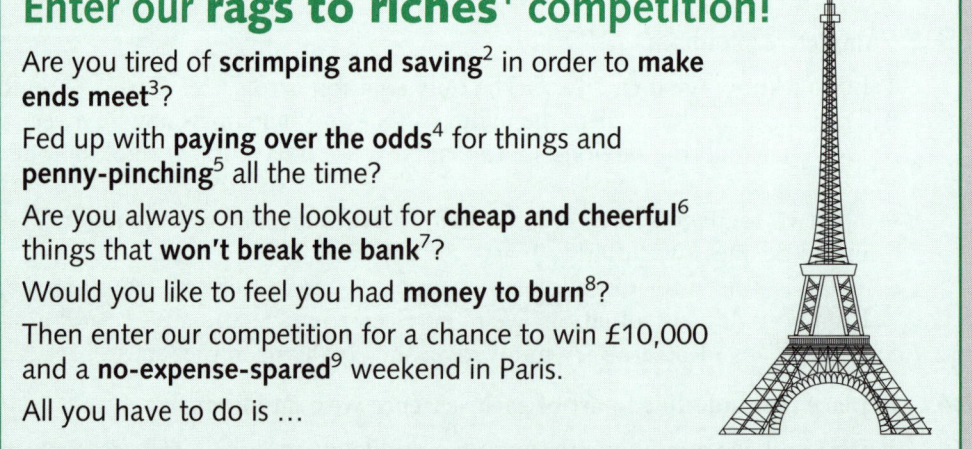

Are you tired of **scrimping and saving**[2] in order to **make ends meet**[3]?

Fed up with **paying over the odds**[4] for things and **penny-pinching**[5] all the time?

Are you always on the lookout for **cheap and cheerful**[6] things that **won't break the bank**[7]?

Would you like to feel you had **money to burn**[8]?

Then enter our competition for a chance to win £10,000 and a **no-expense-spared**[9] weekend in Paris.

All you have to do is …

[1] from poverty to wealth [2] living very economically [3] have just enough money to pay for the things you need [4] paying more than something is worth [5] spending as little money as possible [6] cheap but good or enjoyable [7] don't cost a lot [8] excess money [9] luxury; a lot of money is spent to make it good

Exercises

33.1 Complete each idiom.

1 Working as a security guard is money .... , unless someone actually tries to break in.
2 He went from .... , but he was always afraid he'd end up poor again.
3 A lot of students find it difficult to .... and end up borrowing money from the bank or from their parents.
4 When I was a student, I was always .... cash, so I had to get part-time jobs.
5 He's completely immoral about financial matters. He would ....
6 He sued the newspaper for libel, won his case and took them ....
7 They set up one of those social networking websites. It was an instant success and now they're laughing ....
8 Why do I work so hard and such long hours? Well, someone has to bring .... !
9 Jessie paid me for that job I did last week, so I'm .... We can have a nice meal out tonight!
10 I bought a new guitar at the weekend. It was going for a .... at only £30.

33.2 Correct the mistakes in these idioms.

1 In the current financial crisis, people are finding it harder to make ends match.
2 I'm tired of living on a shoelace. I need to earn more money.
3 You should buy that old house – it's going for a tune.
4 Spending money on ready-made meals is just throwing money down the hole.
5 Did you know he took his girlfriend to the Caribbean for a luxury holiday? He must be absolutely running in it.
6 We had lunch in a cheap and cheesy restaurant.
7 I know you love that dress, but it's so expensive. There's no point in paying over the evens for it – it's just not worth it.
8 Why don't you buy her a bunch of flowers? It won't break the wallet.
9 Kim is the main breadearner in our family.
10 I wish we had more money. I hate being so penny-picking all the time.

33.3 Rewrite each sentence using the word in brackets.

1 The prize is a luxury weekend in a London hotel. (SPARED)
2 Ivana is always going shopping. She must have a huge amount of money. (BURN)
3 Kim has never had much money. She has always had to live economically. (SCRIMP)
4 If you like children, babysitting is a very easy way to earn money. (ROPE)
5 Everyone has to go to work in order to earn enough to live on. (BACON)
6 You sold the car for £200 more than you paid for it, so you've made a good profit. (QUIDS)
7 Sue has no principles when it comes to making money. (GRANDMOTHER)
8 I don't make much money, so I find it almost impossible to live on what I earn. (MEET)

33.4 Answer these questions.

1 What would you buy if you were rolling in it?
2 What would you stop buying if you felt strapped for cash?
3 Have you ever paid over the odds for something?
4 Have you ever bought anything that was going for a song?

34 Society

A People in society

The table below shows some idioms used to describe people in relation to their roles in society.

idiom	example	meaning
a self-made man	Andrew Carnegie is the typical **self-made man**: he was born into a poor family but became one of America's richest men.	person who is rich and successful because they have worked hard, not because they were born into a rich family
the chattering classes	A lot of people find his books boring and pretentious, but he's really popular among **the chattering classes**.	educated people who enjoy discussing social, political and cultural issues
a second-class citizen	Pensioners often feel they are treated as **second-class citizens** by younger people.	someone treated as if they are less important than others in society
the grass roots	Football managers often go to smaller clubs to recruit new players from **the grass roots**.	ordinary people in a political or sporting organisation, not the leaders
the silent majority	I don't think their new policy represents the views of **the silent majority**.	large number of people who do not express their opinions publicly
the (men in) grey suits	**The men in grey suits** have a lot to do if they are to win back public confidence in our banking system.	people in business or politics with a lot of influence or power, although they are not well known to the public
public enemy number one	Smoking has become **public enemy number one** since the introduction of the smoking ban.	something or someone that a lot of people dislike or disapprove of
new kid on the block	I've only been working here for a few weeks, so I really feel like the **new kid on the block**.	someone who is new in a place or organisation and has many things to learn about it (informal)

B Power in society

Bob: Have you seen this newspaper article? It seems like all **the movers and shakers**[1] were at the president's post-election party. All those people who helped him **win by a landslide**[2].
Tim: Or at least helped **rig the election**[3] if you believe what some of the papers say!
Bob: Who knows! Apparently his wife is **the power behind the throne**[4], although she hates **being in the public eye**[5].
Tim: Yes, I'm sure she **pulls the strings**[6]. She's popular with **the grey vote**[7] too, I believe.
Bob: Oh well. It looks like there's another few years for **Mr Big**[8] and his government on **the gravy train**[9].

[1] the people with power and influence
[2] win by a very large majority
[3] arrange an election in a dishonest way
[4] someone with no official position in government or an organisation but who secretly controls it
[5] being famous; written about in the media and seen on TV
[6] is in control, often secretly
[7] the vote of older people (You can also say 'grey pound', the spending power of older people.)
[8] the most important person in a company or organisation (informal)
[9] used to refer to a way of making money quickly, easily and often dishonestly, usually through your position in society

Exercises

34.1 Look at A. Match the words in the box to form five idioms.

> man   citizen   classes   roots   self-made   majority
> second-class   grass   silent   chattering

34.2 Complete each sentence with an idiom from 34.1.

1 Politicians often lose touch with the .... and become isolated from the public.
2 It's time the .... was heard, instead of the more vocal and aggressive minority.
3 My father was a .... He came from a poor background and worked his way up until he became quite rich.
4 I'm sick of listening to the opinions of the .... What about the opinions of ordinary people?
5 If you are poor, you may sometimes think you are a .... in terms of access to university.

34.3 Answer these questions.

1 How do you feel if you are the new kid on the block?
2 What, or who, in your opinion, is public enemy number one?
3 What kind of people are in the public eye?
4 What kind of people make up the grey vote?

34.4 Are these sentences true or false? If the answer is false, say why.

1 'Second-class citizens' are the people with most influence in a society.
2 'The gravy train' refers to the big travel expenses which politicians can claim.
3 'The chattering classes' means very talkative people.
4 If you 'rig' an election, you arrange it in a dishonest or criminal way.
5 If someone wins an election 'by a landslide', they win by just a small number of votes.

34.5 Complete each idiom.

1 It must be hard for that film star's family, being in the public .... all the time.
2 I hate the way some politicians seem more interested in getting on the .... train than in helping ordinary people.
3 After a few days at your new school you won't feel like the new kid on the .... any more.
4 The men – and women – in .... suits have far more influence on our daily lives than we imagine. They pull all the ....
5 The owner of this TV company is the Mr .... of the media world.
6 Sunbathing is public .... number one as far as doctors are concerned.

34.6 Replace the underlined part of each sentence with an idiom.

1 Although Bill receives all the media attention, his mother is really in control.
2 In the election, the Green candidate got far more votes than any other party.
3 Everyone suspects that the elections were not honestly won.
4 Mark has become very successful in business, despite starting out with nothing.
5 Journalists need to establish good contacts with the people who have influence in society.

35 Daily life

A Eating and sleeping

idiom	example	meaning
square meal	You shouldn't just snack – try to have at least one **square meal** every day.	a big meal with all the types of food your body needs
done to a turn	The meat is delicious. It's **done to a turn**.	perfectly cooked
eat like a pig	He has no table manners – he **eats like a pig**.	eats very greedily and unpleasantly (disapproving)
eat like a horse	She's quite thin, even though she **eats like a horse**.	eats a lot
eat like a bird	She's quite fat, even though she **eats like a bird**.	eats very little
burn the midnight oil	Try not to **burn the midnight oil** the night before an exam. It's best to get an early night.	work or study until very late at night
sleep on it	Don't decide now – **sleep on it** and see how you feel in the morning.	postpone making a decision until after a night's sleep
go / be out like a light	The little boy **went out like a light** as soon as he went to bed.	fell asleep very quickly
not lose sleep over sth	It was just a silly argument – I would**n't lose any sleep over** it.	not worry about

B More daily life idioms

Ned: Hi, Liz. Haven't seen you for ages! How are things?
Liz: I've been really busy. In fact, I **don't know whether I'm coming or going**[1]!
Ned: Is that because of work?
Liz: Partly. But I've also got some friends staying with me this week. They're lovely, but they want to **go out on the town**[2] every night. I'm exhausted!
Ned: But surely they could go out on their own?
Liz: Well, last night I suggested I **give it a miss**[3], but they wouldn't listen.
Ned: Sounds like they've **outstayed their welcome**[4]!
Liz: Yes, they have. And also we're so busy at work that I don't have time to eat lunch. I just have a sandwich **on the hoof**[5]. There's not even a spare moment to **pass the time of day**[6] with colleagues. And I'm **having a bad hair day**[7] today too!
Ned: Poor you! You just need to **take each day as it comes**[8]. We're having a difficult week too. We've got no electricity, so the flat's freezing, and we can't cook or have a hot shower. As you know, I like my **creature comforts**[9], so I'm finding it really hard. We were lucky last night, though. We went out for a meal and the owner let us have it **on the house**[10] because I once did a favour for him. Anyway, here's my train. See you soon. Bye.

[1] am unable to think clearly or decide what to do because there are so many things to deal with
[2] spend the evening in bars, restaurants or clubs [3] not take part (informal) [4] stayed longer than the host would like [5] while doing other things [6] have a short, informal conversation or chat
[7] a day when you feel that you look unattractive, especially because of your hair; often used humorously to describe a day when everything seems to go wrong (informal) [8] deal with things as they happen and not worry about the future; often used to describe recovering from an illness
[9] physical comforts like a comfortable bed, hot water, food and warmth [10] given free by the business

Exercises

35.1 Look at A. Match the beginning of each sentence with its ending.

1 Don't worry. There's no point losing any
2 We had a great meal. The meat was done
3 Helen has a lot of homework, so she's been up all night burning
4 My grandmother doesn't want much lunch. She eats
5 I didn't think I was tired, but I went out
6 I feel hungry and tired if I don't eat a square
7 It's late. Let's not talk about this now – we need to
8 I'm embarrassed to go to restaurants with him; he eats

like a light.
meal every evening.
sleep on it.
sleep over it.
like a pig.
the midnight oil.
like a bird.
to a turn.

35.2 Complete the paragraph using idioms from the box.

| on the hoof | square meal | creature comforts | go out on the town |

When Sam first went travelling, he really missed his (1) ...., like hot water and a soft bed. However, he loved being able to (2) .... at night with new friends in different countries. He had such an exciting time that he was usually too busy to eat a (3) ...., and so he just ate (4) .... from street markets. Sam is now back at work but is planning his next trip.

35.3 Complete each dialogue with an idiom.

1 A: How is your new job going?
   B: It's really busy! I don't whether I .... !
2 A: Are you enjoying having Patty and Bob to stay with you?
   B: Well, I was at first, but now I'm fed up. They've ....
3 A: Do you fancy going to some bars and maybe a club or two on Saturday night?
   B: Yes, let's .... together.
4 A: Excuse me. You haven't charged us for our coffee.
   B: It's OK. It's ....
5 A: Are you going to come to chess club this evening?
   B: I was hoping to, but I'm afraid I'm going to have to ....
6 A: Shall we meet for lunch today?
   B: Sorry. I'm too busy at work. I'll just have to have a sandwich ....
7 A: Do you know your neighbours well?
   B: Not really, we just .... sometimes.
8 A: How is your father feeling after his operation?
   B: He's just trying to ....
9 A: Anything wrong? You've been looking miserable all day!
   B: Oh, nothing in particular. I'm just having a ....
10 A: I made a huge amount of food and Nigel ate it all!
    B: Yes, he eats .... !

36 Positive feelings

A Successful events

Read these positive reviews about the arts and note the idioms.

It's difficult to get children interested in sculpture, but the special exhibition at the City Gallery **hits** exactly **the right note**[1].

Wilma Gore's performance of Beatles' songs **went down a treat**[2] with the family audience at the Priory Theatre last night.

The Tara Dance Festival **went with a swing**[3] this year, with a wide variety of fun events.

Everyone **entered into the spirit of**[4] things at the opening of the museum, by dressing up as their favourite historical characters.

Coldplay have certainly **hit the jackpot**[5] with this, their third number one album.

The exciting dishes at the Hantown Food Festival certainly **hit the spot**[6] with everyone.

[1] is suitable and has the right effect (You can also say 'strike the right note'.) [2] everyone enjoyed it very much [3] was successful and exciting [4] showed that they were happy to be there [5] been very successful (and probably made a lot of money) [6] tasted good and made everyone satisfied

B Personal experiences

In these conversations, the second speaker uses an idiom to agree with the first speaker.

Tim: Molly has entered that pop singer contest on TV, The Nation's Best.
Daisy: I know, she's really **got stars in her eyes**, hasn't she! [is very excited about the future and thinks she's going to be famous]

Gina: The new album by Mariah Carey is absolutely amazing! Just fantastic!
Eva: Yeah, it really **blew my mind** the first time I heard it! [made me feel extremely excited or surprised (informal)]

Ciaran: Congratulations on getting the job in Italy. You always wanted that, didn't you?
Fran: Yes, it's **a dream come true**! I can't believe my luck. [it happened, although it was not likely that it would]

Lily: Steve seems so happy ever since he passed his exams.
Anne: Yes, he's **been on a high** ever since he got the news, hasn't he? [been feeling very happy and excited (informal)]

Ken: Hugo seems so happy and contented now that he's married, doesn't he?
Lisa: Yes, he's **as happy as Larry**. [very happy indeed (informal)]

Gerald: William seems very happy today. I wonder why.
Natasha: Yes, he seems to be **full of the joys of spring**! [very happy indeed]

Arnie: The boss has said we can all go home early today!
Hilda: Wow, that's **music to my ears**. Great news! [makes me feel happy]

Stefano: Osvaldo is always so happy and never seems to worry about anything!
Freda: Yes, he's such a **happy-go-lucky** person. [someone who is always happy and never worries]

Exercises

36.1 Look at A. Complete each idiom.

1 The company's new line of sportswear has been incredibly popular, and they've made a lot of money. They really .... jackpot this time.
2 The end-of-term party really went with .... Everyone enjoyed themselves.
3 That apple pie you made went down .... with our dinner guests.
4 We were freezing, so she gave us some hot chocolate to drink – it really .... spot.
5 Everyone was in a happy mood and entered .... the fancy-dress ball.
6 His lecture hit exactly .... Everyone enjoyed it and said it was very informative too.

36.2 Which idioms do these pictures make you think of?

1   2   3   4

36.3 Replace the underlined part of each sentence with an idiom.

1 After winning the race, I was feeling extremely excited for the rest of the day.
2 The decision to cancel the rugby match was very good news to me. I hadn't been looking forward to it at all.
3 Meeting Nelson Mandela was something I had always dreamt of, and now it was real.
4 Shona was looking very happy this morning. Something good must have happened.
5 Jerry's dreaming of becoming famous – he's joined a rock band and given up his job.

36.4 Rewrite each sentence using the word in brackets.

1 Sam Bagg's new album filled me with amazement and excitement. (BLEW)
2 My sister is such a happy and easy-going person. (LUCKY)
3 Iris is incredibly happy today! (SPRING)
4 He's so very happy in his new job. (LARRY)
5 This new series of adventure novels is just perfect for a teenage audience. (STRIKE)

36.5 Correct the mistakes in these idioms.

1 The music festival went on a swing and a lot of money was raised for charity.
2 The song we wrote for the end-of-course party went as a treat for all the teachers.
3 My cousin's got a star on her eye ever since her music teacher told her she could be famous one day.
4 Kevin is such a happy-lucky person; he never worries about anything.

FOLLOW UP Look in a good dictionary or visit Cambridge Dictionaries Online and find at least one idiom referring to positive feelings based on each of these words: *content*, *cheerful*, *moon*.

37 Negative feelings

A Anger

What makes people angry?

- People who are rude to waiters **make my blood boil**[1]!
- Chewing gum in class really **rattles my teacher's cage**[6]!
- People who talk loudly on their mobiles on the train make me **see red**[2]!
- Mum almost **burst a blood vessel**[5] when she saw my brother fighting on the street.
- Phone calls from people trying to sell me things I don't want really **get my goat**[4]!
- People who drive too closely behind me make me **all hot and bothered**[3]!

[1] make me very angry [2] get angry [3] angry and worried (informal) [4] irritates me (informal) [5] got very angry (informal) [6] makes them angry (This idiom is often used to describe someone who has been made angry on purpose.)

B Other negative feelings

idiom	example	meaning
knock someone for six	Losing his job has **knocked** John **for six**.	shocked or upset him very much (informal)
wild horses couldn't make me	**Wild horses couldn't make me** have a filling at the dentist's without an injection.	I would never
have a sinking feeling	I had forgotten to do my homework, so I **had a sinking feeling** when my teacher asked for it.	felt that something bad was about to happen
down in the dumps	Katy has been **down in the dumps** since she failed her exam.	miserable (informal)
not be your bag	Playing cards **is not my bag**. It's really boring!	is not something I am interested in or like (informal)
wouldn't give something house room	The new government **wouldn't give house room** to those outdated policies.	don't like or approve of
kick yourself	I could **kick myself** for forgetting my sister's birthday.	am very cross with myself because I did something stupid
reduce to tears	Her brother's unkind words **reduced** her **to tears**.	made her cry
be a bundle of nerves	Fiona **was a bundle of nerves** before her wedding.	was extremely nervous (informal)
run out of patience	I'm **running out of patience** with these naughty children.	am beginning to feel annoyed

TIP Help yourself remember these idioms by writing sentences about situations where you experienced the feelings they describe.

Exercises

37.1 Look at A. Correct the mistakes in these idioms.

1 Dad almost split a blood vessel when I told him I'd driven into his car.
2 Sally felt all warm and bothered after having to push her way onto the train.
3 Dave saw black when he heard the boy speak so rudely to Janice.
4 You're in a bad temper today. What's rattled your box?
5 What Lily said to her mother really made my water boil.
6 It really gets my dog when you say such stupid things!

37.2 Complete the idioms. What idiom would you use if you felt …

1 very nervous? 'I'm a ....'
2 unhappy? 'I feel .... today.'
3 apprehensive? 'I .... about this exam.'
4 impatient? 'I'm .... with that incompetent company.'
5 upset? 'The argument I had with my best friend has ....'
6 unwilling to do something? '... apologise to Nick.'

37.3 Match the beginning of each sentence with its ending.

1 Going to the opera isn't my   six.
2 I wouldn't give that artist's work   boil.
3 On rainy days I often feel down in the feeling.
4 People dropping litter makes my blood   bothered.
5 Gerry's rudeness made me see   bag.
6 Not getting the job has knocked Ben for house room.
7 Losing his keys made Jim all hot and   dumps.
8 When the phone rang, I had a sinking   red.

37.4 Rewrite the underlined part of each sentence using the word in brackets.

1 Selfish behaviour <u>makes me very angry</u>. (BOIL)
2 The film's sad ending <u>made Stella cry</u>. (TEARS)
3 Cruelty to animals <u>makes me very angry</u>. (RED)
4 I <u>am going to get angry soon</u> with James. (PATIENCE)
5 My brother's laziness <u>makes me very angry</u>. (GOAT)
6 I <u>was angry with myself</u> for missing the train. (KICKED)
7 What's <u>made Paul so annoyed</u>? (CAGE)
8 I shouldn't let him make me so <u>angry</u>. (BOTHERED)
9 Long walks in the countryside <u>are not the sort of thing that appeal to me</u>. (BAG)
10 Your father <u>will be furious</u> if you say you're dropping out of university. (BURST)

37.5 Complete these sentences so that they are true for you.

1 .... reduced me to tears.
2 I wouldn't give .... house room.
3 .... gets my goat.
4 I was a bundle of nerves when ....
5 I could have kicked myself when I ....
6 .... is not my bag.
7 Wild horses couldn't make me ....
8 .... knocked me for six.

38 Problems

A A conversation about a problem

Dev: How are things at work these days, Nadia?
Nadia: It's **a nightmare**[1]. I **took my eye off the ball**[2] when I was trying to negotiate an important deal and managed to lose quite a bit of money.
Dev: Can't you **sweep it under the carpet**[3]?
Nadia: Well, I did wonder about that, but decided I'd just have to own up to **making a pig's ear of**[4] it.
Dev: Was your boss angry?
Nadia: Very! He said I was **losing my touch**[5]. It was quite **a slap in the face**[6] because I've brought in lots of good business until now.
Dev: So are you thinking of looking for another job?
Nadia: That was my first reaction, but I've thought about it again **in the cold light of day**[7], and I think it might be better to stay there for a bit and try to make up for it.
Dev: Well, I'm sure you'll be able to do that without any problems.
Nadia: I certainly hope so. I'd hate to feel I'd really **lost the plot**[8].

[1] is terrible (informal) [2] lost concentration [3] hide what happened [4] doing something very badly (informal) [5] losing my previous skill [6] hurtful; upsetting [7] later, when feeling calmer [8] gone crazy

B Letters to a problem page

Dear Zena,

I work in the same office as my sister. We get on well, but she is very jealous of me. I have now been offered a promotion which would mean earning a much higher salary than her. If I accept it, it will really **put her nose out of joint**[1]. However, I'm **in over my head**[2] with debt just now, and if I don't accept the job I will be **in a tight corner**[3] financially. I **can't see the wood for the trees**[4] at the moment, so please help me. What do you think I should do?

Emma

Dear Zena,

I'm getting married next month, but it's all going wrong! The venue where we wanted to get married has cancelled our booking. This has really **pulled the rug from under our feet**[5], as it's too late to find somewhere else. My fiancé's brother is also refusing to come. I think he's trying to **settle a score**[6] after a big argument they had last year, but it's very upsetting. And now my dress is too small! This is just the latest thing in **a chapter of accidents**[7]. Is this a sign that our marriage won't work? Should I just cancel the wedding?

Megan

[1] upset or offend someone by getting something they wanted
[2] in a difficult situation that you can't deal with
[3] in a difficult position (You can also say 'in a tight spot'.)
[4] be unable to understand a situation because you are too involved in it
[5] do something that causes difficulties for someone, or suddenly take away help or support from them
[6] punish someone for something they did in the past and that you cannot forgive
[7] a series of unlucky events

Exercises

38.1 Look at A. Choose the correct word to complete each idiom.

1 When children help you cook, you can't take your eye off the [TV / car / ball].
2 You're refusing to speak to her now, but I suspect you'll feel differently in the cold [time / air / light] of day.
3 I really don't want to make a speech at my friend's wedding – I'm sure I'll make a total [pig's / dog's / cow's] ear of it.
4 Trying to park in town was an absolute [nightfall / nightcap / nightmare] this morning.
5 Dan's behaving very strangely. Do you think he's finally lost the [map / plot / plan]?

38.2 Which idioms do these pictures make you think of?

1
2
3
4

38.3 Match the beginning of each sentence with its ending.

1 I'm not making as many sales as I used to. I must be losing my	corner.
2 I don't know why Bill is still so determined to settle a	accidents.
3 I wonder if you could help me out of a tight	the ball.
4 His neighbours' expensive new car certainly put Ted's nose out of	touch.
5 He realised he'd made a terrible mistake in the cold light of	score with Jack.
6 No one in this business can afford to take their eye off	day.
7 There have been problems all week – it's just been a chapter of	the trees.
8 You need to stand back from the problem so you can see the wood for	joint.

38.4 Agree with what A says. Complete each dialogue with an idiom.

1 A: This job is really much too difficult for us now.
  B: I agree. We're in ....
2 A: Selina has upset Gemma by going out with her ex-boyfriend.
  B: I know, it's really ....
3 A: It will be impossible to hide our mistake.
  B: Yes, there's no point trying to ....
4 A: That singer's nothing like as popular as he used to be.
  B: You're right, I think he's ....
5 A: We need to get away for a while and think about the situation more clearly.
  B: Good idea. At the moment we ....
6 A: I keep forgetting things recently.
  B: Me too. I feel like I'm .... !
7 A: You have to concentrate all the time in this job.
  B: You're right. You can't ....
8 A: He's got himself into a very difficult position now financially.
  B: Yes, he's ....

39 Journalism

There are many expressions in English which are frequently used in journalism but are rarely used in other contexts. This kind of idiomatic language is sometimes called *journalese*.

A Newspaper articles about politics

MARATHON TALKS[1] COME TO AN END

Several weeks of lengthy talks are coming to an end, and planners are now almost certain to **be given the go-ahead**[2] to build a new housing estate on what is now North Park.

PM FIGHTING FOR HIS POLITICAL LIFE[3]

The prime minister is facing increasing problems today, **amid mounting calls**[4] for his resignation. Many say he **has blood on his hands**[5] after the number of civilian deaths in the recent war.

ELEVENTH-HOUR[6] AGREEMENT REACHED

Management and unions have at last managed to **hammer out**[7] a possible **agreement** on wages. **If, and it's a big if**[8], the final contract is not signed today, workers plan to strike next week.

[1] very long talks [2] get permission [3] in danger of losing his position [4] with more and more people asking [5] is responsible for the death of someone or something [6] last-minute [7] reach (also collocates with other nouns, for example *deal*, *treaty* and *compromise*) [8] used to emphasise that sth is not certain

B A newspaper article about war

VORINLAND ATTACKED

The **war-torn country**[1] of Vorinland has been further **plunged into chaos**[2] by a series of cross-border raids from the Sornak Republic, which took place **under cover of darkness**[3] last night. A number of **bloody confrontations**[4] have resulted in warehouses near the border being **engulfed in flames**[5]. The situation has brought an end to the **uneasy peace**[6] which the two countries had been experiencing for the last few weeks. The immediate motive for the raids is as yet **shrouded in mystery**[7], but one theory is that it was **a last-ditch attempt**[8] to sabotage the peace negotiations currently underway. The international community has appealed for calm.

[1] country which has suffered a lot as a result of war [2] put into an extremely difficult situation [3] protected by the fact that it was dark [4] violent acts of conflict [5] set alight [6] peace that is not stable [7] not known [8] a final try (also collocates with other nouns, for example *challenge* and *effort*)

TIP To find more examples of journalese, type "journalese" into a search engine, e.g Google. You should find both idioms and other language characteristic of modern journalism.

Exercises

39.1 Read the headlines. Are the statements below true or false? If they are false, say why.

1 **CITY MAYOR FIGHTING FOR HIS POLITICAL LIFE**

The mayor is going through a successful period.

2 **NEW ROAD LINK GIVEN THE GO-AHEAD**

The new road link will be built.

3 **ELEVENTH-HOUR AGREEMENT TO SAVE BATTLESHIP**

The agreement to save the battleship was made in plenty of time.

4 **COURT FINDS MAN HAS BLOOD ON HIS HANDS**

The court found the man guilty.

5 **MINISTERS DETERMINED TO HAMMER OUT AGREEMENT**

The ministers want to come to an agreement.

6 **MARATHON TALKS END IN FAILURE**

The talks were brief.

39.2 Complete each idiom.

1 shrouded .... mystery
2 engulfed .... flames
3 .... cover .... darkness
4 plunged .... chaos
5 hammer .... an agreement

39.3 Complete each sentence with an idiom from 39.2.

1 The forest fires resulted in some entire villages being ....
2 The robbers got into the house ....
3 It will not be easy for the two sides to ....
4 The reasons for the bank manager's disappearance are still ....
5 The power cuts .... the whole area ....

39.4 Choose the correct word to complete each idiom.

1 Barbara Matthews, the British actress, has agreed to take the part if, and it's a [big / strong / hard] if, she gets the co-star she has requested.
2 Amid [rising / climbing / mounting] calls for his resignation, the president has not been seen in public today.
3 The [handy / bloody / hearty] confrontations show no sign of coming to an end.
4 There is now an [uncomfortable / unpleasant / uneasy] peace in the area.
5 The councillor is fighting [for / over / to] his political life.
6 There is growing evidence that the CEO himself has [dirt / mud / blood] on his hands.
7 The directors are making a [last-time / last-line / last-ditch] attempt to save the company.
8 It is a [war-worn / war-torn / war-broken] country, with problems of poverty and disease.

39.5 What images do these words make you think of? Why do you think journalists like such images?

1 engulfed
2 plunged
3 shrouded
4 last-ditch
5 eleventh-hour
6 war-torn

40 Advertising

A Idioms to convince people life can be better

Advertisements often claim that products will improve your life or give you special and exciting experiences, and so they use idioms connected with that theme.

The cruise ship *Ocean Comet* offers luxury **beyond** your **wildest dreams**[1]. Holiday in style with our exclusive 21-day winter cruises. Go on, **do** yourself **the world of good**[2] and book now at cometcruiser.com.

In a world where it's getting more and more difficult to **stand out from the crowd**[7], the top-of-the-range Vedra 2000 **beats** other cars in its class **hands down**[8]. *Vedra* – love to be different.

Marjorie Wilkes has a glass of *Corngrass* health drink every day. 'Drinking Corngrass has **taken years off me**[3],' she says. At 85, Marjorie still believes in **living life to the full**[4], and with Corngrass, she does.

'We tried every kind of holiday, but they never quite **hit the mark**[9],' said Ken Stax. 'Then we discovered *Jetaway*. There's **a world of difference**[10] between a normal airline and one that takes care of you from the moment you leave your house.'

The *Vestbook3800T* is a laptop that is truly **ahead of its time**[5]. Less than 1 kg in weight, it **packs an** impressive **punch**[6] with its super-fast Pandros processor.

[1] more than you could ever imagine or wish for
[2] make yourself feel much healthier or happier
[3] made me look and feel much younger
[4] experiencing as many good things as possible in life
[5] has already got features other products will not have for a long time yet
[6] is impressively powerful
[7] be different from and better than others so that everyone notices you
[8] is superior to other cars of its class
[9] were never successful
[10] a very big difference (usually with *between*)

B Idioms and wordplay in advertisements

Advertisers often play with idioms to make a greater impact, for example by basing the names of products and services on idioms to make them more memorable. Here are some examples from recent advertisements. The products and services are shown in the pictures. See Unit 6 for more information on playing with idioms.

Dustbattler 206

It's time to **come clean**[1] and admit you have a dust problem!

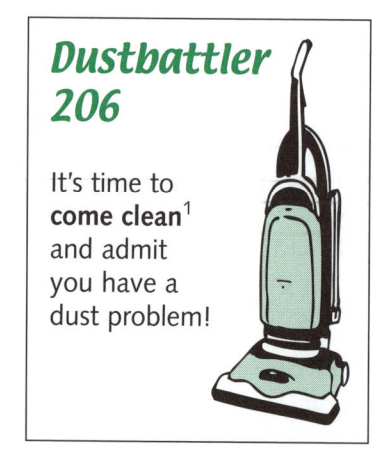

Selling your house was **a smart move**[2]. Now let us do the hard work.

Johnston Removals Ltd

There's **no time like the present**[3] ... and we have the perfect gift for everyone

This week only – free gift wrapping at Lennards

[1] come clean means 'tell the truth', usually about something bad that has been kept secret; the Dustbattler 206 *cleans* carpets [2] a smart move is a wise or clever action; removal companies help people *move* to a new home [3] said if you think it is a good idea to do something immediately; a *present* is a gift

Exercises

40.1 Look at A. Complete each idiom.

1 There's a .... difference .... economy class and business class when you fly long distance.
2 A camera that is ahead .... The new Imagion A64.
3 *Trick me!* The new family fun game that beats other games .... Available now at all good toy shops.
4 A villa in the Mediterranean? Free petrol for life? There are prizes beyond your .... in our new super-lotto competition. Enter online today!
5 Small but perfectly formed, this MP3 player .... an impressive .... , with great sound quality and portability.
6 If your cooking doesn't quite hit .... , why not try our new online home-cookery course at www.foodstermania.com?

40.2 Agree with what A says. Complete each dialogue with an idiom.

1 A: The first hotel was dirty and noisy. The second one was beautiful and really luxurious.
   B: Yes, there was a world .... them.
2 A: Our Caribbean cruise was great. We came home feeling absolutely wonderful.
   B: Yes, it did us ....
3 A: Jake loves meeting new people and trying new things.
   B: Yes, he certainly lives ....
4 A: This new vacuum cleaner is incredibly powerful – look how clean the floor is now!
   B: Yes, it certainly packs ....
5 A: Freya is finding it difficult to get a job in the theatre. There are so many good actors looking for jobs.
   B: Yes, it must be very hard to stand out .... these days.
6 A: Have you seen Edith since she had a facelift? She looks so much younger.
   B: Yes, it's taken .... I think I might have one done myself!

40.3 Which product do you think each idiom would be best suited to advertise using wordplay? Choose the correct answer and say why.

idiom	products
1 a smart move	a) a hair dryer b) an electronic chess game c) a lamp
2 there's no time like the present	a) a watch b) a scarf c) a computer game
3 come clean	a) a mobile phone b) perfume c) washing powder

40.4 Match the advertising slogans on the left (which all contain idioms) with the companies, products or services on the right.

1 PRESENT PERFECT   an airline with beds in its first-class cabin
2 PHOTOGRAPHIC MEMORY   a new gift shop
3 QUALITY TIME   an exhibition of pictures of a village taken 100 years ago
4 SLOWLY BUT SURELY   a new range of luxury watches
5 FLAT OUT TO NEW YORK   a cookery course to encourage people to stop eating fast food

FOLLOW UP Look out for adverts in English and make a note of any idioms used in them, especially any which involve wordplay.

41 Formal writing

Accurate and fluent formal writing is important in advanced-level exams. This unit presents some expressions to help you organise your arguments and ideas in an essay.

A Structuring an argument

First and foremost is a more emphatic form of *first*: **First and foremost**, it must be emphasised that there are several reasons for this change.

On balance, by and large and **in the main** are used to draw a conclusion after evaluating several different facts or opinions: **On balance / By and large / In the main**, the general public seems to be in favour of the proposal.

On no account is an emphatic way of saying *not*. Remember to invert the subject and verb when the phrase is used at the beginning of a sentence: **On no account** should their conclusions be accepted. Their conclusions must **on no account** be accepted.

On the one hand and **on the other hand** are used to present two contrasting ways of looking at the same problem: **On the one hand**, there is some published evidence to support the theory. **On the other hand**, that evidence has been questioned by some recent studies.

Last but not least is used to emphasise that even though something is mentioned last, it is still important: **Last but not least**, the impracticalities of the proposal created many problems.

In the final / last analysis is used to emphasise that you are talking about what is most important or true in a situation: **In the final analysis**, although this is an innovative idea, it is not one that we can consider.

B Indicating relationships between ideas or events

> The **conventional wisdom**[1] is that only children can learn a second language to a really high level. Many people claim that a good adult language learner is **a contradiction in terms**[2]. Young children can be excellent language learners, but that is **not the whole picture**[3]. Adult learners can also master a language. My brother is **a case in point**[4]. He learnt perfect Arabic when he was 30. However, adults, **as a matter of course**[5], have more difficulties than children with pronunciation.

[1] something that people generally believe is true when in fact it is often false [2] an expression that is confusing because the words in it seem to have opposite meanings [3] not taking all the facts into consideration [4] an example of something just described [5] describes what normally happens or what is normally done.

> A recently published Ministry of Education document **points the way**[1] to more teaching of languages at primary schools. This document **sets the stage**[2] for radical changes in language teaching. However, this **begs the question**[3] as to how enough teachers will be found to teach second languages to young learners. Some changes in teacher training are about to be **set in motion**[4], and it is hoped that these will **open the door to**[5] more successful language teaching.

[1] suggests how something might be done in a better way [2] makes something more likely to happen [3] causes you to ask a particular question [4] started [5] let something new start

> **ERROR WARNING**
>
> **On the one hand / On the other hand** do not present two arguments for the same position but are used to present two contrasting ways of looking at the same problem: **On the one hand**, I find life in the country less stressful than living in the city. **On the other hand**, I do miss theatres and cinemas.

Exercises

41.1 Look at A. Complete each idiom.

1 last but not ....
2 .... balance
3 first and ....
4 .... and large
5 .... no account
6 in the final / last ....

41.2 Complete each sentence with an idiom from 41.1. There may be more than one possible answer.

1 .... should we forget the history behind this conflict.
2 .... doctors must trust their own judgement.
3 I can see both arguments, but .... I am in favour of extending the school-leaving age.
4 ...., we must give a definition of family law before we can apply it to the case in question.
5 ...., let us consider the role of the media in this debate.
6 ...., the writer uses traditional poetic style.

41.3 Choose the correct idiom.

1 Liberal right-wing policies sound like [received wisdom / a contradiction in terms].
2 [On no account / In the main], I approve of the government's approach.
3 The reform [begs the question of / opens the door] to an eventual solution of the problem.
4 Once the papers are signed, this legal process is [set the stage / set in motion].
5 [As a matter of course / Last but not least], large companies outperform smaller companies. This is only to be expected.
6 People who fail at school often succeed in later life. Einstein is [a case in point / not the whole picture].
7 The research [points the way / sets the stage] to a future cure for the disease.
8 Saying that boys achieve less at school does not give [a contradiction in terms / the whole picture].
9 Advocating equal opportunity for all [points the way to / begs the question of] how this can be achieved.
10 [On the one hand / On no account], international law exists to protect people from the power of states. [On balance / On the other hand], it can also restrict states from exercising their power to protect the interests of their own people.

41.4 Here are some errors made with idioms by candidates in advanced-level exams. Can you correct them? Looking up the word in brackets in a good idioms dictionary should help you find the correct idiom.

1 The new building <u>stands out like a sore finger</u>. (THUMB)
2 An interesting painting <u>caught my eyeballs</u>. (EYE)
3 It's hard to keep up with government policy, as they seem to <u>choose and change</u> all the time. (CHOP)
4 Business success often goes <u>in pair with</u> good working conditions. (HAND)

> **FOLLOW UP** Find an article relating to your studies. For example, if you study science you could choose an article from the *New Scientist* website at www.newscientist.com. Can you find any examples of idioms? If so, note them down in sentences to show them in context.

42 Advising and warning

A Changing people's attitudes or behaviour

> You've been behaving very badly. It's time to **turn over a new leaf**[1] and start behaving responsibly.

> Well, if you're bored with your job, maybe it's time to **ring the changes**[2] and look for something new.

> You'll never pass your exams if you don't work hard. You need to **put your shoulder to the wheel**[3] and start studying.

> My advice to you is to **reach for the stars**[4]. You can achieve anything you want.

> If I were you, I'd **think twice**[5] before taking the job. It doesn't seem very well paid.

> You keep saying you want to give to charity, but now it's time to **put your money where your mouth is**[6]!

> Don't assume you're going to get into university. Buying all your books before you get a place is **tempting fate**[7].

> If you no longer want to marry Sandra, you need to **bite the bullet**[8] and tell her.

[1] start behaving better [2] make something more interesting by changing it in some way [3] make an effort and work hard [4] try to achieve your ambitions or something that is very difficult (You can also say 'reach for the moon'.) [5] think carefully before making a decision (You can also say 'think long and hard'.) [6] do something practical about something you believe in, especially give money [7] causing bad luck for yourself by talking or acting too confidently about something [8] force yourself to do something difficult or unpleasant

B Other idioms connected with advising and warning

example	meaning
Be careful what you say! I wouldn't **stick my neck out** if I were you.	give an opinion which others might not like or which others are afraid to give
I really think you **are on thin ice** when you criticise your manager so strongly.	taking a risk (You can also say 'be skating on thin ice'; always used in the continuous form.)
Let's just agree with the plan. We don't want to **upset the applecart**.	cause trouble or spoil people's plans
I can't help you financially. I know things are difficult, but you'll just have to **tough it out**.	face a difficult situation without changing your plans or opinions
It's great that you want to start your own business, but don't **bite off more than you can chew**.	try to do more than you are able to
Don't worry about paying for your university studies. We'll **cross that bridge when we come to it**.	face that problem when it happens, not now
Business is not looking good. We have to **trim our sails** and be more realistic about our costs.	spend less money

Exercises

42.1 Look at A. Which idioms do these pictures make you think of?

1   2   3   4

42.2 Complete each sentence with an idiom.

1 The club needs money desperately. Charlie says he wants to help, so he should ....

2 I know you don't want to tell her the bad news, but you have to ....

3 Come on, work harder! You have to .... !

4 The teacher told his students to be ambitious and to ....

5 You need to stop lying and be honest. It's time to ....

42.3 Choose the correct word to complete each idiom.

1 You should think [over / double / twice] before you give anyone your personal details.
2 I wouldn't upset [the applecart / the fruitcart / the apple tree] at work. Just say you agree with your manager.
3 The company realised that it had to [change / tighten / trim] its sails because of the economic recession.
4 Let's not book the holiday until mum has had her operation and she's out of hospital. We don't want to [test / try / tempt] fate.
5 It's going to be a difficult year for us financially, but we'll just have to tough it [out / through / over].
6 You've been wearing the same boring old clothes for years. Come on, let's go shopping. It's time to ring [a change / the changes / the change]!

42.4 What could you say in these situations? Use the idioms in the box.

| be (skating) on thin ice | tough it out | bite off more than you can chew | stick your neck out |

1 A friend buys an old, ruined house, then finds out it will cost a lot of money and take a lot of time to make it habitable.
2 A friend speaks out at a public meeting and gives an opinion that most people do not agree with. You think it was not a good idea to speak out in this way.
3 A friend is in financial difficulties and asks you to help, but you can't. You think they just have to accept their situation.
4 A classmate sends an email to your teacher containing a very strong criticism of her. You think the classmate is taking a big risk.

FOLLOW UP A lot of idioms are based on parts of the human body (for example, *put your shoulder to the wheel* and *stick your neck out* in this unit). Find one more idiom for *shoulder* and one more for *neck* and record them in your vocabulary notebook.

43 Telling stories

A The office party

The office party was embarrassing, **to say the least**[1]. It all went wrong **from the word go**[2], when I couldn't find the venue and was two hours late. I'd only been working at the company for a week, and didn't really know anybody there, so there was a lot **at stake**[3] in terms of getting to know my new colleagues and making a good first impression. I started talking to someone who was, **to put it mildly**[4], one of the most boring people I've ever met, so I escaped quickly and started talking to Alice, who I sit next to at work. I was complaining about the man I'd been talking to and noticed she had gone very quiet. The **penny dropped**[5] when she said, 'He's my husband.' I later discovered that, **for good measure**[6], he's also a director of the company. I can't believe I **dropped** such **a clanger**[7].

[1] expression used to indicate that something is more serious or important than your words may suggest
[2] from the very start
[3] to lose
[4] expression used to describe something as more extreme than your words may suggest
[5] I suddenly understood (informal)
[6] in addition
[7] said something very embarrassing

B Getting a job

I'm sure I got my job **more by luck than judgement**[1]. My CV wasn't very good, **to say nothing of**[2] the disastrous interview. I **nearly fell off my chair**[3] when they offered me the job, and I even got a company car **into the bargain**[4]. There's **a lot to be said for**[5] not worrying about things until you know the final outcome.

[1] by chance rather than skill
[2] and in addition there is / was
[3] I was extremely surprised
[4] as well as other things mentioned
[5] there's a lot in favour of

C Other stories

John told me he'd won the lottery and **for a split second**[1] I believed him!

Between you and me[2], I think Kate's thinking of dropping out of university.

Guess who I bumped into on the way to work? Sara! It **was a real bolt from the blue**[3]. I've not seen her for years.

The exam looked really easy **at first glance**[4], but it was actually really difficult, and I think I've failed.

They may seem a strange couple, but **when all's said and done**[5], they're really happy together.

That's a real **turn-up for the books**[6] – I just got a pay rise I wasn't expecting.

[1] for a very brief moment
[2] said when you are going to tell someone something confidential
[3] an unexpected and very surprising event
[4] when you first look at it
[5] said when you are about to say the most important fact in a situation
[6] strange or surprising event

Exercises

43.1 Complete each idiom.

1 I felt at home in my new flat from the word ....
2 It took a while for the penny to .... , but eventually Joe realised I was joking.
3 Kathy nearly fell off her .... when she saw a film star in her local restaurant.
4 For a .... second I was afraid the car was going to crash.
5 He doesn't like spending money, to .... it mildly.
6 Just .... you and me, I'm thinking of applying for a new job.
7 Be careful what you say in the meeting – there's a lot at ....
8 I dropped a .... at Jane's party: I asked where her cat was, but apparently it died last week!

43.2 Answer these questions about the idioms on the opposite page.

1 Which two idioms talk about the beginning of something?
2 Which three idioms comment on something being surprising?
3 Which three idioms can be used to add extra information to other points mentioned?
4 Which idiom can be used to emphasise that you want to say something significant?
5 Which two idioms relate to chance and risk?

43.3 Replace the underlined part of each sentence with an idiom.

1 There are many advantages to working in an open-plan office.
2 Very briefly, I believed Tom when he said he was moving to Australia; then I realised he was joking.
3 Initially, the project seemed quite simple.
4 He passed his driving test first time, but I'd say it was more thanks to good fortune than to any special ability.
5 Don't tell anyone else, but I think Sue and Larry may be going out together.
6 Their decision to marry came as a complete surprise.
7 It was, at best, a risky thing to do.
8 Both the brothers are very clever, as is their brilliant sister.

43.4 Correct the mistakes in these idioms.

1 The party was fantastic – delicious food, a great band and all my favourite people there for full measure.
2 She's pretty, clever and nice for the bargain.
3 When all's told and done, I think you made the right decision.
4 No one thought the film would be a success, so it was a real turn-up in the books when it won three Oscars.
5 I feel very nervous about this exam; there is a lot at the stake.
6 I didn't understand what he meant at first, but then the pound dropped.
7 We got on really well from the word start.
8 I think you were rather rude to her, to tell it mildly.

> **FOLLOW UP**
> Choose three idioms that you particularly want to learn from this unit. Look them up in an online dictionary, e.g. http://dictionary.cambridge.org/. Write down the example sentences using these idioms that you find there. Then write another example using the idiom in a context relevant to you.

44 Responding to what people say

The idioms in this unit are used mainly in informal spoken language or in informal writing, e.g. emails to friends. They are not used in formal speaking or writing.

A Short responses

In these conversations, the second speaker uses an idiom to react to what the first speaker says.

A: What's Joe doing these days?
B: **You may well ask!** [when someone asks you about something which you think is strange, funny or annoying (humorous)]

A: Do you think Gill will come and help us tomorrow morning?
B: **Fat chance!** She never gets up before ten o'clock! [you think this will definitely not happen]

A: Did you know Nina's boyfriend was a basketball player?
B: Actually, he's a volleyball player.
A: Well, **same difference.** [you admit you were wrong, but think the difference is unimportant]

A: Farah has an amazing job. She travels the world as some millionaire's personal assistant.
B: **Nice work if you can get it!** [an easy job that you would like to have if you could]

A: Teresa and Harry are bringing their four noisy kids and their dog when they come to stay.
B: Oh, no! They're bad enough, but their kids and dog too? **That's all we need!** [something even worse will be added to an already bad situation]

A: Petra has resigned. She's leaving at the end of the month.
B: Well, **good riddance**, I say! I've never liked her. [you are pleased that someone or something you didn't like has gone; you can also say 'good riddance to bad rubbish' (impolite)]

A: Richard says he's going to move to Hollywood and become a famous film star.
B: Oh, **give me a break!** He's the worst actor I've ever seen! [you don't believe what you have just heard]

A: When shall we tell Lily the bad news?
B: Well, **there's no time like the present.** [it's better to do something immediately rather than wait]

B Reacting to news and events

Maria: Hi, Tara. You know Kerry's split up with Matt? Well, **the plot thickens**[1] – she's going out with James!
Tara: **I thought as much**[2]! I saw them together this morning.
Maria: **What is the world coming to**[3]? Matt's lovely! **Don't get me wrong**[4], James is gorgeous, but he's not a very nice person, and he's really boring. He needs to **get a life**[5]!
Tara: I know, **it will all end in tears**[6]! What does she see in him?
Maria: **You've got me there**[7]. Didn't you use to like him?
Tara: **Do me a favour**[8]! **I wouldn't trust him as far as I could throw him**[9]. He cheated on his last girlfriend, you know.
Maria: **Fair enough**[10]. I was only asking!
Tara: Oh well. **Time will tell**[11] whether they stay together or not.

[1] something has happened to make a strange situation even stranger [2] I thought so [3] said when you are shocked by events [4] said before you criticise someone, to make the criticism less severe [5] stop doing boring things and start doing exciting things [6] it will end badly [7] said when you don't know the answer to a question [8] said when you don't believe what someone has said or you disagree very much with it [9] I do not trust him at all [10] I accept your point of view [11] the truth will become clear after a period of time

Exercises

44.1 Look at A. Replace the underlined part of each sentence with an idiom.

1. A: We're already running late, and now I can't find the car keys!
   B: Well, <u>that just makes a bad situation worse</u>!
2. A: You never know, we might win the lottery and become millionaires.
   B: Huh! <u>I don't think that will ever happen</u>!
3. A: Felix says he's joining a rock band and is going to make a number one hit.
   B: Felix? Ha-ha! <u>I don't believe a word of it</u>!
4. A: I wonder why Janet isn't going to work today.
   B: <u>I also think this is strange.</u>
5. A: I hear Toni has emigrated to New Zealand.
   B: <u>I'm glad she's gone</u>! I could never stand her.
6. A: He ended the relationship by email, not text message.
   B: Well, <u>the difference is not important</u>.
7. A: You need to tell your boss that you're resigning today.
   B: You're right. <u>It's better to do it immediately</u>.
8. A: That film star gets paid ten million dollars per film.
   B: <u>I wish I could make money in that easy way</u>.

44.2 Are these sentences true or false? If the answer is false, say why.

1. If you say to someone 'You've got me there', you mean they have convinced you that they are right.
2. If you tell someone to 'get a life', you mean they should find a life partner or marry.
3. If you say 'the plot thickens', you mean that something has happened that makes a strange situation even stranger.
4. If you say 'Nice work if you can get it', you mean you would hate to have to do that work.

44.3 Complete each idiom.

1. They may be enjoying themselves now, but in the long run it will all ....
2. It says here in the paper that children prefer playing computer games alone to playing with their friends. What is the world .... !
3. I think Tara's unreliable and a liar. I wouldn't trust her ....
4. So Janice has been lying about how much money she makes? I thought ....
5. The new manager may make a difference to the company, or he may fail. Only time ....
6. We should act now, and not delay. There's no ....

44.4 Match each statement with a suitable response.

1 So you're saying she's selfish?	You've got me there. I really can't remember.
2 Erik says Johnny Depp is his best friend.	Good riddance to bad rubbish!
3 I didn't invite her because she upset me.	Do me a favour! How absurd!
4 What time did Granny say she was arriving?	Well, there's no time like the present.
5 That useless manager got the sack.	No, don't get me wrong; that's not the problem.
6 Should we go and tell her now or later?	Fair enough. I'm sorry to hear that.

45 Agreeing and disagreeing

A Agreeing

Maria doesn't approve of letting children eat sweets and chocolate, and her husband is **of the same mind / of like mind**. [has the same opinion]

The four people are all agreeing in an informal way with the man in the centre.

- You're not wrong!
- Tell me about it!
- We're overworked and underpaid!
- That's about the size of it!
- You **took the words right out of my mouth**!

I thought you didn't approve of people who drive cars to work instead of using public transport.

Well, yes, but **if you can't beat 'em, join 'em!**[1]

[1] something that you say when you decide to do something bad because other people are getting an advantage from doing it and you cannot stop them (informal)

You must **be on message**[2] in anything you say to the press and express agreement with the party's position. We won't win the next election unless we're all **singing from the same hymn sheet**[3].

[2] support the official view of the organisation [3] saying the same things in public

B Disagreeing

Manager: The only choice is to introduce my plan for longer working hours. It'll increase our productivity levels, which will be good for us all.
Bill: **I beg to differ**[1]. I think the staff will get very tired, and that will reduce productivity.
Manager: There's **a world of difference**[2] between expecting people to work twelve hours a day and asking them to occasionally work ten hours, which is all I'm asking.
Bill: Ten hours and fifteen minutes actually.
Manager: Now you're just **splitting hairs**[3].
Bill: Well, you're **at odds with**[4] your staff on this one. Everyone thinks you're **barking up the wrong tree**[5]! They say that paying people more would be a far better way to increase productivity.
Manager: Hey, I'm not exactly **a lone voice**[6]! Joanna, you backed my plan yesterday.
Joanna: Yes, well, now **I'm torn**[7]. **I'm in two minds**[8] as to whether it'd work or not.
Manager: Well, I'm sorry this **note of discord**[9] has crept into our discussions. I know it's a difficult decision to make. Tom, what do you think? You're usually good at **pouring oil on troubled waters**[10].

[1] I disagree (formal) [2] a big difference [3] arguing about whether unimportant details are exactly correct [4] have a different opinion from [5] trying to achieve something in the wrong way or being wrong about the reason for something (informal) [6] the only person with a specific opinion [7] undecided [8] unable to decide [9] disagreement (formal) [10] calming down a difficult situation

Exercises

45.1 Look at A. Correct the mistakes in these idioms.

1. A: I think we should go home now.
   B: You took the sentence right out of my mouth.
2. A: This project is a total disaster, isn't it?
   B: Yes, that's about the shape of it!
3. A: I think Jack is arrogant and rude.
   B: Talk about it!
4. A: I think they were wrong to sack George just for being late a few times.
   B: I think most of us are of the same meaning about that.
5. A: I'd never have expected to see you at a casino. I thought you didn't approve of gambling.
   B: Well, in the end I thought, 'If you can't win 'em, join 'em.'

45.2 Complete each idiom.

1. They were having a terrible row, so I tried to pour oil on troubled ....
2. Frank's convinced he's right, but I think he's barking up the wrong ....
3. The CEO wants to ensure we're all are singing from the same ....
4. It's part of a lawyer's job to be pedantic, to spend time splitting ....
5. Absolutely. You took the words right out of my ....
6. Our normally friendly meetings have been spoilt by a note of .... recently.
7. You may think it's a good idea, but I beg to ....
8. I don't know what to think. I'm in two ....

45.3 Choose the correct word to complete each idiom.

1. He certainly is a nasty person. You're not [untrue / wrong / false]!
2. When everyone else was ignoring the situation, Kate was a(n) [lone / only / alone] voice pointing out the danger we were in.
3. It's so hard to decide – I'm really [worn / torn / broken] about what to do.
4. As twins, Una and I tend to be of [alike / similar / like] mind over most issues.
5. That politician is at [difference / minds / odds] with his party over their economic policy.
6. The company's spokespeople were briefed before talking to the press to ensure they were all on [note / tone / message].

45.4 Replace the underlined part of each sentence with an idiom.

1. There's <u>a big difference</u> between being poor and not having as much money as you'd like.
2. I <u>have a different opinion from</u> everyone else in my family about where we should go on holiday.
3. Please do all you can to <u>calm things down</u>. I hate it when people argue.
4. The politician was sacked for not <u>following the party line</u>.

45.5 Do you agree or disagree with these statements? Respond to each statement with an idiom.

1. Men are better drivers than women.
2. Learning grammar rules is a waste of time.
3. Footballers deserve to be paid a lot more money than politicians.
4. TV has a bad effect on family life.
5. I couldn't live without my mobile phone.

46 Expressing success and failure

A Success

Look at these newspaper headlines about sport and business success. The meaning of the idiom in the headline is explained in the story that follows.

JACKSON WINS HIS SPURS[1]
Jackson's performance last night proved that he deserves his place in the team. He is clearly a very talented young player.

COUNTY TEAM IS ON A ROLL[4]
Red County basketball team has been having a very successful season, with six wins in a row.

PCL IS RIDING HIGH[2] **IN POPULARITY POLL**
PCL is one of the most popular businesses to work for this year, according to the results of a major survey.

NEW COLLECTION GOES DOWN A STORM[5]
The designer's exclusive dresses sold out within minutes at the New York fashion show.

BLAKE COMES UP TRUMPS[3]
The young player did far better than anyone would have expected in last night's match, scoring three goals to win the game for City.

VENCO STAY AHEAD OF THE GAME[6]
Shoe company Venco have maintained their lead in the industry for the third year running.

[1] do something to show that you deserve a particular position and have the skills needed for it; *spurs* are sharp, metal, wheel-shaped objects fixed to the heel of boots worn by people riding horses, and used to make the horse go faster [2] is very successful [3] complete an activity successfully or produce a good result, especially when you were not expected to [4] is having a successful period [5] is very popular [6] know more about the most recent developments than the people or companies with whom they are competing

B Failure

The comedian's performance at the Variety Show **went down like a lead balloon**. [people did not like it at all]

The disastrous attempt at a military campaign revealed the country as **a paper tiger**. [country or organisation which seems strong but is actually weak]

The president is dealing with the **double whammy** of losing the election and having his private life discussed in the press. [two bad things happening at the same time (informal)]

Starting a new business without careful planning is **a recipe for disaster**. [sure to become a disaster]

Unfortunately, it soon became clear that the new CEO **couldn't cut the mustard**. [couldn't deal with any difficulties or problems]

The economic crisis will have a huge impact on any business that **is built on sand**. [not firmly established]

> **TIP** The idioms in this unit are all based on vivid metaphors, which is one reason why they are particularly popular in journalism. Draw (or even just imagine) pictures to help you remember the idioms.

Exercises

46.1 Look at A. Match the beginning of each sentence with its ending.

1 Our team's been practising hard, so I hope we'll come	storm, both with critics and the public.
2 Negotiating that important deal makes me feel I have won	high.
3 His excellent IT skills have helped him stay ahead	a roll now.
4 I found it hard to get started with my thesis, but I'm on	my spurs in my new job.
5 Her latest book has gone down a	up trumps in the match tomorrow.
6 After some initial problems, the pop group is now riding	of the game.

46.2 Which idioms do these pictures make you think of?

46.3 Rewrite each sentence using the word in brackets.

1 The chef's new recipes <u>were very popular</u> with the clientele. (STORM)
2 My ideas for restructuring the company <u>were met with total silence</u>. (BALLOON)
3 The new prime minister <u>is extremely popular</u> at the moment. (RIDING)
4 I'm quite worried about starting my new job. I'm afraid I won't be able <u>to cope</u>. (MUSTARD)
5 I've been studying hard all year, so I hope I will <u>know a lot about the subject</u> when it comes to taking my exams. (GAME)
6 Poor Carl has been hit by <u>two problems at the same time</u> – losing his job and having a flood in his house. (DOUBLE)

46.4 Complete each idiom in this review of a play.

> Although Lucy James's disappointing first play went down like a (1) ....
> balloon, she has come up (2) .... with her second play, now showing at
> West Theatre. The dramatic plot went down a (3) .... with the first-night
> audience. I thought it would be a (4) .... for disaster casting the young Bill
> Catlin as an old man, but I was proved wrong. Catlin is (5) .... a roll at the
> moment; his last play also delighted critics.

> **FOLLOW UP** Look at Units 56 and 59, which are based on the keywords *dead* and *fall*. Which other idioms relating to failure can you find there?

47 Emphasising

In this unit we look at the way certain nouns and adjectives combine to form idiomatic compounds which emphasise the second word in the compound.

A Emphasis of adjectives

The words before each adjective express the idea of *very / completely / extremely*.

My trousers got soaked. I laid them on the sand and, in the hot sun, they were soon **bone dry**.

The cakes I made were a disaster. They were **rock hard** and nobody could eat them!

He lost his shorts in the water and came out of the river **stark naked**.

Derek has a **razor-sharp** sense of humour; he's so funny.

The oven broke down and our dinner was **stone cold** instead of **piping hot**.

The new prime minister is trying to project a **squeaky-clean** image of herself.

My granddad is 87, but he's **fighting fit** and goes for a long walk every day.

It's **crystal clear** to me that we need to raise money urgently.

His uncle Reginald is **filthy rich**. He owns houses in England, Italy and the Caribbean.

B Emphatic noun phrases

Read this phone conversation between Lou and Mary-Jo and note the idioms.

Lou: Have you heard about Yolanda? She was robbed **in broad daylight**[1] in the city centre yesterday. It really scared her.

Mary-Jo: Oh no! Things have really hit **rock bottom**[2] here if people are getting mugged in the middle of the day in crowded places!

Lou: Yes. Nobody has any respect any more. The city spent **a small fortune**[3] on surveillance cameras, but nobody ever gets caught. The police do nothing.

Mary-Jo: Well, even if they do get caught, they have no respect for the courts. They just tell **bare-faced lies**[4] and walk away free, or get fined **a mere pittance**[5].

Lou: Well, I think anyone who mugs someone should go to prison, **full stop**[6].

[1] during the day when people could have seen it [2] the lowest and worst possible level [3] a large sum of money [4] obvious untruths [5] a very small sum of money [6] there is nothing more to say about the subject

> **TIP** There are a large number of emphatic compounds with idiomatic meanings like the ones above. Always make a special note of them in your vocabulary notebook when you find new ones.

Exercises

47.1 Match the beginning of each idiom with its ending.

1 razor   clear
2 fighting   hot
3 crystal   sharp
4 stark   fit
5 piping   naked

47.2 Look at A. Replace the underlined part of each sentence with an idiom.

1 My old auntie May is very fit, even though she had an operation two months ago.
2 She's very rich: she owns a private jet and a massive yacht.
3 A man jumped into the fountain completely naked and was arrested by the police.
4 The new government had a completely clean image until the recent scandal broke.
5 Henrietta has a very sharp mind and is the most intelligent person I know.
6 My feet and hands were completely cold, so I sat in front of the fire, had a bowl of very hot soup and soon felt better.
7 I overcooked the meat and it was very dry.
8 We can't put the tent up here. The ground's very hard.

47.3 Correct the mistakes in these idioms.

1 Things have hit stone bottom between my parents and their neighbours; they don't speak to each other any more.
2 I couldn't sleep on that mattress – it was stone hard.
3 This vase is stark dry and the poor old flowers are dying!
4 It is glass clear to me that she is trying to deceive us all.
5 They've spent a filthy fortune on furniture for their new house.
6 Police report that more crimes are taking place in full daylight.

47.4 Answer these questions.

1 Which idiom in this unit means you have a lot of money?
2 Which idiom means 'There's nothing more to say about it!'?
3 Which idiom means a) 'a very small sum of money' and b) 'a very large sum of money'?
4 Which idiom 'means in the middle of the day, when everyone can see what is happening'?

47.5 Complete the crossword.

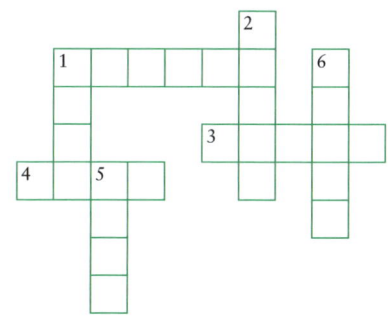

Across
1 goes with *rock*
3 goes with *crystal*
4 goes with *pittance*

Down
1 goes with *-faced lies*
2 goes with *fortune*
5 goes with *filthy*
6 goes with *naked*

48 Play and game

A Play

I went out with my brother and his girlfriend. They didn't really want me there, and it was really boring **playing gooseberry**. [being an unwanted third person in a romantic situation]

If you really like him, don't make it too obvious. Try to **play it cool**. [behave in a calm way, pretending to be less interested in someone than you really are]

I always take an umbrella with me, even if it's not raining. I like to **play it safe**! [be extra careful and not take any risks]

I run a restaurant. Another restaurant in town **plays dirty** – saying there are rats in our kitchen, and so on. [behaves dishonestly] But I'm not stupid – they can't **play me for a fool**. [treat me as if I am stupid] At the moment we're just waiting and **playing for time**, [waiting until we're ready] but we'll get our revenge in the end.

In my opinion, scientists have no right to **play God** by experimenting on embryos. [act as if they have control over other people's lives]

I'm tired of **playing second fiddle** to my brother [being in a less important or weaker position]

The police **played cat and mouse** with the suspect before arresting him. [tried to defeat someone by tricking them so that they had an advantage over them]

B Game

idiom	example	meaning
raise your game	Our competitors won an award this week. We're really going to have to **raise our game**.	work harder to achieve something
the game's up	He's got away with lying for a long time, but **the game's up** now.	used to say that someone's secret activities are known and must now stop
a game plan	The marketing campaign isn't working. We need a new **game plan**.	plan for achieving success
the name of the game	Good customer service is **the name of the game** for successful companies.	the most important part of an activity or quality needed for that activity

C Idioms with *play* and *game*

idiom	example	meaning
play games	They're never going to sign the contract. They're just **playing games**.	trying to deceive someone about what they intend to do
play the game	I don't agree with the changes at work, but I'm not going to complain; I'll just **play the game**.	behave in a way that is expected or demanded by those in authority.
play a / the waiting game	The banks are **playing a / the waiting game** until they see how their customers react to the financial crisis.	delaying taking action until they see how things develop

ERROR WARNING: It is important to use articles correctly in idioms. We always say 'play second fiddle' and 'play gooseberry', NOT 'play a second fiddle' and 'play a gooseberry'.

Exercises

48.1 Which idioms do these pictures make you think of?

1 2 3

48.2 Replace the underlined part of each sentence with an idiom.

1 We want the directors to agree to our proposals, so we need to discuss our <u>strategy</u>.
2 OK, kids – <u>that's enough</u>. I know where you've been hiding my glasses!
3 Martha has decided to apply to be the shop manager. She's been an assistant manager for five years and is tired of <u>not being fully in charge</u>.
4 When you're looking for a new flat, location is <u>the most important thing to consider</u>.
5 I went to the cinema with Elena and her new boyfriend, but it was horrible <u>being there with them when they just wanted to be alone</u>.
6 I think that doctors sometimes go too far in their attempts to <u>control what happens in our lives</u>.
7 We're still not ready to decide, so we need to <u>try to delay things a bit</u> and not sign the contract yet.

48.3 Complete each dialogue with an idiom.

1 A: Have you seen this email? I don't have time to do all of this extra work!
   B: I know, I know. Just .... for now. There's nothing we can do about it.
2 A: I really like him. Why won't he answer any of my texts?
   B: Maybe he's just ....
3 A: The new mayor seems fair and honest, doesn't he?
   B: Yes. He's promised not to ....
4 A: I don't think we should take any risks or experiment.
   B: No, much better to ....
5 A: I think we need a new plan to improve sales and increase profits.
   B: Yes, it's definitely time we ....

48.4 Rewrite each sentence using the word in brackets.

1 I'm fed up with him treating me as if I were stupid. (FOOL)
2 When people ask how the interview went, just answer calmly. (COOL)
3 I think he behaves dishonestly because he enjoys tricking people. (GAMES)
4 Some businesses behave dishonestly just to make more money. (DIRTY)

49 Half

A Meaning 'not full' or 'not complete'

In a number of idioms, *half* conveys the idea of something not being complete or full. For example, if you **listen** to something **with half an ear,** you are not fully concentrating on it:
I was **listening** to the radio **with half an ear** as I cooked dinner.
Similarly, you might watch something **with half an eye.**

If something is described as a **half-baked scheme** (informal), it has not been thought through fully:
This is another **half-baked scheme** of the government. They haven't considered any of its implications.

Half-measures are actions that will only achieve part of what they are they are intended to achieve:
There can be no **half-measures** when confronting this serious problem.

To **have half a mind to** do something is to think that you might do something (though you probably won't), often because someone or something has annoyed you:
I can't believe my boss said that! I've **half a mind to** just walk out of the office and never come back.
Note that I've **a good mind to** is an alternative form of this idiom. **See Unit 57 for more idioms with** *mind*.

If someone **doesn't know the half of it** (informal), they know a little about something that happens, especially something bad, but they do not know everything about it:
His mother thought she knew all about what happened when he was in Spain, but she **doesn't know the half of it.**

If you **meet someone halfway,** you do some of the things that someone would like you to do in order to show that you want to reach an agreement or improve your relationship:
I didn't want to spend a week at the conference, but I decided to **meet my manager halfway** and agreed to go for a couple of days.

B *Half* as emphasis

Read these conversations and note the emphatic idioms. All of the idioms in this section are informal.

A: Did you enjoy the party last night?
B: **Not half!** [said to agree emphatically]

A: It **isn't half** busy in here! [is very]
B: You're right. Let's go somewhere less crowded.

A: It's important to keep a positive attitude when you're recovering from an operation.
B: Yes, they say that's **half the battle.** [is the most difficult part of the process]

A: That was **a game and a half,** wasn't it! [something very special, surprising or that took a long time]
B: Yes, it was fantastic!

A: Would you like to visit Canada again?
B: **Given half a chance,** I'd move there tomorrow. [if I had the opportunity]

A: Linda is always correcting the teacher, isn't she?
B: Yes, she's **too clever by half.** [confident and smart in an annoying way]

Exercises

49.1 Look at A. Complete each idiom.

1 Whoever thought up such a stupid, half-................................. scheme?
2 I know we can't agree to all their requests, but I'd like to .... them halfway if possible.
3 I spent the evening reading the newspaper and watching TV with half an ....
4 I've half a .... to tell him exactly how unkind I think he's being!
5 They'll never solve the problem if they only try half-................................. .
6 The company is in very serious trouble. It's probably just as well that most of our employees don't .... the half of it.

49.2 Correct the mistakes in these idioms.

1 Julie was doing a crossword and listening to the radio with half her ear.
2 Giving half a chance, I'd leave my job and stay at home with the children.
3 We had a really good plan, but Sally pointed out all the things that were wrong with it. I find her just too clever in half.
4 Writers say that coming up with a good idea for a novel is half a battle.
5 I've the good mind to write a letter of complaint to your manager.
6 I'm a perfectionist. I have no time for half-measurements.
7 I know it's hard to compromise but you should try to join him halfway.

49.3 Complete each dialogue with an idiom.

1 Sam: Pat's little brother seems very confident, doesn't he?
   Ben: He's .... in my opinion!
2 Daisy: Our new boss is really good-looking, isn't he?
   Laura: .... !
3 Katy: Would you give up your job if you won the lottery?
   Mark: .... , I'd leave tomorrow, lottery or no lottery!
4 May: It .... hot in here!
   Tim: Yes, it's boiling!
5 Sue: What a fantastic dinner they gave us!
   Rick: Yes, it was a meal .... , wasn't it?
6 Liz: Our boss has no idea what we get up to while he's away, does he?
   Meg: No, he ....
7 Ali: We need to stay focused if our business is going to succeed.
   Jamie: Yes, I'm sure that's ....

49.4 Replace the underlined part of each sentence with an idiom.

1 <u>It's extremely</u> noisy here – shall we go somewhere quieter?
2 Having a clear structure and plan for your essay is <u>the most important thing</u>.
3 It'll be to management's advantage to <u>come to a compromise with the union</u>.
4 There was a lot of bad behaviour on the school trip, but the teachers <u>didn't find out about everything that happened</u>.
5 Well, that was certainly <u>an extremely long walk</u>!

50 Two

A People in pairs

Read these problem page letters and note the informal idioms in the responses.

> My friend won't text, phone or see me now that I have a boyfriend. I think she's wrong to behave like this.
>
> Fizz says: **That makes two of us**[1]. Your friend needs to accept your new boyfriend and act more like an adult.

> My friend Rick and I are always in trouble at school. The teachers say we just mess about and act stupidly. Any advice?
>
> Fizz says: Sounds like you and Rick **are two of a kind**[4]. My advice: stay away from each other at school.

> My boyfriend is chatting to girls he doesn't know online, and I'm jealous. Should I chat to strangers online too so he can see how I feel?
>
> Fizz says: They say that **two can play at that game**[2], but it'd be better to tell him how you feel.

> My best friend is getting married next month, and I can't decide what to wear. Everything I try on looks terrible. What should I do?
>
> Fizz says: Well, **two heads are better than one**[5] – why not ask a friend or family member to help you choose something?

> Things have been going really badly with me and my girlfriend lately. She's always starting arguments. Any advice?
>
> Fizz says: Remember, **it takes two to tango**[3]. Maybe some of it is your fault.

> My best friend has a new boyfriend, but I'm lonely. Should I ask if I can go out on dates with them?
>
> Fizz says: No. Remember, **two's company, three's a crowd**[6]

[1] we have the same opinion about a situation [2] you can hurt that person in the same way they hurt you [3] both people are responsible for the bad situation [4] are very similar in character [5] it is better to have two people trying to solve the same problem [6] it's better that two people should be alone

B Other idioms with two

Young people these days just **put / stick two fingers up at**[1] authority.
School tests **cut both / two ways**[2]: they let teachers monitor progress, but they also prevent teachers from teaching freely.
Barbara **knows a thing or two about**[3] local history – let's ask her.
Anger and frustration are **two sides of the same coin**[4].

[1] show that they are angry or have no respect (informal) [2] have positive and negative effects [3] knows a lot about (informal) [4] two different aspects of the same problem

C Other two idioms for people and things

Don't ask me to dance – **I've got two left feet**[1]!
When my parents first got married, they **didn't have two pennies to rub together**[2].
Let's ask Mr Ross for a donation to the club. He's **not short of a bob or two**[3].
Mobile phones **are two a penny**[4] these days. In the 1980s, nobody had one.
When he heard he'd passed all his exams, he was **like a dog with two tails**[5].
Gloria and Manuela **are like two peas in a pod**[6] – you can tell they're sisters.
Anna's so arrogant. She needs to **be brought down a peg or two**[7].

[1] am a very bad dancer [2] were very poor [3] is quite rich (informal) [4] very common [5] very happy [6] very similar [7] have sth happen to her to show her she is not as good as she thinks she is

> **TIP**
> Many idioms are informal. The ones marked *informal* here are particularly informal. Always make a special note about formality, and be careful not to use very informal idioms in formal writing.

Exercises

50.1 Look at A. Complete each idiom.

1 Lou told our boss that I left work early yesterday, so I told him that she's looking for a new job. Two can ....
2 The director and department head are both very arrogant. They're two ....
3 You hate meetings and I hate meetings, so that makes ....
4 When a couple breaks up, it is hardly ever the fault of just one person. It takes ....
5 Avril, can you help me with this? Two heads ....
6 I'm not going to the restaurant with Dave and Mary. I can see they want to be alone. Two's ....

50.2 Read these statements and answer the questions.

Tony: No, sorry. Ask someone else. I've got two left feet.
Amy: My cousin has just bought an amazing new house. She's not short of a bob or two.
Lotta: Sam has been like a dog with two tails since he got that new job.
Adam: I just don't have two pennies to rub together these days.

Who is ...	name
1 short of money?	
2 a bad dancer?	
3 talking about someone who has a lot of money?	
4 talking about someone who is feeling very happy?	

50.3 Which idioms do these pictures make you think of?

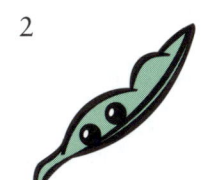

1   2   3   4

50.4 Rewrite the underlined part of each sentence using the word in brackets.

1 Richard is knowledgeable on the subject of finance. (THING)
2 Losing the race made him realise he wasn't as good as he thought. (PEG)
3 A lot of kids nowadays disrespect the police and do what they want. (FINGER)
4 Political power has positive and negative effects: it enables people to change things, but it tempts them to become corrupt too. (CUT)
5 Einstein sees time and space as two aspects of the same phenomenon. (COIN)
6 Sat Nav systems in cars are very common these days. (PENNY)

51 All

A Having a chat

Clare: You look tired, Ella. Is everything OK?

Ella: It's just our new neighbours. They come and go **at all hours**[1] of the day and night. I don't know how my husband manages to sleep through it. But **that's him all over**[2] – he sleeps really heavily, but I wake up each time they come in or out. Last night, they woke me up seven times, **all told**[3]!

Clare: He sounds like my husband! Once he's asleep, the house could be burning down **for all he cares**[4]. Anyway, can't you speak to your neighbours about it?

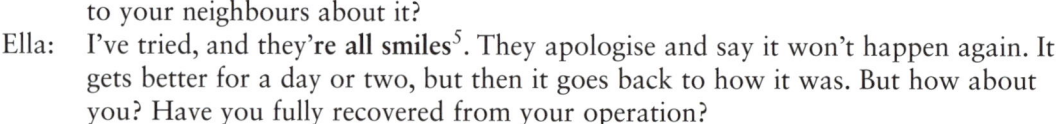

Ella: I've tried, and they're **all smiles**[5]. They apologise and say it won't happen again. It gets better for a day or two, but then it goes back to how it was. But how about you? Have you fully recovered from your operation?

Clare: Almost, but I won't **get the all-clear**[6] to go back to work for another couple of weeks, I don't think.

Ella: Oh well. **All in good time**[7]! It won't be too long before **it's all systems go**[8] again.

[1] at all sorts of unusual times [2] that's typical of (informal) [3] in total [4] and it wouldn't bother him [5] unexpectedly friendly and pleasant [6] get official permission, usually medical [7] you just have to be patient [8] everything is busy again

B Other idioms with *all*

idiom	example	meaning
all in all	**All in all**, I think the concert was a success.	taking everything into consideration
all or nothing	Tim either loves something or hates it – it's **all or nothing** with him.	completely or not at all
to cap it all	I've had a really stressful week, and **to cap it all** I've got to work over the weekend.	in addition to all the other bad things that have happened
in all but name	Vera runs the business **in all but name**.	existing as a fact, but not officially described that way
an all-time high / low	Share prices reached **an all-time high / low** yesterday.	a record high / low point
be all in the mind	His doctor told him that he isn't really ill – his symptoms **are all in the mind**.	are imagined; not physically real
be all things to all men	The show would have been better if it hadn't tried to **be all things to all men**.	please everyone even when this is not possible
all-singing, all-dancing	There's a new **all-singing, all-dancing** version of the software, but it's expensive.	ambitious and modern, with lots of special features

Exercises

51.1 Look at A. Complete each idiom with one word.

1 get the all-..............................
2 be all ....
3 all systems ....
4 .... all she cares
5 at all ....
6 all in .... time
7 all ....
8 that's him all ....

51.2 Complete each sentence with an idiom from 51.1. You may need to change the form of the verb.

1 The office never stops. It's .... from 8 am to 6 pm.
2 There were eighteen of us for dinner, ...
3 Don't be in such a hurry to pass your driving test. .... !
4 My sister isn't interested in what I'm doing. I could be homeless ....
5 Barry went out to celebrate .... from his doctor.
6 Some parents allow their children to come home .... of the day and night.
7 My brother's really forgetful, so I'm not surprised he forgot your birthday. .... !
8 My dad was really grumpy this morning, but .... now.

51.3 Match the beginning of each sentence with its ending.

1 There are over a hundred thousand books in the library, all   high.
2 The new government is trying to be all things to all   smiles.
3 He claims that he is the boss of his company in all but   told.
4 She's said some terrible things about me, but to my face she's all   nothing.
5 The banks raised interest rates yesterday to an all-time   name.
6 You can't give up smoking slowly – it has to be all or   men.

51.4 Choose the correct idiom.

1 I want to get a new [all-time high / all-singing, all-dancing / all-clear] mobile phone.
2 I was late for work, I argued with my friend and, [in all but name / all in good time / to cap it all], my bike got stolen.
3 She's the head of the school [all in all / all or nothing / in all but name].
4 They're trying to be [all things to all men / all told / at all hours], but it's an impossible aim.
5 The atmosphere at work seems to be at [an all-time low / all or nothing / all systems go].
6 I've got thirteen uncles, [in all but name / all told / all smiles].

51.5 Correct the six mistakes with idioms in this email.

> I'm training to be a vet, and I've got ten exams, all said, to prepare for. It means I've been studying at all minutes of the day and night. I'm exhausted, and to hat it all I've got three exams on the same day this week! I just want to relax and go on holiday, but all in nice time – I'll be finished next month. I told my friend I was feeling stressed, but he just laughed – that's him all off; he never takes anything seriously, and even when he's worried or anxious he's all smile.

52 No

A Conversational expressions using *no*

- I'll be home **in next to no time**[1].
- I found **no end of**[2] bargains in the sales.
- It'd help me **no end**[3] if you did the shopping.
- She was spending money **like there's no tomorrow**[4].
- You must come to my party. **I won't take no for an answer**[5].
- **No prizes for guessing**[6] who arrived last.
- Let's ask her now. **No time like the present**[7].
- Go and wash your hands. **No ifs and buts**[8].
- I'll help you. **No strings attached**[9], I promise.
- Don't believe their promises. **There's no such thing as a free lunch**[10].
- Some parts of the city are **no-go areas**[11] at night.
- He's not phoned or emailed, but **no news is good news**[12].
- She told me **in no uncertain terms**[13] that she thought I was making a foolish mistake.

[1] very quickly [2] lots of [3] very much [4] quickly [5] won't let you refuse to come [6] it's obvious [7] now is the perfect time [8] do it without arguing (usually used to a child) [9] there'll be no unpleasant or inconvenient demands [10] if someone gives you something, they always expect something in return [11] dangerous places [12] we'd hear something if there were a problem [13] strongly and directly

B *No for dramatic effect*

Note these idioms with *no*. In each one, the idiom is used in place of a more direct word or expression. For example, *Rome is no ordinary city* actually means *Rome is an extraordinary city*.

idiom	example	meaning
be no oil painting	Kay is a beautiful woman, but her daughter **is no oil painting**.	is ugly
be no spring chicken	She loves windsurfing and paragliding, even though she'**s no spring chicken**.	is not young any more
be no / nobody's fool	He'll never believe your lies – he'**s no / nobody's fool**.	is clever and not easily deceived
be no joke	It'**s no joke** driving on those steep, narrow mountain roads.	is serious or difficult
be no picnic	Trekking across the desert in temperatures of over 100 degrees **was no picnic** for the explorers.	was difficult and unpleasant

Exercises

52.1 Look at A. When would you use the idioms in the box? Match the idioms with the situations.

> I won't take no for an answer!
> Go at once – no ifs and buts!
> No time like the present!
> There's no such thing as a free lunch!
> No news is good news!
> No strings attached – I promise!

1 Someone tells you about an email they received promising them a free dream holiday.
2 You are determined that someone will accept your invitation to dinner.
3 A friend asks you when to do something. You think they should do it immediately.
4 You want to reassure a friend that you won't ask anything in return for taking them to an expensive restaurant.
5 You want your child to go to bed immediately.
6 You want to reassure a friend who is worried that she hasn't heard from her teenage daughter who is travelling round Australia.

52.2 Read these statements and answer the questions.

1 Richard said it was no picnic for someone of his age to get used to a new job.
Was it easy or difficult for Richard when he started his new job?
2 Lena is very nice, but she's no oil painting.
Is Lena pretty?
3 John is very good at squash, even though he's no spring chicken.
Is John still a young man?
4 People often laugh at Mary, but she's nobody's fool.
How easy would it be to deceive Mary?
5 Charles's boss told him in no uncertain terms that he'd be dismissed immediately if he didn't work hard enough.
How direct was Charles's boss with his threats?
6 It's no joke trying to bring up a family on the minimum wage.
How easy is it to look after a family if your only income is the minimum wage?

52.3 Correct the mistakes in these idioms.

1 There's no such thing as a free gift.
2 She loves going shopping and spending like there's no future.
3 We were told in no uncertain words that we must always be punctual for work.
4 He said he would lend me €2000 with no strings involved.
5 He's a very good squash player, even though he's no spring onion.
6 The new housing development caused no finish of problems.

52.4 Replace the underlined part of each sentence with an idiom.

1 The town was full of people partying <u>madly</u> on New Year's Eve.
2 <u>You won't be surprised when I tell you</u> who won the cookery competition.
3 The journey was very easy, and we got to our destination <u>very quickly</u>.
4 There are <u>lots and lots of</u> places to eat in our town.
5 The police have declared the zone <u>a dangerous place</u>.
6 It would help your grandma <u>a lot</u> if you cut the grass for her.

53 Hand

A Positive situations

In these comments, the speakers use an idiom to repeat and sum up what they say.

> He was the only candidate for the job, and he got it; it **was handed to him on a plate**[1].

> Let's ask Nora to be club president as she has so much experience. She's **an old hand at**[4] running organisations.

> Our team played well from the start and we soon **had the upper hand**[2].

> Laura's opponent in the badminton final played badly, so she **won hands down**[5].

> I know she's arrogant, but she *has* broken three world records. **You have to hand it to her**[3]!

> He's a great comedian. He **had** the audience **eating out of the palm of his hand**[6].

[1] he got it very easily and did not have to work for it [2] gained power and control [3] you have to admire what she did, even if you don't admire everything about her [4] is very experienced at [5] won very easily [6] had complete control of them (You can also say he had the audience 'in the palm of his hand'.)

B Negative situations

Refusing to speak to your uncle when he has been so generous to you is **biting the hand that feeds you**. [treating somebody badly who helps you in some way, often by giving you money]

I'd like to pay you more, but **my hands are tied**. [I'm not free to do what I'd like to do]

The minister's accidental reference to tax increases in an interview **played into** the opposition's **hands**. [unintentionally gave someone an advantage over him]

The government have rejected **out of hand** the allegation that torture has been used in prisons. [completely]

If you **lay a hand on** me, I will report you to the police. [hurt or physically attack]

He lost his job, then his house was flooded. Some people **are dealt a lousy hand**. [are very unlucky in life]

They gave their opponents an advantage by naming the team before the final. They shouldn't have **shown their hand** so early. [told people their plans when they were a secret before]

Very few people supported her. You **could count them on the fingers of one hand**. [they were very small in number]

C Other idioms with *hand*

If you **give somebody a big hand**, you applaud them by clapping.

If you **hand over the reins to** someone, you give the power you had (for example, over a business or an organisation) to another person.

If you say 'Her children **are off her hands** now. One is married and the other is at university', you mean she is not responsible for them any more.

If you just **sit on your hands**, you do nothing about a problem that needs to be solved.

If you say 'I know I have a map of Dublin somewhere, but **I can't lay my hands on it** at the moment', you mean you can't find it.

If you ask someone to **put their hand on their heart** and tell you something, you ask them to tell you something truthfully.

Exercises

53.1 Look at A. Complete each idiom.

1 He doesn't know anything about business, but he's made a success of his internet company – you have to .... him.
2 In the tennis final, Dennis Roxley had the .... for the entire match and won easily.
3 Katarina is always complaining that a lot of children with rich parents have everything handed to them ....
4 We scored 230 points. No other team got more than 120, so we won the competition ....
5 What a brilliant speaker! She had everyone eating .... of her hand.
6 Adam is an .... at dealing with lawyers – he used to be one himself!

53.2 Correct the mistakes in the idioms in these news cuttings.

1 By publishing their tax plans a year before the election, the opposition have shown hand too early.

2 Mr Mills has gone right into the hands of his critics by admitting that he made errors in the past.

3 You can count on your fingers of one hand the number of times this government has done anything to help the poor.

4 In court, the accused said he had never laid his hand on anyone and denied the charges.

5 The minister claimed that her hand was tied by European regulations, and that she could not act to change the situation.

6 The minister of education rejected out off hand the claim that small schools would be closed.

53.3 Match the beginning of each sentence with its ending.

1 I think you've been dealt
2 It's crazy to bite
3 My sister feels relieved that her kids are
4 If you do that, you'll play
5 You mustn't expect things to be handed
6 You've got everyone eating

into the hands of your enemies.
off her hands and are independent.
out of the palm of your hand.
a lousy hand. You've had so much bad luck.
the hand that feeds you.
to you on a plate.

53.4 What would you say in these situations? Use an idiom from the opposite page in your answer.

1 You are the chairperson of an informal lecture. The guest speaker, Professor Ward, has given a wonderful lecture, and you want everyone to applaud her.
2 Someone asks if they can borrow your dictionary. You know you have one somewhere, but you can't find it at the moment. Explain.
3 Tell your colleagues that you think you should all do something positive about a bad situation instead of doing nothing.
4 You have been the secretary of a sports club for ten years. Tell the other members that you are ready to pass the job to someone else.
5 Your friend says they have never told a lie. Ask them if they would swear this is the truth.

FOLLOW UP Make a special page in your vocabulary notebook for *hand* idioms and see how many you can collect in one month. Check their meanings in a dictionary if you are not sure.

54 Heart

A Heart idioms in dialogues

In these conversations, the second speaker uses an idiom to repeat and sum up what the first speaker says.

A: She's always dreamt of being a ballet dancer, hasn't she?
B: Yes, it's been **her heart's desire** ever since she was three years old.

A: She sometimes seems a bit rude, but she's very kind really.
B: I know. She's **got a heart of gold**, hasn't she?

A: The teacher is only strict with his students because he thinks it will help them.
B: That's right. He only **has their best interests at heart**.

A: Only the coldest, most unfeeling person could fail to be moved by such a sad story.
B: I agree. You'd have to **have a heart of stone** not to be upset by it.

A: The movement wants to attack our society's most important values.
B: That's right. It aims to **strike at the heart of** freedom and democracy.

A: I don't want to go to her party, but it would be unkind not to, don't you think?
B: Yes, I **don't have the heart to** say no.

A: Was Jill very upset when she told you about Peter leaving?
B: Yes, she certainly was. She **cried her heart out**!

A: I feel so sorry for everyone who lost their homes in the flood.
B: Me too. **My heart goes out to** them.

A: Jo says she's exhausted after going on that luxury cruise.
B: **My heart bleeds** for her! [I don't feel sorry for her at all; this idiom is often used ironically to mean the opposite, but is sometimes used in a non-humorous way, e.g. my heart bleeds for the victims of the tragedy]

B Heart idioms in horoscopes

	You always show your emotions, but this week it would be better for you not to **wear your heart on your sleeve**[1].		You are worried about something difficult you have to do this week, but **take heart**[5] – it won't be as bad as you expect.
	Try not to show that **your heart isn't in**[2] your work this week. You may find that things soon start to improve.		**Your heart is in your boots**[6] when you think of all the work you have to do today, but just get on with it. Once you get started, you may even enjoy it.
	You say that you are not sure where your relationship is going, but in **your heart of hearts**[3] you know that it is unlikely to last much longer.		You keep telling someone close to you about their faults. **Have a heart**[7]! Tell them what you like about them too.
	You don't want to hurt your friend by giving them some bad news, but it's important that you tell them soon. **Harden your heart**[4] and do it now.		

[1] make your feelings obvious [2] you are not interested in [3] in your true, most secret thoughts
[4] don't let your feelings stop you [5] don't be anxious or afraid [6] you feel unhappy [7] be kind

Exercises

54.1 Look at A. Choose the correct answer.

1 If someone is very kind to others, do they have a) a heart of stone or b) a heart of gold?
2 If your heart bleeds for someone, does this always mean you feel sorry for them? a) Yes b) No
3 If you cry your heart out, are you a) shouting or b) sobbing?
4 If someone has your best interests at heart, are they concerned about a) your general well-being or b) your finances?
5 Is your heart more likely to go out to someone who is a) suffering or b) very successful?
6 Are you more likely to say 'I don't have the heart to' do something a) pleasant or b) unpleasant?

54.2 Correct the five mistakes with idioms in this letter to a problem page.

> I've been offered a job that all my friends and family think I should take. The problem is that in my heart of heart I really don't want it. It's always been my heart's wish to leave this city and work abroad, but I don't get the heart to tell my family this, as I know they'll be upset. I know you will tell me to keep heart and be strong, but I really don't want to hurt them. After all, I know they have my best interests by heart. What should I do?

54.3 Replace the underlined part of each sentence with an idiom.

1 Don't expect so much of him – he's only four! <u>Be kind to him</u>!
2 You'll only get hurt if you <u>make your feelings so obvious</u>.
3 <u>He felt very miserable</u> as he thought about the difficult week ahead.
4 You know your parents <u>want what is best for you</u>.
5 He showed her round the city, but she could tell that <u>he was not really interested in it</u>.

54.4 Complete the crossword.

Across

3 Alan knew he hadn't studied enough, and his heart was in his .... as he entered the exam room.
6 So you only have two cars now, not three? My heart .... for you.
7 He's trying to be enthusiastic, but you can tell his heart isn't really .... it.
9 Rosa was frightened, but she .... her heart and entered the room.
10 When I saw the film about the refugees, my heart .... out to them, and I had to do something to help.

Down

1 Kasia didn't have the heart .... refuse to help her little brother.
2 The article strikes .... the heart of the problem when it talks about child poverty.
4 You always know how Daniela feels – she wears her heart on her ....
5 Few people in life are lucky enough to achieve their heart's ....
8 .... heart, Irma! Lots of people fail their driving test the first time.

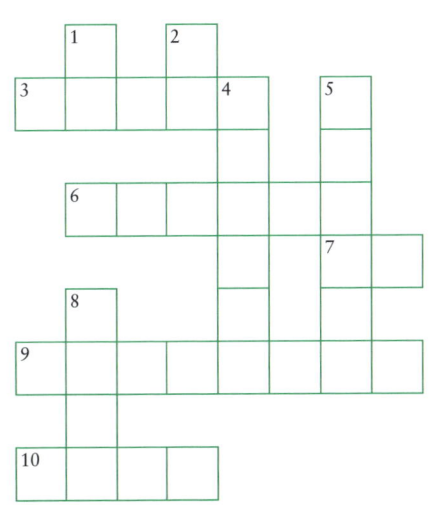

55 Life and live

A Idioms with life

Mandy: Did you have a good holiday in New Zealand?
Sophie: Yes, thanks. We **had the time of our life**[1]! Did I tell you I bumped into my next door neighbour there? I **got the shock of my life**[2]!
Mandy: What a surprise! So, what did you do on holiday?
Sophie: We did lots of sailing, and my husband even went bungee jumping.
Mandy: Wow! That'd **scare the life out of me**[3].
Sophie: Me too. There's no way I'd **risk life and limb**[4] like that. Anyway, we had some friends round last night, and he **was the life and soul of the party**[5] telling them all about his bungee jump. He claims he came **within an inch of his life**[6] doing it!
Mandy: Oh dear!
Sophie: Still, we both feel we've **got a new lease of life**[7].
Mandy: Oh, I'd love to go travelling and **see life**[8]! I'm going to **make my husband's life a misery**[9] until he agrees that we can go to Canada. I've always wanted to go there.
Sophie: Do you think he'll agree?
Mandy: Of course. He'd **do anything for a quiet life**[10]!

[1] enjoyed ourselves very much
[2] was very shocked
[3] frighten me very much
[4] do something physically dangerous
[5] was the centre of attention
[6] nearly died
[7] become more energetic and active; can also be used to describe objects or places as seeming like new again
[8] experience different, often unexpected things
[9] make things difficult for someone, e.g. by talking about something all the time
[10] agree to anything to avoid problems

B Idioms with live

idiom	example	meaning
be / live in a dream world	He's **living in a dream world** if he thinks he'll become a famous pop star.	has unrealistic hopes (usually used in continuous form)
live a charmed life	James has **lived a charmed life**; everything he does works out well.	been very lucky in life
live a lie	You must tell her you're married – you can't go on **living a lie**.	living dishonestly by pretending to be something that is not true
live out of a suitcase	After a month sleeping on a friend's floor, Jane is tired of **living out of a suitcase**.	not having a permanent place to live
live on borrowed time	The government is **living on borrowed time** at the moment and is unlikely to survive the next election.	existing longer than expected
live to tell the tale	Our walking holiday was awful! We got lost on the mountains, and it rained all the time. But at least we **lived to tell the tale**.	successfully dealt with a difficult or frightening experience
live and let live	I wouldn't want to have as many pets as they do but, hey, **live and let live**!	accept how others live and behave, even though it is different from your way of life

Exercises

55.1 Look at A. Match the beginning of each sentence with its ending.

1 Mum finally said I could go to the party – she'd do
2 When he retired, Steve got
3 The children had the time
4 That film scared the life
5 Firefighters risk life
6 Melanie is always the life
7 He threatened to make her life
8 Diana got the shock of

a misery if she spoke to the police.
and soul of the party.
her life when she saw the snake.
anything for a quiet life.
of their lives at the party.
and limb every day to help others.
out of me!
a new lease of life.

55.2 Correct the mistakes in these idioms.

1 We were within a mile of our lives when the lightning struck the tree beside us.
2 I don't like cycling to work. I feel like I'm risking life and legs in all that traffic.
3 The operation has given my grandmother a new licence of life.
4 Taking your final exams won't be easy, but I'm sure you'll live to tell the news.
5 Clare felt the shock of her life when she saw the police officer at her door.
6 Some people find living out of some luggage away from home very stressful.
7 The company chairman is living on lent time after the latest fall in profits.
8 Lewis is really shy and isn't usually the life and heart of the party.

55.3 Replace the underlined part of each sentence with an idiom.

1 Your life will be based on deceit if you don't tell him you were once in prison.
2 In this life we have to accept people for what they are, even if they are very different from us.
3 Not many people have lived such a happy and successful life as Ed has.
4 We had a fantastic holiday in California last year.
5 Travelling is the best way to discover different things about the world.
6 The explorers faced many challenges in the Arctic but came back safely and told us all about it.
7 The sudden scream gave me a terrible fright.
8 Jenny thinks she'll have a career as a model, but she's being totally unrealistic in my opinion.
9 The naughty child made things very unpleasant for his teacher.
10 The full service has made our old car feel like new again.

55.4 Complete each idiom with a preposition.

1 Ever since they lost the competition, United's coach has felt he is living .... borrowed time.
2 We were .... an inch of our lives when the falling rock just missed our car.
3 I got the shock .... my life when I switched on the TV and saw my mum being interviewed.
4 Travelling round the world living .... of a suitcase can be exciting at first but soon loses its novelty.
5 I'm sure your parents will have the time .... their lives on the cruise.
6 My dad hates confrontation. I think he'd do anything .... a quiet life!

56 Dead and death

A Dead and death as the end of something or as failure

In these conversations, the second speaker uses an idiom to react to what the first speaker says.

A: I wanted to talk to you about your plan to start a hiking club.
B: I don't want to talk about it. As far as I'm concerned, that idea is now **dead and buried**[1].

A: It was a pity that house prices rose so much last year.
B: Yes. That was **the kiss of death to**[2] our plan to buy a place in the city centre.

A: Did anything happen about that scheme to build a centre for the homeless?
B: No. The city council ran out of money, and the whole plan is **dead in the water**[3].

A: I tried to buy *Zoom* magazine today but couldn't get it anywhere.
B: Oh yes. That's **as dead as a dodo**[4]. They stopped publishing it about a year ago.

A: Your committee doesn't seem to achieve much. Why is that?
B: If you want my opinion, there's too much **dead wood**[5]. We need some new people.

A: What happened to the party's manifesto for change?
B: Oh, it's **a dead duck**[6]. Everyone voted against it.

A: Many companies are struggling financially at the moment.
B: Yes. The economic recession has dealt **a death blow**[7] to many small businesses.

[1] finished or ended completely [2] event that caused our plan to fail (informal) [3] failed and will never succeed [4] not existing or popular or important any more (informal; a *dodo* is an extinct bird) [5] members of a group who are not useful any more and who should be removed [6] not successful or useful (informal) [7] an event that causes something to fail completely

B Other idioms with dead and death

If you are **dead to the world**, you are in a deep sleep.

If you are **sick to death** of something, you are annoyed by it because you have experienced it for too long. (You can also say 'bored *or* worried to death'.)

If something is **a fate worse than death** (humorous), it is the worst thing that can happen to you.

If someone endures **a living death**, they have a life so full of suffering that it would be better to be dead.

If something is **a matter of life and / or death**, it is a serious situation where people might die.

If you do something **in the dead of night**, you do it in the middle of the night.

If you say something will happen '**over my dead body!**', you mean you will do everything you can to prevent it.

If you say a vehicle, a building or a machine is **a death trap**, you think it is so dangerous it could cause people to die.

If someone **is at death's door**, they are nearly dead.

> **TIP**
> There are many idioms based on *dead* and *death* in English. Make a special page for *dead* / *death* idioms in your vocabulary notebook and record any new ones you find.

Exercises

56.1 Look at A. Rewrite the underlined part of each sentence using the word in brackets.

1 There are a lot of useless people in my office. They should sack some people. (WOOD)
2 Putting Bernard in charge was the event that caused the project to fail. (KISS)
3 His idea of building a plane and flying round the world has been abandoned. (DODO)
4 The old family quarrel has now ended completely, and they live in harmony. (BURIED)
5 The planning committee's decision was an event that caused the failure of the proposal to build the new airport. (BLOW)

56.2 Which *dead* or *death* idioms do these pictures make you think of?

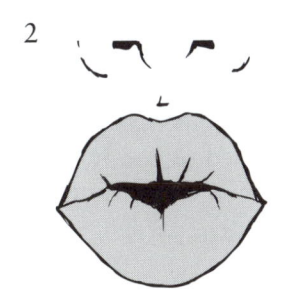

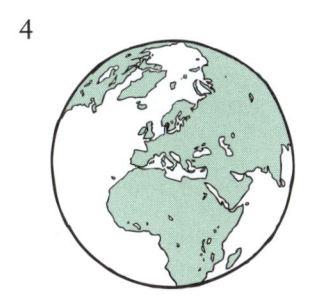

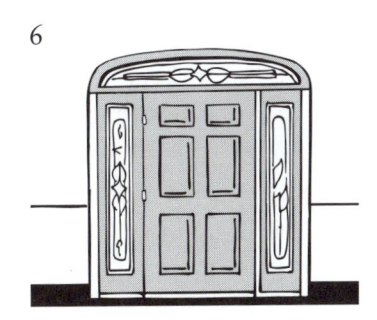

1
2
3
4
5
6

56.3 Complete each sentence with an idiom from 56.2.

1 The burglars came ...., when everyone was sleeping.
2 The bank refused to lend him the money. That was the .... to his plan to open a restaurant.
3 I was .... and didn't hear her enter the room.
4 The negotiations have broken down, and the deal is ....
5 I don't think people will pay to have their computers cleaned every three months. That idea is .... if you ask me.
6 Poor old Jesse is .... I don't think he'll last another year.

56.4 Correct the mistakes in the idioms.

1 You should only call an ambulance if it is the matter of death and life.
2 The thieves stole the painting in the death of night.
3 I am sick to the dead of people complaining all the time. It's not my fault!
4 That old car is so dangerous; it's the dead trap.
5 Having to sit next to my boring uncle at the restaurant was the fate like death.
6 Many people suffered a death in life in prison camps during the civil war.
7 The council are planning to demolish my house to build a motorway. On my dead body!
8 There are too many dead woods on the school committee. They never do anything useful.

57 Mind

A Mind as a noun

Mind as a noun means 'thoughts' or 'imagination'. In these conversations, the second speaker uses an idiom to repeat and sum up what the first speaker says.

A: I'm fed up with listening to the teacher and not doing anything, aren't you?
B: Yes, I'm **bored out of my mind**.

A: Vikki should pass her maths exam, provided she makes an effort.
B: Yes, she certainly should, **if she puts her mind to it**.

A: The concert was absolutely spectacular, wasn't it!
B: Yes, it **blew my mind**!

A: No sane person would want to be prime minister.
B: That's true. **Nobody in their right mind** would want that responsibility.

A: He must be crazy to spend all that money on a car.
B: Yes, he's **out of his mind**!

A: I'm really tired of this boring party. Shall we go home?
B: You **read my mind** – let's go!

A: We must do something to stop your sister thinking about her operation tomorrow.
B: Let's take her to the cinema. That should **take her mind off** it.

A: I can't stop worrying about Hamid's accident.
B: I know. It's been **preying on my mind** all day.

A: I can't believe the wedding has been cancelled. They seemed so happy.
B: Yes, I can't **get my mind round** it either! (You can also say 'I can't get my head round it'.)

A: Whatever I say, he always brings the conversation back to sport!
B: I know. He **has a** terrible **one-track mind**.

A: Try to remember what happened next.
B: I'm trying to **cast my mind back**, but I just can't remember a thing.

A: Tell yourself you can do it, and you'll easily manage to swim that distance.
B: I know. It's just a question of **mind over matter**. [your thoughts influencing your body]

B Mind as a verb

Mind can also be a verb and is often used when warning people to be careful.

A: My dad hates bad manners, so **mind your Ps and Qs** when you meet him. [be polite – *p* stands for *please* and *q* represents the /kju:/ sound at the end of *thank you*]
B: Don't worry! I will.

A: The pavement is very uneven here.
B: Yes, you need to **mind your step**. [walk carefully]

A: Why did you come back so late last night?
B: **Mind your own business**! [it's got nothing to do with you]

A: See you later, Grandma.
B: OK. **Mind how you go**! [take care; used when saying goodbye (informal)]

A: Nathan doesn't trust his colleagues. He thinks they're telling lies about him to his boss.
B: Yes, he needs to **mind his back** in that office. [be careful because others are trying to cause problems for him; you can also say 'watch your back']

Exercises

57.1 Look at A. Are the idioms in these sentences used correctly? If not, correct them.
1 Nobody in their correct mind would lend him money again. He never pays it back.
2 Dom had always said he wanted to study law, so his mother is finding it hard to get her mind round his decision to leave university and join a rock band.
3 He's always talking about cars. I've never met anyone with such a one-way mind.
4 I'm sure you can mend your own bike if you put your mind to it.
5 What can we do to take Marco's mind out of his problems?
6 Now, I'd like you all to throw your mind back to your very first day at school.

57.2 Complete each dialogue with an idiom.
1 Pete: I'm off now then. See you in a couple of hours.
   Beth: Bye. ....
2 Harry: You've bought another pair of shoes?! How much were they?
   Tina: .... !
3 Nathan: Why are you yawning?
   Molly: I'm ....
4 Lisa: I'm thinking of taking a year off to cycle round the world.
   Rita: You must be .... !
5 Joe: Were you able to forget about the exam today?
   Lou: No, it's .... all day.
6 Police officer: Please .... and tell us exactly what happened on the night in question.
   Vera: Well, it's a long time ago now ...

57.3 Which idioms do these pictures make you think of? Complete the captions.

1 He needs to ....

2 I can ....

3 Come on – .... !

4 That singer .... !

57.4 Replace the underlined part of each sentence with an idiom.
1 <u>Walk carefully</u> on the ice – it's very slippery.
2 The actor's performance <u>was amazing</u>!
3 It goes without saying that you should always <u>be very polite</u> at an interview.
4 People who drink and drive must be <u>totally crazy</u>.
5 My twin brother can <u>tell exactly what I'm thinking</u>.
6 I'm always <u>so bored</u> in physics lessons!
7 Their argument <u>worried Fiona</u> for a long time.
8 You'll find it quite easy to learn the guitar if you <u>make a bit of an effort</u>.

58 Hard

A Letters to a problem page

Dear Bella

I've just started working in a clothes shop, but it's proving much **harder than I had bargained for**[1]. I've realised that I'm no good at **giving people the hard sell**[2], and there don't seem to be any **hard and fast rules**[3] for what I should be doing. I thought I would love it, but I'm finding it really **hard going**[4]. Will it get better or is this it?

Liz

Dear Bella

My partner and I have just split up. It was a mutual decision, and we agreed there would be **no hard feelings**[5], but it has **hit me much harder**[6] than I expected. My ex seems to be going out a lot and is perfectly happy, which I find **hard to swallow**[7]. Am I being unreasonable?

Ali

Dear Bella

I lost my job last month, so my family has **fallen on hard times**[8]. My wife is still working, but we're struggling, and we're really **hard up**[9]. I'm finding it difficult to find a new job, and I'm **hard put**[10] to see a solution. What should I do?

Simon

[1] more difficult than expected [2] trying very hard to persuade people to buy something [3] clear rules
[4] difficult and tiring [5] no anger towards each other [6] affected me much worse [7] difficult to accept
[8] are finding life difficult because we have no money [9] without much money [10] finding it difficult

B Horoscopes

This week you will **learn the hard way**[1] that things are not always what they seem.

A problem at work this week will turn out to be **a hard nut to crack**[4].

Someone you don't know very well will do their best to **drive a hard bargain**[2] with you, but make sure you do not agree to anything without taking advice.

Try not to **make hard work of**[5] something that is really quite simple to solve.

You will **be hard-pressed**[3] to finish all the work you have to do this week, but keep going and it will all be worthwhile.

A friend's behaviour makes you feel **hard done by**[6], but you will soon understand that they are not treating you unfairly.

[1] discover something through a difficult experience [2] demand a lot in exchange for what they do for you [3] find it difficult [4] a difficult problem to solve [5] make something into a major problem
[6] unfairly treated

Exercises

58.1 Look at A. Correct the mistakes in these idioms.

1 I hate it when people try to give you the hard sale over the phone.
2 Her grandfather's illness has really struck her very hard.
3 I'm so glad we're friends again. No hard feels, OK?
4 Walking home in the heavy snow was really hard go.
5 I find his constant criticism of me very hard to drink.
6 Learning how to skate turned out to be much harder than Nina had bargained by.

58.2 Read this letter to a problem page. Are these sentences true or false? If the answer is false, say why.

I'm feeling very hard-pressed at work at the moment. I have a long report to finish, but I'll be hard put to get it done in time. I'd love to hand in my notice, but I'm far too hard up to be able to manage without a salary even for a week or two. I guess I'm learning the hard way that money doesn't grow on trees! Can you help me? Kira

1 Kira is very busy at work.
2 She will easily meet her deadline for the report.
3 She can't afford to leave her job.
4 She is learning a fun lesson about life.

58.3 Complete each idiom.

1 .... on hard times
2 a hard .... to crack
3 hard to ....
4 .... a hard bargain
5 hard and .... rules
6 learn the hard ....
7 .... hard work of
8 feel hard .... by

58.4 Complete each sentence with an idiom from 58.3. You may need to change the form of the verb.

1 The truth is unpleasant, and I'm worried you'll find it ....
2 Although Jack's grandfather used to be rich, he .... and the family lived in poverty.
3 There are no .... as to how you should behave in circumstances like these.
4 I'm sure Suzi will .... when she discovers that her uncle has bought her twin sister a new sports car.
5 Children eventually .... that life is not always fair.
6 I have no idea how we're going to solve this problem. It's going to be .... , I'm sure.
7 Ruby always complains and seems to .... any little problem.
8 You want me to reduce the price by £200? You certainly ....

> **FOLLOW UP**
> Look up *hard* in the Cambridge Idioms Dictionary at http://dictionary.cambridge.org/. Make a note of three other interesting idioms that you find there. Write them down in example sentences.

59 Fall

A When things go wrong

Many idioms with *fall* refer to situations where things go wrong, people encounter problems, or where something fails. Read these news cuttings and note the idioms.

> The minister of education seems to have **fallen from grace**[1]. There are rumours that the pwresident is planning to sack her next week when ...

> The village carnival **fell foul of**[5] health and safety regulations and was cancelled. A spokesperson said that ...

> Occasionally, secret documents **fall into the wrong hands**[2] and national security is threatened. One such case has raised fears ...

> The minister's statement **fell short of**[6] an apology, though he did admit that some ...

> Last year, a petition with 10,000 signatures demanding an end to the tax **fell on deaf ears**[3], so yesterday protesters took to the streets and ...

> The government has **fallen into the trap of**[7] creating committee after committee, thinking that will solve the problems of social ...

> House prices have **fallen through the floor**[4] in the last six months, leaving many homeowners worrying about how ...

> The global banking system seemed to **be falling apart at the seams**[8] in 2009 ...

[1] done something which made people in authority stop liking or admiring them
[2] the wrong people obtain and control them
[3] was ignored
[4] dropped to a very low level
[5] broke a law or regulation
[6] did not come up to the standard of
[7] done something which seemed like a good idea but was not wise
[8] be in a very bad state and about to fail

B Other idioms with *fall*

People were **falling over themselves to** volunteer as helpers for the president's visit. [very keen and eager]

She never seems to have to work to get what she wants. Everything just seems to **fall / drop into her lap**. [happen or be given to her without any effort on her part]

Kevin seems to have **fallen for** Gloria **hook, line and sinker**! [fallen madly in love with]

My colleagues at the office played a joke on me, and I **fell for it hook, line and sinker**. [completely believed something which was not true]

I'm afraid you will have to **fall into line** and accept the company's rules and policy. [start to accept the rules of an organisation]

Here are two proverbs which include *fall*:
Pride comes before a fall. [if someone is too confident or arrogant, something bad will happen which will show that they are not as good as they think they are]
The bigger they are / come, the harder they fall. [the more power or success someone has, the harder it will be for them to lose it]

See Unit 11 for more proverbs.

Exercises

59.1 Look at A. Complete each idiom in these work emails.

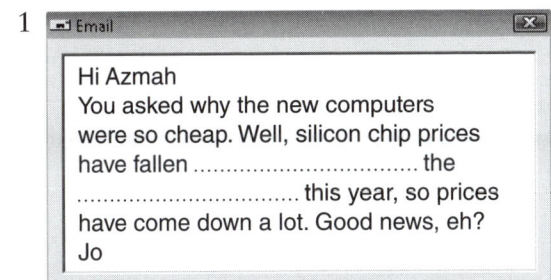

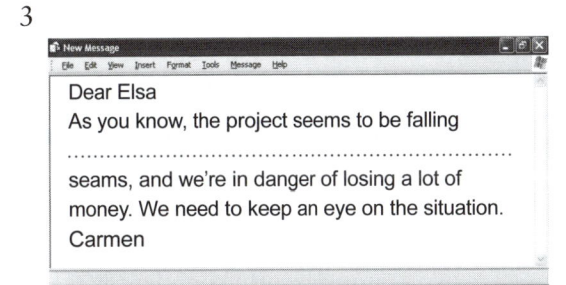

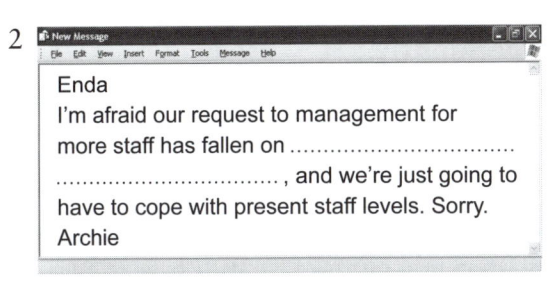

1. Hi Azmah
You asked why the new computers were so cheap. Well, silicon chip prices have fallen .... the .... this year, so prices have come down a lot. Good news, eh?
Jo

2. Enda
I'm afraid our request to management for more staff has fallen on ...., and we're just going to have to cope with present staff levels. Sorry.
Archie

3. Dear Elsa
As you know, the project seems to be falling .... seams, and we're in danger of losing a lot of money. We need to keep an eye on the situation.
Carmen

4. Dear all
A memory stick with sensitive information on it is missing. We don't want it to fall into .... Can you all check your desks, please? It's vital that we find it.
Brian

59.2 Rewrite the underlined part of each sentence using the word in brackets.

1. It seems that the prime minister's special adviser, Anne Sparks, is not liked or respected any more, and she is expected to resign soon. (GRACE)
2. Everyone had to accept the decision and work longer hours for the same pay. (LINE)
3. The deal broke the export regulations and had to be cancelled at the last minute. (FOUL)
4. The report is not really an outright condemnation of the government's actions, but it does contain strong criticism. (SHORT)

59.3 Complete each idiom.

1. I didn't realise she was deceiving me, and I fell for it hook, ...
2. It looks as if the whole system is falling apart ....
3. I didn't really have to do anything to get the job. It just fell ....
4. Sally may not like the new rules, but she'll just have to ....

59.4 Answer these questions.

1. What is the difference between falling for something hook, line and sinker and falling for a person hook, line and sinker?
2. What proverb could you use about someone who is over-confident and arrogant, and you suspect something bad will happen to them as a result?
3. True or false? If someone falls over themselves to do something, it means they have an accident.
4. What proverb could you use about a billionaire who lost all their money in one day and had to beg in the streets?

60 Own

A Own as adjective, noun and verb

Own is frequently used as an adjective:

She's **a woman after my own heart**. [having the same opinions or interests as me]

Own is occasionally used as a noun:

Bicycles **come into their own** in rush hour, as they end up moving much faster than cars or buses. [are very useful or successful in a particular situation]

Own can also be used as a verb:

She's only worked here for a week, but she behaves **as if she owns the place**. [in an unpleasantly confident way]

B Own suggesting acting independently

idiom	example	meaning
be your own person	Rajiv **is his own person**. Nobody can make him do anything he doesn't want to.	behaves as he wants to without being influenced by others
take matters into your own hands	The police didn't do anything about the situation, so we decided to **take matters into our own hands**.	deal with something ourselves because others are failing to act
in your own time	There's no need to hurry. Just give me an answer **in your own time**.	when you are ready
save your own skin	Don't expect her to support you – she's only wants to **save her own skin**.	protect herself from danger or difficulty, regardless of others
go their own ways	They've decided they can't live together any longer and are going to **go their own ways**.	separate (verb)
hold your own	Fazia is only fourteen, but she can **hold her own** in any adult conversation.	be as successful as anyone else

C Own in idioms criticising people

Pilar: Mario's always saying how wonderful he is.
Maya: I know. He never stops **blowing his own trumpet**.
Pilar: His behaviour will cause him a lot of trouble.
Maya: Yes, he's **digging his own grave**, isn't he!
Pilar: It's his own fault that he's so unpopular.
Maya: I know, it'**s of his own making**.
Pilar: Everyone thinks he's using his position to make money dishonestly.
Maya: Yes, they suspect him of **feathering his own nest**.
Pilar: The trouble is, it encourages others to use the same methods as he does.
Maya: That's right. I suppose they're trying to **play him at his own game**.
Pilar: Yes, they want to get revenge by showing him how unpleasant it is.
Maya: That's exactly it. They're trying to **get their own back**.

> **ERROR WARNING**
> We always use *own* with a possessive form before it (e.g. *his own making*), not an article, e.g. *the* or *an*. The only exception to this rule is the idiom *an own goal*, e.g. The government's decision to raise taxes just before the election was very much **an own goal**. [something which helped the other side rather than themselves]

Exercises

60.1 Choose the correct word to complete each idiom.

I like Tina. She's her own [*girl / person*]. In fact, she's very much a woman after my own [*heart / head*]. But I'm not keen on her boyfriend, Karl. He's always blowing his own [*trumpet / trombone*], and when they come to my flat, he behaves as if he owns the [*space / place*]. I think it's time they went their own [*roads / ways*]. In fact, I really think she'd [*come / get*] into her own if they did.

60.2 Replace the underlined part of each sentence with an idiom.

1 I must think of a way of taking my revenge on Matt for playing that trick on me.
2 He told the police who had really planned the burglary in order to get out of trouble himself.
3 Tim was smaller than the other judo players, but he was as successful as anyone else.
4 You're making trouble for yourself by putting your boss in such a difficult position.
5 If women want to succeed in politics, they have to use the same methods as men.

60.3 Complete the crossword.

Across

2 The newspaper accused the politician of trying to .... his own nest.
4 You can't blame him for trying to save his own .... He really can't afford to lose his job.
5 You're .... your own grave by going on strike.
9 My problems may be .... my own making, but that doesn't make it any easier.
10 Just answer in your own .... There's no rush.
11 The company has managed to .... its own, despite fierce competition.

Down

1 I admire Faye for always being her own .... , even when it makes her unpopular.
3 If the town council has no plans to improve the appearance of our street, why don't we take matters into our own .... ?
6 If we want to beat our competitors, we'll have to play them at their own ....
7 Henry had never been into such a luxurious hotel before, but he walked in as .... he owned the place.
8 I'm afraid I scored an own .... when I told my boss that I didn't really need a pay rise.

> **FOLLOW UP** Note uses of *own* that you see in the course of your reading over the next week. In each case, think about whether it is being used ordinarily or idiomatically and write down any new idiomatic uses of *own* that you find.

Key

Unit 1

1.1 In 2009, I **set off** (phrasal verb) on a long journey. As I left my house, my neighbour shouted, '**Good luck!**' (greetings and good wishes) I didn't know **at that moment** (prepositional phrase) that I would not see him again for three years. I **boarded** the **plane** (collocation) at Heathrow, and soon it **took off** (phrasal verb) for Malaysia. When we **touched down** (phrasal verb) in Kuala Lumpur, I couldn't wait to **get off** (phrasal verb) the plane. I **took a bus** (collocation) to the **city centre** (compound) and **spent the night** (collocation) at a **youth hostel** (compound). The first person I met was someone I had been **at school** (prepositional phrase) with years ago. '**It's a small world!**' (saying or proverb) he said when he saw me.

1.2 My friend suggested that we <u>join forces</u>. '<u>There's safety in numbers</u>,' he said. 'Let's <u>hit the road</u> together.' I <u>was in two minds</u> whether to go with him but finally decided to say yes. We travelled together for six months and <u>had a whale of a time</u>. We spent money <u>like there was no tomorrow</u>, so I had to <u>twist my dad's arm</u> and persuade him to send me some more money so I could travel further.

1.3
1 c) a flash in the pan
2 b) taken a shine to
3 c) safe and sound
4 b) put my foot in it
5 b) as quiet as a mouse

1.4 1 b   2 c   3 a   4 a

Unit 2

2.1
1 False. Many idioms stay in frequent usage for a long time.
2 True.
3 True.
4 True.
5 False. Headline writers often play with idioms for humorous or dramatic effect, or to catch the reader's eye.
6 False. They can be found in most types of speaking and writing (although they may be more frequent in some types, such as popular journalism and informal conversation).
7 True.
8 False. Idioms are used in academic writing, although these idioms are different from typical idioms used in speech or informal writing.

2.2
1 shape
2 licking
3 stone
4 effect
5 course
6 pricked

2.3
1 go up in the world
2 lick your wounds
3 prick up your ears
4 open the door to

2.4
1 a mountain-climbing organisation
2 a boxing club
3 be patient
4 the person's conscience
5 a hi-fi company

Unit 3

3.1
1. It gives information – where necessary – about the usage of the idiom (e.g. whether it is used in a literary or an informal context), and it gives examples of the idiom in a typical context.
2. There are over one billion words of international English (i.e. British, American and Australian) taken from both spoken and written contexts.
3. It is informal.

3.2
1. very informal (*Get off your backside* means 'stop being lazy'.)
2. formal (*Know no bounds* means 'be extreme'.)
3. taboo (*The shit hits the fan* means 'there is serious trouble'.)
4. informal (*Know something inside out* means 'know thoroughly'.)
5. literary (*Curl your lip* means 'to sneer; to show you feel no respect for someone or something'.)
6. old-fashioned (*Kith and kin* means 'relatives'.)
7. humorous (*Know your place* means 'accept your low position within society without trying to improve it'.)

3.3
1. Henry will help you deal with these forms. He **knows** the system **inside out**.
2. There is a growing interest in genealogy, as people increasingly want to discover all they can about their **kith and kin**.
3. Joey can be so lazy. I wish he'd **get off his backside**.
4. Don't worry. I'll behave properly when I meet your boss. **I know my place**!
5. If Greg finds out what you've done, **the shit will hit the fan**.
6. Don't you dare **curl your lip** at me, young lady!
7. The old woman's kindness to us all **knows / knew no bounds**.

3.4 At the time of writing, the first site does not have its own entry for this phrase, but it connects you to a range of other online sites which do have information about it.

The British National Corpus finds five examples of the idiom in its corpus.

The search engine Google finds 482,000 sites using this idiom. Some of these sites are directly discussing the idiom, while many provide examples of it in a range of different contexts.

3.5 SPORTS MINISTER HOPPING MAD
John Hamilton has made a name for himself by running a tight ship at the Ministry of Sport. So it was no surprise to his staff that he reportedly 'went spare' when he learnt what had been going on behind his back. Two of his leading advisors had been feathering their own nests with government money intended for young people's sports organisations. 'Such behaviour is quite beyond the pale,' said Hamilton, 'and the two people concerned have already been given the sack'.

Meaning of idioms from 'Sports Minister hopping mad':
hopping mad = very angry
make a name for = become famous or respected for
run a tight ship = control something firmly and effectively
went spare = was extremely angry
behind one's back = without someone knowing
feather one's own nest = dishonestly use your position to get money for yourself
be beyond the pale = be unacceptable
get the sack = be dismissed from your job

Unit 4

4.1
1. They make a comparison.
2. In literary writing, e.g. poetry.
3. Those used in literary contexts are original, and the comparison is intended to make the reader think; those used in idioms have become so much part of the language that speakers rarely still notice the original comparison.
4. It can help to make sense of the meaning of the idiom, and thinking about the image underlying the idiom may help you to learn and remember the idiom.

4.2
1. have something up your sleeve
2. get / be given your marching orders / pull rank on
3. uncharted waters
4. take centre stage

4.3
1. minefield
2. launch
3. mark
4. see
5. point, light
6. pull
7. at
8. bluff

4.4
1. Everyone else was laughing, but Katie couldn't <u>see the joke</u>.
2. Jean <u>is going / getting nowhere</u> with her research.
3. BritTel is going to <u>join forces with</u> SatCom to lobby the government.
4. The teacher <u>saw red</u> when Matt refused to do his homework.
5. The errors in the report really weren't Ned's fault, but he <u>took / got the flak for</u> them.
6. Tina is hoping her father will eventually <u>see reason / sense</u> and let her drive the family car.
7. Unfortunately, my brother's transport business was <u>a casualty of</u> the rise in fuel prices.
8. As the president of a major company, Gary is used to <u>taking centre stage</u>.

Unit 5

5.1
1. from the cradle to the grave
2. to clip someone's wings
3. the tip of the iceberg
4. paying out of your own pocket

5.2
1. My sister is always buying up-to-<u>the</u>-minute gadgets.
2. Correct.
3. My granddad's always talking about <u>the</u> good old days.
4. They've been engaged for six months but haven't made any plans about when they're going to tie the <u>knot</u>.
5. Correct.
6. Engineering isn't the kind of job that every Tom, Dick or <u>Harry</u> could do.

5.3
1. mountain
2. numbered
3. spirit
4. pocket
5. bear

5.4
1. You'll pass your driving test if you really want to – <u>where there's a will, there's a way</u>.
2. I get bored if I always do the same things at the weekend – <u>variety is the spice of life</u>.
3. Shh! Be quiet! There's no need to talk <u>at the top of your voice</u>.
4. He never saves any money. He spends whatever he has. <u>Easy come, easy go</u> is his motto.
5. I was so upset when I failed the exam. I <u>cried my eyes out</u>.
6. She's a total optimist – she always manages to <u>look on / see the bright side</u>.

Unit 6

6.1
1. be blown away by
2. be on the same wavelength
3. fringe benefits

6.2
1. *Fringe benefits* are extra benefits you get with a job apart from your pay, and a *fringe* is hair that hangs down over your forehead.
2. Radio stations use FM or AM *wavelengths* to send their radio signals. If two people are *on the same wavelength*, they think in the same way.
3. If you are *blown away* by a performance, you are amazed and impressed because it is so good. A trumpet is an example of a *wind* instrument. A strong wind can also 'blow you away'.
4. *Part and parcel* refers to a necessary part of the job, and postmen have to deliver *parcels*.
5. Film stars *act*, and *get your act together* means to organise yourself and resolve a problem.

6.3
1. The money was burning **a hole in** my pocket.
2. Her two brothers don't see **eye to eye** and haven't spoken to each other for over a year.
3. Learning how to manage your finances is part **and parcel** of becoming an adult.
4. It's time you got **your act together** and found a job!
5. The president refused to make a decision, and was accused of sitting **on the fence**.
6. My computer crashed, so I'm back to **square one** with my assignment.

6.4
2. a local drama club
3. a delivery firm
4. a gardening company

Follow-up *Possible answers:*
fighting fit: a judo club, a boxing club, a gym
two left feet: a dance school
it never rains but it pours: a company that makes raincoats, umbrellas or wellington boots

Unit 7

7.1
1. You'd need to tidy the room.
2. No, you'd probably feel upset because your friend is saying you're crazy.
3. Your friend thinks her brother is often silly.

7.2
1. catch
2. fresh
3. dropped
4. bat
5. worth
6. thousand
7. throw

7.3
1. US
2. Britain
3. Britain
4. US
5. US
6. Britain
7. Britain

7.4
1. You have to pay the deposit for hiring the boat in <u>hard</u> cash. (British)
2. Rhiannon and her sister have always fought like <u>cats and dogs</u>. (US)
3. It was such a sad film / movie – I <u>cried</u> buckets. (US)
4. There's a lot of <u>donkey</u> work to be done before we can open the new restaurant. (British)
5. Having such perfect weather on holiday was the <u>icing</u> on the cake. (British)
6. Having to stay late at work on a holiday weekend really took the <u>cake</u>. (US)
7. What's happened? You look like the cat that <u>ate the canary</u>. (US)

7.5
1. donkey work
2. the icing / frosting on the cake
3. fight like cat and dog / like cats and dogs

Unit 8

8.1
1 You have to be prepared to go the **extra** mile if you want to get promoted.
2 Correct.
3 This shampoo is great – it does exactly what it **says** on the tin.
4 I'd never share an apartment with her – she'd be the flatmate **from** hell.
5 Correct.

8.2
1 Too much information
2 whatever floats your boat
3 big time
4 I'm cool with that
5 Don't even go there
6 End of

8.3
1 doesn't float my boat
2 like nailing jelly to the wall.
3 go the extra mile
4 big time

Possible answers:

8.4
1 This doesn't make sense – it would be annoying or upsetting to live next door to the neighbours from hell.
2 This doesn't make sense – being happy about something is the same as being cool with it.
3 This makes sense, as loving the painter's work is the opposite of it not floating the speaker's boat.
4 This doesn't make sense – nailing jelly to a wall means that something is hard to do; if someone is honest and open, then it is easy to see and understand their feelings and opinions.

Unit 9

9.1
1 My new dress fits **like** a glove.
2 You'll need to run **like** the wind to catch the train.
3 She's as thin **as** a rake.
4 Sandra always looks as fresh **as** a daisy.
5 He drove off **like** a maniac.
6 Her mouth felt as dry **as** a bone.
7 Their son is as bright **as** a button.
8 Her hair felt as smooth **as** silk.

9.2
1 dust
2 two short planks
3 crystal
4 thieves
5 a bone
6 mud

9.3
1 Tom and Rosa have been <u>fighting like cat and dog</u> recently.
2 Amy <u>went as red as a beetroot</u> when Lasse commented on her new dress.
3 When our teacher asks the class a difficult question, Hatsuki usually answers <u>as quick as a flash</u>.
4 It was early Sunday morning and the house was <u>as silent as the grave</u>.
5 Emma <u>was all over Jakob like a rash</u> at the barbecue last week.
6 All her sisters are <u>as poor as church mice</u>. (Notice how this simile is made plural to match the plural subject.)
7 Caterina felt <u>as fresh as a daisy</u> after her shower.
8 The students in my class are great – hardworking, punctual and <u>keen as mustard</u>.

9.4
1 Yes, he had **a face like thunder**.
2 Yes, he's **as stubborn as a mule**.
3 Yes, he was driving **like a maniac**.
4 Yes, I've been **working like a dog**.
5 Yes, she's **as keen as mustard**.

Unit 10

10.1 black and blue
neck and neck
little by little
bumper to bumper
here, there and everywhere
give or take (Notice that we also say *give and take*, but it has a different meaning: *For a relationship to work, you need a lot of **give and take**.* [compromise])
nook and cranny
hit and miss (*Hit or miss* is also possible and has the same meaning.)
neat and tidy
wear and tear

10.2
1 bumper to bumper
2 here, there and everywhere
3 wear and tear
4 little by little
5 nook and cranny
6 neat and tidy
7 neck and neck
8 give or take

10.3
1 'The **hustle and bustle** of market day.'
2 'He's a United supporter **through and through**.'
3 '**Heads or tails**?'
4 'Her two dogs are like **chalk and cheese**.'

10.4
1 People started to enter the room **in dribs and drabs**.
2 Jack's commitment to work **waxed and waned** throughout the year.
3 Have a few days' rest and you'll be **out and about** in no time.
4 I've told him **time after time** (also *time and time again*) not to leave his car unlocked.
5 The work required a lot of **blood, sweat and tears** but it was worth it.
6 The whole team's been **at sixes and sevens** since Kay resigned.
7 I keep dropping things today – I'm **all fingers and thumbs**.
8 My mum and I are **like chalk and cheese**, but we get on well.

Unit 11

11.1
1 Every cloud has a silver lining.
2 Nothing ventured, nothing gained.
3 Necessity is the mother of invention.
4 Where there's a will, there's a way.
5 Variety is the spice of life.

11.2
1 It takes two to tango.
2 It never rains but it pours.
3 All's fair in love and war.
4 Every cloud has a silver lining.
5 Rome wasn't built in a day.
6 Where there's a will, there's a way.

11.3
1 We had no tent, so we made a shelter out of branches and leaves to protect ourselves from the storm. It was a case of **necessity** is the mother of invention.
2 I'm doing three jobs at the moment to pay for my studies. Still, they say that **variety** is the spice of life!
3 I went to the gym every day for three months and felt so much fitter. It was very hard work but **no pain, no gain**.
4 I decided that bungee-jumping was too dangerous and didn't go with my friends – better to be safe than **sorry**.
5 We've got ten laptops at half-price. But hurry – it's first come, first **served**.
6 Three big bills at the same time? It never **rains** but it **pours**!

11.4   1 When we got there they had given away all the free CDs – it was a case of first **come**, first **served**.
2 Take your time and don't be impatient; Rome wasn't **built** in **a day**!
3 It's a shame you missed your flight, but at least we can spend more time together. They do say every **cloud** has **a** silver **lining**.
4 All my problems seem to come at the same time. It's true what they say: it never **rains but** it pours!
5 It's going to be a lot of hard work, but nothing **ventured**, nothing **gained**.
6 They are both in the wrong. It takes **two** to **tango**.

Unit 12

12.1   1 bun in the oven   3 in his birthday suit
2 spend a penny

12.2   1 The poet breathed his **last** on 20 January 1891.
2 Older dogs need to be let out more often to answer the **call** of nature.
3 He'd only been married for a year before he found himself a bit on the **side**.
4 For one dreadful moment I thought my number was **up**.
5 I hate my daughter's taste in music – it's full of **four**-letter words.
6 The old lady asked where she could go to powder her **nose**.
7 Did you know Marta had a **bun** in the oven?
8 Don't be such a bloody fool, pardon my **French.**

12.3   1 blinding   2 sacrifice   3 spend   4 under   5 long   6 nose

12.4   1 She's got a bun in the oven.
2 He's in the altogether / in his birthday suit.
3 I'm just going to spend a penny / powder my nose / answer the call of nature.
4 The old man knew he would soon breathe his last / was not long for this world.
5 He plays the field.
6 He's always effing and blinding.
7 Pardon my French!
8 We must reduce the number of friendly fire incidents.

12.5   1 The doctors have just told him he's got **cancer**.
2 I think you're **lying**.
3 The cat was so badly injured we had to have it **killed by the vet**.
4 Why didn't you tell me your sister was **pregnant**?
5 Shall we pause the meeting **so people can use the lavatory if they wish** now?

Unit 13

13.1   1 the fat lady   4 pebbles   7 a horse
2 enough   5 bliss   8 fish
3 the bright side   6 after the event   9 it will out

13.2   1 B: No, I promise. <u>Mum's the word</u>.
2 B: That's not fair! <u>Give me a break</u>! It's only the third time this week.
3 B: Hmm. <u>I'll believe it when I see it</u>.
4 A: <u>Get your skates on</u>! We need to leave in five minutes.
5 B: Not at all. <u>Good riddance</u>!
6 B: <u>Take it easy</u>! Don't panic! I'll help you if you like.
7 B: Just <u>give her a break</u>. It's only her second day here.
8 B: <u>So far, so good</u>. But it's early days yet.
9 B: I don't know. It's a complex situation. I suspect <u>there's more to it than meets the eye</u>.
10 B: I don't know but I'm sure we'll find out. <u>Truth will out</u>.

13.3
1 <u>Give</u> me a break!
2 There are plenty more <u>fish</u> in the sea.
3 So <u>far</u>, so good.
4 It's not over until the fat lady <u>sings</u>.
5 Truth will <u>out</u>.
6 <u>Mum's</u> the word. Note that *mum* in this expression has nothing to do with mothers. It comes from an old word meaning 'silent'.

Follow-up *Possible answers:*
Any friend of yours is a friend of mine: I like you so I am sure I will like any friend of yours too.
Beauty is only skin deep: People who are good-looking do not always have good characters.
Money is the root of all evil: The reason why people do illegal and immoral things is often money.

A: Would it be all right if I bring my friend Jack to your birthday party?
B: Of course. *Any friend of yours is a friend of mine.*

A: I'm amazed that someone so beautiful can say and do such terrible things.
B: Well, *beauty is only skin deep*, remember.

A: I just can't understand why anyone would want to set fire to their own house.
B: Well, *money is the root of all evil*. Perhaps they were hoping to claim on the insurance.

Unit 14

14.1
1 We don't receive many complaints, so we just deal with them on an **ad hoc** basis.
2 The **de facto** government will remain in power until the election results are finalised.
3 This sentence in your essay is a **non sequitur** – it's not logically connected to your previous point.
4 I could go on **ad infinitum** about the advantages of moving to the countryside.
5 Whenever a new person takes over as manager, they disturb the **status quo**, at least to some extent.
6 His lawyer claims he wasn't fully **compos mentis** when he admitted he was guilty.

14.2
1 There were no opportunities for discussion; the reform was presented as a **fait accompli**.
2 All players must be **au fait with** the rules of the game.
3 I can't come out tonight because I have to work late. Oh well, **c'est la vie**.
4 Of course I love being a movie star, but I must say that awards ceremonies are **my bête noire**.
5 So Dan has been arguing with his boss again. **Plus ça change!**
6 A lot of the parents are not very happy about the new headmaster's **laissez-faire** attitude to behaviour.

14.3
1 False. A laissez-faire approach is relaxed.
2 False. A de facto leader is a leader who has not been officially recognised as such.
3 True.
4 False. It is important not to include non sequiturs in your writing.
5 True.
6 False. If you are compos mentis, you are in control of your actions.
7 False. A fait accompli is a completed action that cannot be changed.
8 True.

Follow-up *Possible answers:*

cream of the cream – the crème de la crème

The expression is used to describe the very best examples of people or things; the cream sits on top of the milk.

it does not follow – non sequitur

The expression is used to refer to a statement which does not follow on logically from what was previously said.

a done deed – a fait accompli

If a deed is done, then it cannot be changed. Note that we do also use the expression *a done deed*.

Unit 15

15.1 1 a 2 b 3 a 4 a 5 b 6 a 7 b 8 a 9 b

15.2
1 deck   3 in   5 high   7 storm
2 wind   4 taken   6 board   8 weathering

15.3
1 There's trouble ahead, so we'd better batten down the hatches.
2 It's a long journey, but we're making good headway.
3 The business is doing so badly that I'm tempted to cut and run.
4 There are some interesting plans for new projects in the offing.
5 The film star left the room with a group of journalists in her wake.
6 It's about time someone took the wind out of Marco's sails.

15.4
1 I try to **give** the city centre **a wide berth** on Saturdays if I possibly can.
2 Jamie's mother was **taken aback** by his decision to leave school.
3 Amy's plans to buy a new car **went by the board** when she lost her job.
4 Their relationship has been **on the rocks** for some months.
5 Asim **runs a tight ship**.
6 The cost of home insurance has risen **in the wake of** last summer's floods.
7 We were **left high and dry** when the babysitter didn't turn up.
8 I know it's been hard for you, but I'm sure you'll **weather the storm**.

Unit 16

16.1
1 warpath   3 arms   5 fighting
2 bombshell   4 shell   6 beat

16.2
shoot down in flames   a battle of wills
baptism of fire   run the gauntlet
a flash in the pan   hang fire

16.3
1 hang fire   4 run the gauntlet
2 baptism of fire   5 shot down in flames
3 a flash in the pan   6 a battle of wills

16.4 When Ali graduated, he decided he didn't want to **join the ranks** of commuters struggling to work every day. He wanted to set up his own online gift-ordering business so that he could work from home. He knew it was a risk but felt he would have at least **a fighting chance** of success. Initially, he and a college friend planned to start the business together. Ali had the idea and Igor, his friend, had the money to invest in the company. But then just weeks before the launch, Igor **dropped a bombshell**: he said he no longer wanted to be part of Ali's plans. Despite Ali's attempts to persuade him to **hang fire** on his decision, Igor said he was no longer prepared to take the risk and was going to **beat a retreat** before it was too late. However, two weeks later Igor **stole a march** on Ali by launching his own online gift-ordering company. Ali was **shell-shocked** by this betrayal, but he soon **came out fighting**. He took Igor's behaviour as **a call to arms** and has persuaded a bank to lend him the money he needs. Ali's introduction to the business world has certainly been a **baptism of fire**, but I'm sure he will be really successful on his own.

Follow-up

Here are some examples of sentences found through the British National Corpus website:

The last thing he needed at the moment was an outraged husband *on the warpath*.

It took a while for the true magnitude of his achievement to dawn on the crowd, *shell-shocked* as they were by the defeat of their hero.

On November 1 they told us that normal Christmas arrangements would apply – that we would work for most of the holiday period – then they *dropped this bombshell* on November 22 and said we would be off for two weeks.

Freshers were obliged to *run a gauntlet* of computer software, insurance and Student Railcard salesmen and a host of banks seeking their overdrafts, before reaching the union societies' billeted in the sports hall.

Unit 17

17.1
1 go off the rails
2 run out of steam
3 do a U-turn

17.2
1 life in the slow lane
2 done a complete U-turn
3 gone off the rails
4 run out of steam
5 go / move / step up a gear
6 at / behind the wheel

17.3
1 I'm glad to say that things are now back on track.
2 We don't know what could happen a year down the line.
3 Things are out of control. Nobody seems to be in the driving seat any more.
4 Profits of internet-based companies have taken a nosedive recently.
5 I think the employers and the unions are on a collision course.
6 Nothing's happening. Things have come to a complete standstill.

17.4 1 c   2 a   3 c   4 a

Follow-up *Possible answers:*

Drive someone round the bend means to annoy or irritate someone: *Be quiet! You're driving me round the bend!*

A back-seat driver is a passenger in a car who keeps giving advice to the driver that the driver has not asked for. It also means someone trying to control what happens, even though it is not their responsibility: *Even though we have a new director, the old one still seems to be a back-seat driver in the company.*

Step on it means to drive faster or to hurry up (informal). We can also say 'step on the gas', meaning put your foot on the accelerator in a car to make it go faster: *Step on it! We have to be there in five minutes!*

Put the brakes on means to slow down or stop an activity: *The government has put the brakes on airport expansion because of climate change.*

Give / get the green light means give / get permission for someone to do something or for something to happen: *The architects have been given the green light to build a new bridge over the River Handa.*

Unit 18

18.1
1. Yes, she thinks **she's the cat's whiskers**.
2. Yes, it's **a dog's life**!
3. No, I haven't got **a cat in hell's chance**.
4. Yes, he has a real **dog-in-the-manger** attitude. (Notice the use of hyphens when the idiom is used as an adjective.)

18.2
1. the elephant in the room
2. a wolf in sheep's clothing
3. straight from the horse's mouth
4. to sort (out) the sheep from the goats
5. shedding crocodile tears
6. unil the cows come home

18.3
1. horse
2. leopard
3. cows
4. parrot
5. sheep, lamb

18.4
1. Don't **cry wolf** or no one will help when you really need it.
2. The Minister **sheds crocodile tears** about homelessness, but does nothing about it.
3. I hate our neighbours' **dog-in-the-manger** attitude – they don't want the parking space but they won't let us have it.
4. We can discuss it **until the cows come home**, but I won't change my mind.

Follow-up *Possible answers:*
A snake in the grass: someone who pretends to be your friend but is really an enemy.
A big fish in a small pond: an important person in a not very important place.
To smell a rat: to suspect something.

Unit 19

19.1
1. I wonder what is really behind the president's decision. I'm sure there's more to it than meets the **eye**.
2. Melissa is head and **shoulders** above her brother when it comes to maths.
3. I'm sure we can think of a good present for Jim if we put our **heads** together.
4. Kasia really loves getting her **teeth** into a new project.
5. You mustn't bury your **head** in the sand – problems don't go away if you ignore them.
6. It was one in the **eye** for Liliana's brother when she passed her driving test first time – it had taken him five attempts.

19.2
1. respect
2. to speak
3. starting
4. respect
5. less nice

19.3
1. Let's talk about planning the party. Yes, let's put our heads together.
2. Bruno was upset when he lost the race to his rival. Yes, it was one in the eye for him.
3. Ahmed's been so arrogant since he won that competition. Yes, it's really gone to his head.
4. He didn't want people to think less of him. Yes, he was afraid of losing face.
5. They never really liked him in his old job. That's right, his face didn't fit.
6. It's a very complicated issue, I think. Yes, there's more to it than meets the eye.
7. Everyone says that Ian's to blame. Yes, they're all pointing the finger at him.
8. I read a newspaper every day. Well, it's good to keep your finger on the pulse.

19.4
1. **I'd give my right arm to** go to Japan with you!
2. After some **teething troubles**, the business began to do well.
3. I find it very hard to **get my tongue round** some Welsh place names.
4. I don't know why they're **pointing the finger at** me – I'm not guilty.
5. I'm not very good at maths, but my brother **has a good head for** figures.
6. I hope I'm not **treading on your toes**, but could I suggest you try a different approach?
7. Paulo's speech at the wedding **made my toes curl**!
8. I don't see how you can **keep your finger on the pulse** if you never watch TV or listen to the radio.

136 English Idioms in Use Advanced

Unit 20

20.1
1 play / keep your cards close to your chest
2 hold all the cards
3 monopoly money
4 the dice are loaded against (someone)
5 dicing with death
6 play your ace / play your trump card

20.2
1 I felt I was **dicing with death** riding at high speed on the back of his motorbike.
2 I **played / kept my cards close to my chest** and didn't mention that I was going to resign soon.
3 He's so rich. He spends money as if it were **monopoly money**.
4 The barrister **played his ace / played his trump card** and revealed the final piece of evidence.
5 I wanted a job in politics, but felt **the dice were loaded against me** as I had no personal contacts in the political world.
6 Masa is so much more qualified and experienced than I am. He **holds all the cards** if we both apply for the same job.

20.3 1b Ivana   2c Jung   3d Gina   4a Joseph

20.4
1 Jin's in a very powerful position; he **holds** all the **cards**.
2 The teacher has **moved** the **goalposts** so many times that none of the students knows what the rules are any more.
3 Simon is very direct with people; he never **pulls** any **punches**.
4 What? The headteacher changed the holiday from a whole day to a half day! Poor kids! It's just not **cricket**, is it?
5 The two presidential candidates have played **hardball** recently and have made quite personal attacks on each other.
6 Advertising on TV is not the same as it was 20 years ago; it's a whole **new ball game** now.
7 Everyone felt **punch-drunk** after six hours of political debate.
8 At 10 pm on the night of the election, the president threw **in the sponge / towel** and admitted he had lost.

Unit 21

21.1
1 a Trojan horse
2 Achilles' heel
3 the sword of Damocles
4 Pandora's box

21.2
1 New financial regulations are hanging over the banking industry like **the sword of Damocles**. Bankers are extremely worried.
2 One famous type of computer virus works like **a Trojan horse**. It attacks your computer from inside the system.
3 He's a good worker in many ways, but planning is his **Achilles heel**. He's so disorganised.
4 She opened **Pandora's box** when she started investigating corruption in the building industry.

21.3

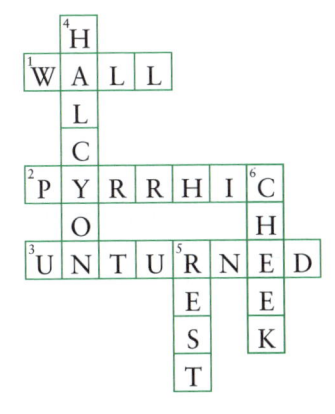

		⁴H			
¹W	A	L	L		
		C			
		²P	Y	R	R	H	I	⁶C
		O			H
³U	N	T	U	⁵R	N	E	D
				E		E
				S		K
				T		

21.4 1 Julia's **parting** shot as she walked out of the room was to say that she never wanted to see any of us ever again.
2 The police left no **stone** unturned in trying to trace the missing child.
3 Piero fell **on** his sword and accepted full responsibility for the disaster.
4 She really has the **Midas** touch – everything she does is hugely successful.
5 It was a task of epic **proportions**, but everyone tried their hardest to succeed.
6 We should continue to work hard and not **rest** on our laurels.
7 If we are faced with a violent attack, we should just turn the other **cheek** and not react.
8 Doing nothing at this stage would be like **fiddling** while Rome burns.

Unit 22

22.1 1 The film is about two **star-crossed lovers** and their relationship.
2 Dom and his friends **ate me out of house and home**.
3 Harry's driving **made my hair stand on end**, but we arrived safely.
4 He set off on **a wild-goose chase** to find the buried treasure he'd read about.
5 Having criticised the previous government for their financial scandals, the new president was **hoist with his own petard** when he was arrested for fraud.
6 Masha prepared a delicious meal **in the twinkling of an eye**.
7 **The green-eyed monster** is responsible for many crimes of passion.
8 The reviewer didn't praise the play subtly – he **laid it on with a trowel**.

22.2 1 true, smooth 2 end 3 house 4 eye 5 swoop

22.3 1 make your hair stand on end
2 a wild-goose chase
3 lay it on with a trowel
4 the green-eyed monster

22.4 1 The bank robbers left the country after they had cleverly managed to send the police off on a **wild-goose chase**.
2 The ghost story David told made **my hair stand on end**.
3 Maya and Harry's relationship was destroyed by **the green-eyed monster**.
4 Simply tell your daughter that you like her work. There's no need to **lay it on with a trowel**.

Follow-up

pound of flesh: something owed but which it is unreasonable to demand, e.g. *People accuse the taxman of always making sure he gets his pound of flesh.*

send someone packing: ask someone to leave at once, e.g. *I can't face any visitors, so if anyone comes to the door, just send them packing.*

Unit 23

23.1 1 Man Friday 3 Prince Charming 5 Aladdin
2 Hyde 4 Big Brother

23.2 1 My sister's getting married next week. I'm so happy she's found her **Prince Charming**.
2 The internet service providers know exactly which websites we visit – **Big Brother** is watching us all the time.
3 My life is totally chaotic. I need a **Man Friday / Girl Friday** to help me with everything.
4 The old cupboard was an **Aladdin**'s cave of valuable objects.
5 Roberto is a real Jekyll and **Hyde** character. You can never predict how he's going to behave.

23.3
1. Don't worry, it's just **a storm in a teacup**.
2. He wants to borrow a lot of money to go travelling, but paying it back could become **an albatross around his neck**.
3. Why are you just getting a new fridge and cooker? Why not **go the whole hog** and get a new kitchen?
4. He's always got some new money-making plan or scheme, but most of the time they're just **castles in the air**.
5. I met him ten years ago and then saw him again last year. We seem to **be like ships that pass in the night**.

23.4
1. She's very direct and always calls a spade a spade.
2. I found myself in a ridiculous Catch-22 situation.
3. People say that academics live in ivory towers.
4. There's nothing to worry about; it's just a storm in a teacup.

23.5
1. castles in the air
2. storm in a teacup
3. ships that pass in the night
4. ivory tower

Unit 24

24.1

Who is talking about ...	name
1 something that is at the cutting edge of technology?	Clara
2 something that was hot off the press?	Rob
3 something that pushes the right buttons?	Matthew
4 something that was the brainchild of someone?	Julian

24.2
1. I try my best to do my job well, but sometimes I feel as if I'm just **a cog in the machine**.
2. I don't want to **throw a spanner in the works**, but I think you should apply for official permission first.
3. I worry sometimes that we're just **reinventing the wheel** in our research.
4. I'm afraid I couldn't print the document; our printer is **on the blink**.
5. There was a power failure and everything **went haywire**.
6. She should be able to write a simple text message. I mean, it's not **rocket science**, is it?
7. I think we're **light years away from** finding a cure for this terrible disease.
8. Why change the system? **If it ain't broke, don't fix it!**

24.3 1 b 2 c 3 a 4 c

24.4
1. My school was new. We had all kinds of **cutting-edge** technology.
2. Suddenly, everything went **haywire** and there was complete chaos.
3. She felt she was just a cog in the **machine** and that no one ever noticed her.
4. The city council set the **wheels in motion** for the construction of the new park.

Unit 25

25.1
1. The critics didn't hesitate to pick holes in the actor's performance.
2. The hero's dying words sent shivers down my spine.
3. The comedian's jokes brought the house down.
4. It took me all of my holiday to wade through that novel.
5. The singers were all great, but the young soprano stole the show.
6. The play was so funny it had the audience rolling in the aisles.
7. The film was really exciting and kept us on the edge of our seats.
8. The *Sunday News* critic hated the book and did a hatchet job on it.

25.2
1 an armchair critic
2 waiting in the wings
3 have your name in lights
4 do a hatchet job on something
5 rolling in the aisles
6 keep you on the edge of your seat

25.3 *Possible answers:*
1 support / admire
2 reassure / calm
3 stage in a theatre
4 A lot of / Lots of
5 Shy / Unconfident

25.4
1 Richard is **a leading light** in the local tennis club.
2 The teacher **picked holes in** my essay.
3 Don't worry about your presentation. **It'll be all right on the night**.
4 The dog **stole the show**.
5 She spent years **treading the boards** before getting a part in a TV soap.
6 The new manager is good at **playing to the gallery**.
7 The book was very **heavy going**.
8 I can't believe that the *Sunday News* critic described such a boring novel as a **page-turner**.

Unit 26

26.1
1 They invited their nearest and dearest to the wedding.
2 We don't live in each other's pockets, but we're a happy family.
3 He has deserted his own flesh and blood and gone to join the army.
4 Young Walter is the spitting image of his grandfather.
5 She was just a twinkle in her father's eye three years ago!
6 When he turned 18, he flew the nest and went to live in Australia.
7 Harry is a real chip off the old block – he's just like his uncle Rex.
8 Kay and her mum are pretty. Good looks run in the family.

26.2
1 Heather is the **spitting image of** her mother – she looks just like her.
2 How could you harm your brother? He's your own **flesh** and **blood**.
3 She was born in 1986. In 1983, she was just a **twinkle** in **her father's eye**.
4 All her **nearest** and **dearest** gathered round her for a family photo on her 90th birthday.
5 I'd hate the sort of family where everybody lives **in each other's pockets**.
6 He's 42 and still living with his parents. Most people **fly the nest** a lot earlier.
7 All of her sisters are really musical too. It must **run in the family**.
8 Max is as generous as his dad. He's a **chip off the old block**.

26.3

1 Who has known someone for many years?	Chelsea
2 Who has a friend who is only there when things are going well?	Zenab
3 Who has a friend who won't speak to her?	Lidia
4 Who has a friend who has given a lot of support in difficult times?	Connor
5 Who knows powerful and influential people?	Ashley

26.4
1 If **he has the ear of the boss**, we should let him represent us.
2 Joanna was **a tower** (or *pillar*) **of strength** when I was going through a bad time.
3 Hilda has invited **an old flame** of hers to the party on Saturday.
4 My friend Roger has stood by me **through thick and thin**.
5 He was **footloose and fancy-free** until he was 25; then he got married.
6 Raisa and I **go back a long way**.

Unit 27

27.1 1 up 2 parts 3 kids 4 strings 5 mine

27.2
1 Concentrate on your homework and stop playing **the** fool!
2 I hope Joe doesn't come to the party – he's such a **wet** blanket.
3 I suppose that everyone ultimately has to look out for **number** one.
4 Kate volunteers for all the jobs that no one else will do – she's a real glutton for **punishment**.
5 I always said she was a loose **cannon**, so I'm not surprised she's causing trouble.
6 The newspapers are claiming that the prince is a **love-rat**.
7 Be extra kind and calm with Jarek – he's very **highly** strung.
8 Everyone admires the young entrepreneur for his get-up and **go**.

27.3
1 a wet blanket
2 a man of many parts
3 have (plenty of) strings to your bow
4 a love-rat

27.4
1 I'm really scared about meeting them. I'm sure they'll **eat me for breakfast**.
2 I don't want to be **a wet blanket**, but please can you turn the music down? It's too loud.
3 Some say that to succeed in business, you need to **look out for number one**.
4 There always seems to be a child in every class who **plays the fool** to make the other pupils laugh.
5 Martina would be easier to live with if she weren't so **highly strung**.
6 Some see him as **a loose cannon**, but this is unfair.

Unit 28

28.1
1 Her new boyfriend is really attractive, but he's so boring! He's just eye **candy**.
2 Beauty is in the eye of the **beholder**.
3 Of course my idea's a good one! I'm not just a pretty **face**!
4 I've never met my brother's boss, but my brother says she's not much **to look** at.
5 I love that film star. He's **drop**-dead gorgeous!
6 His new girlfriend is really pretty; she's very **easy** on the eye.

Possible answers:

28.2
1 c) both a and b mean attractive
2 b) both a and c suggest she is attractively dressed, whereas b suggests she is inappropriately dressed
3 c) this is the only one that sounds positive rather than critical
4 c) a and b are focusing on his body rather than his clothes

28.3 1 dinner 2 glad 3 part 4 kill 5 mutton 6 pretty

28.4
1 We'll need to leave for the wedding soon. Hurry up and put **your glad rags** on.
2 She's 50, but she dresses like a teenager. She looks like **mutton dressed as lamb**.
3 If you want to get a good job in a bank, you'll have to stop dressing like a student and make an effort to **look the part**.
4 Even on an ordinary day at work, Gemma is **dressed to kill** in high heels and a smart suit. I wonder who she's trying to impress!
5 As well as being extremely good-looking, that actor is a very good businessman. He's **not just a pretty face!**
6 The actress looked ridiculous at the film premiere – too much jewellery and a very short dress. She really was **done up / dressed up like a dog's dinner**.

28.5
1 Yes, he's getting a real **middle-age spread**.
2 Absolutely. He's **the spitting image of him**.
3 That's right. She's never normally so **down-at-heel**.
4 No, she's **not much to look at**.
5 No, he looks as if **butter wouldn't melt in his mouth**.

English Idioms in Use Advanced   141

Unit 29

29.1
1 counter
2 lining their, pockets
3 job
4 fiddle, wool, eyes
5 taking, ride

29.2 1 f 2 e 3 c 4 h 5 g 6 d 7 a 8 i 9 b

29.3
1 True.
2 False. They themselves run away, usually from trouble.
3 True.
4 False. They spend time in prison.

Unit 30

30.1
1 at the top of the ladder
2 a golden handshake
3 a sleeping / silent partner
4 a foot in the door

30.2
1 She founded the company, but she's not very active in it now. She's just **a sleeping / silent partner**.
2 He desperately wanted to work in the film industry, so he got a job carrying camera equipment to get **a foot in the door**.
3 When he retired, the company gave him a **golden handshake**.
4 It took him years to become chief executive, but he's **at the top of the ladder** now.

30.3
1 No. If you have a good track record, you have a history of success, not failure.
2 No. A cushy number is a very easy job.
3 Yes.
4 Yes.
5 No. If you are doing a roaring trade, you are selling lots of goods.
6 No. If a company goes belly up, it has failed and usually closes.
7 No. If a company corners the market, they are very successful and do not have any serious competitors.
8 Yes.

30.4
1 Our new online business is **going great guns**.
2 Some airlines are in danger of **going to the wall**.
3 That new farmers' market seems to be **doing a roaring trade**.
4 Mr Olsen decided to **shut up shop** and retire to the coast.
5 Another insurance company **went bust** last week.
6 She realised she had hit a **glass ceiling** at work.

Unit 31

31.1
1 saddled with debt
2 throw someone a lifeline
3 big fish in a small pond
4 cloud on the horizon

31.2
1 rein in spending (riders use reins to guide the horse and control its speed)
2 soar sky-high and take a nosedive
3 birds soar sky-high and a plane can take a nosedive
4 receive a windfall (the image is that of a strong wind blowing fruit off the trees unexpectedly early)
5 a ballpark figure (the idiom comes from baseball)
6 the bottom drops / falls out of the market (the image is of the bottom coming off a box, thus spilling all its contents)

31.3
1 The speaker said he was concerned about the way in which young people **worship** at the altar of instant gratification.
2 Correct.

3 Receiving a sizeable **windfall** from one of our investments allowed us to extend our premises.
4 Changes in the company's structure will take place across the **board**.
5 Jackson was **under** no illusions about how long it would take his business to get established.
6 Correct.
7 It's time we considered how we can take our business to the next **level**.
8 The senior staff all **fell** into line with the new CEO's demands.

31.4
1 The latest crisis at work means that heads will roll.
2 I can't tell you the exact price, but I can give you a ballpark figure.
3 No one will want to take over a company so saddled with debt.
4 As our profits have fallen, we'll have to rein in spending.
5 Jake likes being a big fish in a small pond.
6 There are fears that the bottom may fall out of the market.
7 For the first time in ages there are no clouds on the company's horizon.
8 The plan is to implement substantial changes across the board.

Unit 32

32.1
1 The speaker wants to know when Sandra will be free, e.g. to meet.
2 The speaker is suggesting that they make contact with each other, or meet.
3 Because it uses several words ('at this moment in time') where one ('now') would do equally well.
4 Yes, it does.

32.2
1 have a window
2 the gloves are off
3 push the envelope
4 blue-sky thinking

32.3
1 suck   3 box   5 dog   7 rock
2 fact   4 off   6 up   8 envelope

32.4
1 Do you have any points that you would like **to bring to the table** today?
2 We need to prove that our products are **at the cutting edge** if we are to stay competitive.
3 They've been working **24 / 7** to complete the project.
4 **The fact of the matter is** that our previous advertising campaign was not as successful as we had hoped.
5 I have **a window** on Thursday afternoon if that suits you.
6 They chose Mark for the job because he **ticked all the boxes**.

Unit 33

33.1
1 Working as a security guard is money **for old rope**, unless someone actually tries to break in.
2 He went from **rags to riches**, but he was always afraid he'd end up poor again.
3 A lot of students find it difficult to **make ends meet** and end up borrowing money from the bank or from their parents.
4 When I was a student, I was always **strapped for** cash, so I had to get part-time jobs.
5 He's completely immoral about financial matters. He would **sell his own grandmother**.
6 He sued the newspaper for libel, won his case and took them **to the cleaners**.
7 They set up one of those social networking websites. It was an instant success and now they're laughing **all the way to the bank**.
8 Why do I work so hard and such long hours? Well, someone has to bring **home the bacon**!
9 Jessie paid me for that job I did last week, so I'm **quids in**. We can have a nice meal out tonight!
10 I bought a new guitar at the weekend. It was going for a **song** at only £30.

33.2
1. In the current financial crisis, people are finding it harder to make ends **meet**.
2. I'm tired of living on a **shoestring**. I need to earn more money.
3. You should buy that old house – it's going for a **song**.
4. Spending money on ready-made meals is just throwing money down the **drain**.
5. Did you know he took his girlfriend to the Caribbean for a luxury holiday? He must be absolutely **rolling** in it.
6. We had lunch in a cheap and **cheerful** restaurant.
7. I know you love that dress, but it's so expensive. There's no point in paying over the **odds** for it – it's just not worth it.
8. Why don't you buy her a bunch of flowers? It won't break the **bank**.
9. Kim is the main **breadwinner** in our family.
10. I wish we had more money. I hate being so penny-**pinching** all the time.

33.3
1. The prize is a no-expense-spared weekend in a London hotel *or* The prize is a weekend in a London hotel, no expense spared.
2. Ivana is always going shopping. She must have money to burn.
3. Kim has never had much money. She has always had to scrimp and save.
4. If you like children, babysitting is money for old rope.
5. Everyone has to go to work in order to bring home the bacon.
6. You sold the car for £200 more than you paid for it, so you're quids in.
7. (When it comes to making money), Sue would sell her own grandmother.
8. I don't make much money, so I find it almost impossible to make ends meet.

33.4 *Answers for the author who wrote this unit*
1. a very expensive violin
2. electronic gadgets
3. Yes, a meal in a London restaurant
4. Yes, a second-hand bicycle

Unit 34

34.1
self-made man   grass roots
second-class citizen   silent majority
chattering classes

34.2
1. Politicians often lose touch with the **grass roots** and become isolated from the public.
2. It's time the **silent majority** was heard, instead of the more vocal and aggressive minority.
3. My father was a **self-made man**. He came from a poor background and worked his way up until he became quite rich.
4. I'm sick of listening to the opinions of the **chattering classes**. What about the opinions of ordinary people?
5. If you are poor, you may sometimes think you are a **second-class citizen** in terms of access to university.

34.3 *Possible answers:*
1. Probably a bit nervous and apprehensive.
2. Big cars which use an excessive amount of fuel and damage the environment.
3. Celebrities, politicians, sports people, etc.
4. Elderly people.

34.4
1. False. They have very little influence or power in society.
2. False. The gravy train refers to ways of making money quickly, easily and often dishonestly, usually through your position in society.
3. False. It means educated people who enjoy discussing social, political and cultural issues.
4. True.
5. False. They win by a very large number of votes or a very large majority.

34.5
1 eye
2 gravy
3 block
4 grey, strings
5 Big
6 enemy

34.6
1 Although Bill receives all the media attention, his mother is **the power behind the throne**.
2 In the election, the Green candidate **won by a landslide**.
3 Everyone suspects that **the elections were rigged**.
4 Mark **is a self-made man**.
5 Journalists need to establish good contacts with **the movers and shakers**.

Unit 35

35.1
1 Don't worry. There's no point losing any sleep over it.
2 We had a great meal. The meat was done to a turn.
3 Helen has a lot of homework, so she's been up all night burning the midnight oil.
4 My grandmother doesn't want much lunch. She eats like a bird.
5 I didn't think I was tired, but I went out like a light.
6 I feel hungry and tired if I don't eat a square meal every evening.
7 It's late. Let's not talk about this now – we need to sleep on it.
8 I'm embarrassed to go to restaurants with him; he eats like a pig.

35.2 When Sam first went travelling, he missed his **creature comforts**, like hot water and a soft bed. However, he loved being able to **go out on the town** at night with new friends in different countries. He had such an exciting time that he was usually too busy to eat a **square meal**, and so he just ate **on the hoof** from street markets. Sam is now back at work but is planning his next trip.

35.3
1 It's really busy! I don't know whether **I'm coming or going**!
2 Well, I was at first, but now I'm fed up. They've **outstayed their welcome**.
3 Yes, let's **go out on the town** together.
4 It's OK. It's **on the house**.
5 I was hoping to, but I'm afraid I'm going to have to **give it a miss**.
6 Sorry. I'm too busy at work. I'll just have to have a sandwich **on the hoof**.
7 Not really, we just **pass the time of day** sometimes.
8 He's just trying to **take each day as it comes**.
9 Oh, nothing in particular. I'm just having a **bad hair day**.
10 Yes, he eats **like a horse**!

Unit 36

36.1
1 The company's new line of sportswear has been incredibly popular, and they've made a lot of money. They really **hit the** jackpot this time.
2 The end-of-term party really went with **a swing**. Everyone enjoyed themselves.
3 That apple pie you made went down **a treat** with our dinner guests.
4 We were freezing, so she gave us some hot chocolate to drink – it really **hit the** spot.
5 Everyone was in a happy mood and entered **into the spirit of** the fancy-dress ball.
6 His lecture hit exactly **the right note**. Everyone enjoyed it and said it was very informative too.

36.2
1 stars in your eyes
2 full of the joys of spring
3 music to my ears
4 be on a high

36.3
1 After winning the race, I was **on a high** for the rest of the day.
2 The decision to cancel the rugby match **was music to my ears**. I hadn't been looking forward to it at all.
3 Meeting Nelson Mandela was **a dream come true**.
4 Shona was **full of the joys of spring** this morning. Something good must have happened.
5 Jerry's **got stars in his eyes** – he's joined a rock band and given up his job.

36.4
1 Sam Bagg's new album blew my mind.
2 My sister is such a happy-go-lucky person. / My sister is so happy-go-lucky.
3 Iris is full of the joys of spring today!
4 He's as happy as Larry in his new job.
5 This new series of adventure novels strikes (exactly) the right note for a teenage audience.

36.5
1 The music festival went **with** a swing and a lot of money was raised for charity.
2 The song we wrote for the end-of-course party went **down** a treat **with** all the teachers.
3 My cousin's got **stars in her eyes** ever since her music teacher told her she could be famous one day.
4 Kevin is such a **happy-go-lucky** person; he never worries about anything.

Follow-up *Possible answers:*
You can play football **to your heart's content** when the exams are over, but now you must study! [do something pleasant for as long as you want to]

It's not a luxury hotel; it's **cheap and cheerful**. [cheap, but pleasant and attractive]

I was **over the moon** when I heard the news! [very happy indeed]

Unit 37

37.1
1 Dad almost **burst** a blood vessel when I told him I'd driven into his car.
2 Sally felt all **hot** and bothered after having to push her way onto the train.
3 Dave saw **red** when he heard the boy speak so rudely to Janice.
4 You're in a bad temper today. What's rattled your **cage**?
5 What Lily said to her mother really made my **blood** boil.
6 It really gets my **goat** when you say such stupid things!

37.2
1 I'm a **bundle of nerves**.
2 I feel **down in the dumps** today.
3 I **have a sinking feeling** about this exam.
4 I'm **running out of patience** with that incompetent company.
5 The argument I had with my best friend has **knocked me for six**.
6 **Wild horses couldn't make me** apologise to Nick.

37.3
1 Going to the opera isn't my bag.
2 I wouldn't give that artist's work house room.
3 On rainy days I often feel down in the dumps.
4 People dropping litter makes my blood boil.
5 Gerry's rudeness made me see red.
6 Not getting the job has knocked Ben for six.
7 Losing his keys made Jim all hot and bothered.
8 When the phone rang, I had a sinking feeling.

37.4
1 Selfish behaviour makes my blood boil.
2 The film's sad ending reduced Stella to tears.
3 Cruelty to animals makes me see red.
4 I am running out of patience with James.
5 My brother's laziness gets my goat.
6 I (could have) kicked myself for missing the train.
7 What's rattled Paul's cage?
8 I shouldn't let him make me so hot and bothered.
9 Long walks in the countryside are not my bag.
10 Your father will burst a blood vessel if you say you're dropping out of university.

37.5 *Possible answers:*
1 That TV programme about child poverty reduced me to tears.
2 I wouldn't give that politician's opinions house room.
3 Amos's arrogance gets my goat.
4 I was a bundle of nerves when I was waiting for my exam results.
5 I could have kicked myself when I let your secret slip.
6 Watching cricket is not my bag.
7 Wild horses couldn't make me sing in public.
8 My friend's accident knocked me for six.

Unit 38

38.1
1 ball
2 light
3 pig's
4 nightmare
5 plot

38.2
1 pull the rug from under (my feet)
2 can't see the wood for the trees
3 a slap in the face
4 sweep it under the carpet

38.3
1 I'm not making as many sales as I used to. I must be losing my touch.
2 I don't know why Bill is still so determined to settle a score with Jack.
3 I wonder if you could help me out of a tight corner.
4 His neighbours' expensive new car certainly put Ted's nose out of joint.
5 He realised he'd made a terrible mistake in the cold light of day.
6 No one in this business can afford to take their eye off the ball.
7 There have been problems all week – it's just been a chapter of accidents.
8 You need to stand back from the problem so you can see the wood for the trees.

38.4
1 I agree. We're in **over our heads**.
2 I know, it's really **put her nose out of joint**.
3 Yes, there's no point trying to **sweep it under the carpet**.
4 You're right, I think he's **lost / losing his touch**.
5 Good idea. At the moment we **can't see the wood for the trees**.
6 Me too. I feel like I'm **losing the plot!**
7 You're right. You can't **take your eye off the ball**.
8 Yes, he's **in a tight corner / spot**.

Unit 39

39.1
1 False. The mayor is going through a difficult period.
2 True.
3 False. It was made at the last minute.
4 True.
5 True.
6 False. 'Marathon' means that they were long.

39.2
1 in
2 in
3 under, of
4 into
5 out

39.3
1 The forest fires resulted in some entire villages being **engulfed in flames**.
2 The robbers got into the house **under cover of darkness**.
3 It will not be easy for the two sides to **hammer out an agreement**.
4 The reasons for the bank manager's disappearance are still **shrouded in mystery**.
5 The power cuts **plunged** the whole area **into chaos**.

English Idioms in Use Advanced 147

39.4
1. big
2. mounting
3. bloody
4. uneasy
5. for
6. blood
7. last-ditch
8. war-torn

39.5 *Possible answers:*
1. something totally covered by fire or water
2. something going down very fast, often into water
3. something totally covered – a shroud is the cloth that traditionally covers a dead body
4. a battle (The last ditch is the last part of an army's defences, i.e. the last point at which it can avoid defeat.)
5. something being saved in the last few moments before disaster strikes (at twelve o'clock)
6. a country divided into pieces by war.

They are all dramatic images, which is why journalists like them.

Unit 40

40.1
1. world of, between
2. of its time
3. hands down
4. wildest dreams
5. packs, punch
6. the mark

40.2
1. Yes, there was a world **of difference between** them.
2. Yes, it did us **the world of good**.
3. Yes, he certainly lives **life to the full**.
4. Yes, it certainly packs **a punch**.
5. Yes, it must be hard to stand out **from the crowd** these days.
6. Yes, it's taken **years off her**. I think I might have one done myself!

40.3
1. b) in chess, the players make moves
2. a) you use a watch to tell the time
3. c) washing powder makes clothes clean

40.4
1. a new gift shop (a shop which has the perfect presents for people)
2. an exhibition of pictures of a village taken 100 years ago (if you have a photographic memory, you remember everything perfectly, just like a photograph in your mind)
3. a new range of luxury watches ('quality time' is time you spend doing things you like and which are important to you, for example being with your family, doing a hobby, etc.)
4. a cookery course to encourage people to stop eating fast food ('slowly but surely' means that something is happening, usually positive, but it takes time)
5. an airline with beds in its first-class cabin ('flat out' means at high speed, so the flight is fast, and the beds are flat)

Unit 41

41.1
1. least
2. on
3. foremost
4. by
5. on
6. analysis

41.2 *Possible answers:*
1. **On no account** should we forget the history behind this conflict.
2. **In the final analysis**, doctors must trust their own judgement.
3. I can see both arguments, but **on balance** I am in favour of extending the school-leaving age.
4. **First and foremost,** we must give a definition of family law before we can apply it to the case in question.
5. **Last but not least,** let us consider the role of the media in this debate.
6. **By and large,** the writer uses traditional poetic style.

41.3
1 Liberal right-wing policies sound like **a contradiction in terms**.
2 **In the main**, I approve of the government's approach.
3 The reform **opens the door** to an eventual solution of the problem.
4 Once the papers are signed, this legal process is **set in motion**.
5 **As a matter of course**, large companies outperform smaller companies. This is only to be expected.
6 People who fail at school often succeed in later life. Einstein is **a case in point**.
7 The research **points the way** to a future cure for the disease.
8 Saying that boys achieve less at school does not give **the whole picture**.
9 Advocating equal opportunity for all **begs the question of** how this can be achieved.
10 **On the one hand**, international law exists to protect people from the power of states. **On the other hand**, it can also restrict states from exercising their power to protect the interests of their own people.

41.4
1 The new building **stands out like a sore thumb**.
2 An interesting painting **caught my eye**.
3 It's hard to keep up with government policy, as they seem to **chop and change** all the time.
4 Business success often goes **hand in hand with** good working conditions.

Unit 42

42.1
1 put your shoulder to the wheel
2 reach for the stars
3 turn over a new leaf
4 put your money where your mouth is

42.2
1 The club needs money desperately. Charlie says he wants to help, so he should **put his money where his mouth is**.
2 I know you don't want to tell her the bad news, but you have to **bite the bullet**.
3 Come on, work harder! You have to **put your shoulder to the wheel**!
4 The teacher told his students to be ambitious and to **reach for the stars**.
5 You need to stop lying and be honest. It's time to **turn over a new leaf**.

42.3
1 twice
2 the applecart
3 trim
4 tempt
5 out
6 the changes

42.4 *Possible answers:*
1 I think you've bitten off more than you can chew. / Don't bite off more than you can chew.
2 I don't think it's a good idea to stick your neck out. / You shouldn't stick your neck out like that.
3 I'm sorry, I can't help. I think you'll just have to tough it out.
4 I think you're (skating) on thin ice criticising her so strongly.

Follow-up: Look up these idioms in a good dictionary or at Cambridge Dictionaries Online if you do not know their meanings.
Examples of idioms with *shoulder*:
a shoulder to cry on
have a chip on your shoulder
shoulder to shoulder
give someone the cold shoulder

Examples of idioms with *neck*:
breathe down someone's neck
be a pain in the neck
be up to your neck in something
have the brass neck to do something

Unit 43

43.1
1. go
2. drop
3. chair
4. split
5. put
6. between
7. stake
8. clanger

43.2
1. from the word go; at first glance
2. nearly fell off my chair; a bolt from the blue; a real turn-up for the books
3. for good measure; into the bargain; to say nothing of
4. when all's said and done
5. a lot at stake; more by luck than judgement

43.3
1. **There's a lot to be said for** working in an open-plan office.
2. **For a split second**, I believed Tom when he said he was moving to Australia; then I realised he was joking.
3. **At first glance**, the project seemed quite simple.
4. He passed his driving test first time, but I'd say it was **more by luck than judgement**.
5. **Between you and me**, I think Sue and Larry may be going out together.
6. Their decision to marry **was a real bolt from the blue**.
7. It was, **to say the least / to put it mildly**, a risky thing to do.
8. Both the brothers are very clever, **to say nothing of** their brilliant sister.

43.4
1. The party was fantastic – delicious food, a great band and all my favourite people there for **good** measure.
2. She's pretty, clever and nice **into** the bargain.
3. When all's **said** and done, I think you made the right decision.
4. No one thought the film would be a success, so it was a real turn-up **for** the books when it won three Oscars.
5. I feel very nervous about this exam; there is a lot **at stake**.
6. I didn't understand what he meant at first, but then the **penny** dropped.
7. We got on really well from the word **go**.
8. I think you were rather rude to her, to **put** it mildly.

Unit 44

44.1
1. Well, **that's all we need!**
2. Huh! **Fat chance!**
3. Felix? Ha-ha! **Give me a break!**
4. **You may well ask!**
5. **Good riddance (to bad rubbish)!** I could never stand her.
6. Well, **same difference**.
7. You're right. **There's no time like the present.**
8. **Nice work if you can get it.**

44.2
1. False. It means you don't understand what they mean or who / what they are referring to.
2. False. It is something you say to someone who has a boring life or does boring things; it means they should do more exciting things.
3. True.
4. False. It means you would love to have the same job if it were possible.

44.3
1. They may be enjoying themselves now, but in the long run it will all **end in tears**.
2. It says here in the paper that children prefer playing computer games alone to playing with their friends. What is the world **coming to!**
3. I think Tara is unreliable and a liar. I wouldn't trust her **as far as I could throw her**.
4. So Janice has been lying about how much money she makes? I thought **as much**.
5. The new manager may make a difference to the company, or he may fail. Only time **will tell**.
6. We should act now, and not delay. There's no **time like the present**.

44.4
1 So you're saying she's selfish?
No, don't get me wrong; that's not the problem.

2 Erik says Johnny Depp is his best friend.
Do me a favour! How absurd!

3 I didn't invite her because she upset me.
Fair enough. I'm sorry to hear that.

4 What time did Granny say she was arriving?
You've got me there. I really can't remember.

5 That useless manager got the sack.
Good riddance to bad rubbish!

6 Should we go and tell her now or later?
Well, there's no time like the present.

Unit 45

45.1
1 You took the **words** right out of my mouth.
2 Yes, that's about the **size** of it!
3 **Tell me** about it!
4 I think most of us are of the same **mind** about that.
5 Well, in the end I thought, 'If you can't **beat** 'em, join 'em.'

45.2
1 waters	4 hairs	7 differ
2 tree	5 mouth	8 minds
3 hymn sheet	6 discord	

45.3
1 wrong	3 torn	5 odds
2 lone	4 like	6 message

45.4
1 There's **a world of difference** between being poor and not having as much money as you'd like.
2 I **am at odds with** everyone else in my family about where we should go on holiday.
3 Please do all you can to **pour oil on troubled waters**. I hate it when people argue.
4 The politician was sacked for not **being on message**.

45.5 *Possible answers:*
1 I beg to differ.	4 You're not wrong.
2 I'm in two minds about that.	5 Tell me about it.
3 I'm torn over that.	

Unit 46

46.1
1 Our team's been practising hard, so I hope we'll come up trumps in the match tomorrow.
2 Negotiating that important deal makes me feel I have won my spurs in my new job.
3 His excellent IT skills have helped him stay ahead of the game.
4 I found it hard to get started with my thesis, but I'm on a roll now.
5 Her latest book has gone down a storm, both with critics and the public.
6 After some initial problems, the pop group is now riding high.

46.2
1 a paper tiger	3 win your spurs
2 built on sand	4 on a roll

46.3
1 The chef's new recipes **went down a storm** with the clientele.
2 My ideas for restructuring the company **went down like a lead balloon**.
3 The new prime minister **is riding high** at the moment.
4 I'm quite worried about starting my new job. I'm afraid I won't be able to **cut the mustard**.
5 I've been studying hard all year, so I hope I will **be ahead of the game** when it comes to taking my exams.
6 Poor Carl has been hit by **a double whammy** – losing his job and having a flood in his house.

46.4
1 lead
2 trumps
3 storm
4 recipe
5 on

Unit 47

47.1 1 razor sharp   2 fighting fit   3 crystal clear   4 stark naked   5 piping hot

47.2
1 My old auntie May is **fighting fit**, even though she had an operation two months ago.
2 She's **filthy rich**: she owns a private jet and a massive yacht.
3 A man jumped into the fountain **stark naked** and was arrested by the police.
4 The new government had a **squeaky-clean** image until the recent scandal broke.
5 Henrietta has a **razor-sharp** mind and is the most intelligent person I know.
6 My feet and hands were **stone cold**, so I sat in front of the fire, had a bowl of **piping hot** soup and soon felt better.
7 I overcooked the meat and it was **bone dry**.
8 We can't put the tent up here. The ground's **rock hard**.

47.3
1 Things have hit **rock** bottom between my parents and their neighbours; they don't speak to each other any more.
2 I couldn't sleep on that mattress – it was **rock** hard.
3 This vase is **bone** dry and the poor old flowers are dying!
4 It is **crystal** clear to me that she is trying to deceive us all.
5 They've spent a **small** fortune on furniture for their new house.
6 Police report that more crimes are taking place in **broad** daylight.

47.4
1 filthy rich
2 full stop
3 a) a mere pittance b) a small fortune
4 in broad daylight

47.5

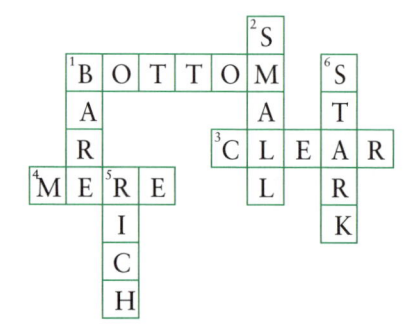

Crossword:
1 across: BOTTOM
2 down: SAAL (S-A-A-L...) — 2 down: STALL?
3 across: CLEAR
4 across: MERE
5 down: REICH
6 down: STARK
1 down: BAR

Unit 48

48.1
1 play cat and mouse
2 play gooseberry
3 play second fiddle

48.2
1 We want the directors to agree to our proposals, so we need to discuss our **game plan**.
2 OK, kids – **the game's up**. I know where you've been hiding my glasses!
3 Martha has decided to apply to be the shop manager. She's been an assistant manager for five years and is tired of **playing second fiddle**.
4 When you're looking for a new flat, location is **the name of the game**.
5 I went to the cinema with Elena and her new boyfriend, but it was horrible **playing gooseberry**.
6 I think that doctors sometimes go too far in their attempts to **play God**.
7 We're still not ready to decide, so we need to **play for time** and not sign the contract yet.

48.3
1 I know, I know. Just **play the game** for now. There's nothing we can do about it.
2 Maybe he's just **playing it cool**.
3 Yes. He's promised not to **play dirty**.
4 No, much better to **play it safe**.
5 Yes, it's definitely time we **raised our game**.

48.4
1 I'm fed up with him playing me for a fool.
2 When people ask how the interview went, just play it cool.
3 I think he behaves dishonestly because he enjoys playing games with people.
4 Some businesses play dirty just to make more money.

Unit 49

49.1
1 baked
2 meet
3 eye
4 mind
5 measures
6 know

49.2
1 Julie was doing a crossword and listening to the radio with half **an** ear.
2 **Given** half **a** chance, I'd leave my job and stay at home with the children.
3 We had a really good plan, but Sally pointed out all the things that were wrong with it. I find her just too clever **by** half.
4 Writers say that coming up with a good idea for a novel is half **the** battle.
5 I've **a** good mind to write a letter of complaint to your manager. *Or* I've **half a mind** to write …
6 I'm a perfectionist. I have no time for **half-measures**.
7 I know it's hard to compromise but you should try to **meet** him halfway.

49.3
1 He's **too clever by half** in my opinion!
2 **Not half!**
3 **Given half a chance**, I'd leave tomorrow, lottery or no lottery!
4 It **isn't half** hot in here!
5 Yes, it was a meal **and a half**, wasn't it?
6 No, he **doesn't know the half of it**.
7 Yes, I'm sure that's **half the battle**.

49.4 1 **It isn't half** noisy here – shall we go somewhere quieter?
2 Having a clear structure and plan for your essay is **half the battle**.
3 It'll be to management's advantage to **meet the union halfway**.
4 There was a lot of bad behaviour on the school trip, but the teachers **didn't know the half of it**.
5 Well, that was certainly **a walk and a half**!

Unit 50

50.1 1 Lou told our boss that I left work early yesterday, so I told him that she's looking for a new job. Two can **play at that game**.
2 The director and department head are both very arrogant. They're two **of a kind**.
3 You hate meetings and I hate meetings, so that makes **two of us**.
4 When a couple breaks up, it is hardly ever the fault of just one person. It takes **two to tango**.
5 Avril, can you help me with this? Two heads **are better than one**.
6 I'm not going to the restaurant with Dave and Mary. I can see they want to be alone. Two's **company, three's a crowd**.

50.2

Who is …	name
1 short of money?	Adam
2 a bad dancer?	Tony
3 talking about someone who has a lot of money?	Amy
4 talking about someone who is feeling very happy?	Lotta

50.3 1 two sides of the same coin
2 like two peas in a pod
3 it takes two to tango
4 two heads are better than one / that makes two of us

50.4 1 Richard **knows a thing or two about** finance.
2 Losing the race **brought him down a peg or two**.
3 A lot of kids nowadays **put / stick two fingers up at** the police and do what they want.
4 Political power **cuts two / both ways**: it enables people to change things, but it tempts them to become corrupt too.
5 Einstein sees time and space as **two sides of the same coin**.
6 Sat Nav systems in cars are **two a penny** these days.

Unit 51

51.1 1 clear   4 for   7 told
2 smiles   5 hours   8 over
3 go   6 good

51.2 1 The office never stops. It's **all systems go** from 8 am to 6 pm.
2 There were eighteen of us for dinner, **all told**.
3 Don't be in such a hurry to pass your driving test. **All in good time!**
4 My sister isn't interested in what I'm doing. I could be homeless **for all she cares**.
5 Barry went out to celebrate **getting the all-clear** from his doctor.
6 Some parents allow their children to come home **at all hours** of the day and night.
7 My brother's really forgetful, so I'm not surprised he forgot your birthday. **That's him all over!**
8 My dad was really grumpy this morning, but **he's all smiles** now.

51.3
1 There are over a hundred thousand books in the library, all told.
2 The new government is trying to be all things to all men.
3 He claims that he is the boss of his company in all but name.
4 She's said some terrible things about me, but to my face she's all smiles.
5 The banks raised interest rates yesterday to an all-time high.
6 You can't give up smoking slowly – it has to be all or nothing.

51.4
1 all-singing, all-dancing
2 to cap it all
3 in all but name
4 all things to all men
5 an all-time low
6 all told

51.5 I'm training to be a vet, and I've got ten exams, all **told**, to prepare for. It means I've been studying at all **hours** of the day and night. I'm exhausted, and to **cap** it all I've got three exams on the same day this week! I just want to relax and go on holiday, but all in **good** time – I'll be finished next month. I told my friend I was feeling stressed, but he just laughed – that's him all **over**; he never takes anything seriously, and even when he's worried or anxious he's all **smiles**.

Unit 52

52.1
1 There's no such thing as a free lunch!
2 I won't take no for an answer!
3 No time like the present!
4 No strings attached – I promise!
5 Go at once – no ifs and buts!
6 No news is good news!

52.2
1 It was difficult.
2 No, she isn't.
3 No, he's not young any more.
4 It would be difficult.
5 He was very direct.
6 It's difficult.

52.3
1 There's no such thing as a free **lunch**.
2 She loves going shopping and spending like there's no **tomorrow**.
3 We were told in no uncertain **terms** that we must always be punctual for work.
4 He said he would lend me €2000 with no strings **attached**.
5 He's a very good squash player, even though he's no spring **chicken**.
6 The new housing development caused no **end** of problems.

52.4
1 The town was full of people partying **like there's no tomorrow** on New Year's Eve.
2 **No prizes for guessing** who won the cookery competition.
3 The journey was very easy, and we got to our destination **in next to no time**.
4 There are **no end of** places to eat in our town.
5 The police have declared the zone **a no-go area**.
6 It would help your grandma **no end** if you cut the grass for her.

Unit 53

53.1
1 hand it to
2 upper hand
3 on a plate.
4 hands down
5 out of the palm
6 old hand

53.2 1 By publishing their tax plans a year before the election, the opposition have shown **their** hand too early.
2 Mr Mills has **played** right into the hands of his critics by admitting that he made errors in the past.
3 You can count on **the** fingers of one hand the number of times this government has done anything to help the poor.
4 In court, the accused said he had never laid **a** hand on anyone and denied the charges.
5 The minister claimed that her **hands were** tied by European regulations, and that she could not act to change the situation.
6 The minister of education rejected out **of** hand the claim that small schools would be closed.

53.3 1 I think you've been dealt a lousy hand. You've had so much bad luck.
2 It's crazy to bite the hand that feeds you.
3 My sister feels relieved that her kids are off her hands and are independent.
4 If you do that, you'll play into the hands of your enemies.
5 You mustn't expect things to be handed to you on a plate.
6 You've got everyone eating out of the palm of your hand.

53.4 *Possible answers*:
1 Professor Ward has given a wonderful lecture. Please give her a big hand.
2 I know I have one somewhere, but I can't lay my hands on it at the moment.
3 I think we should all act and do something, not just sit on our hands.
4 I'm ready to hand over the reins to someone else.
5 Hand on heart, have you never told a lie?

Unit 54

54.1 1 b) a heart of gold
2 b) No. It is often used ironically.
3 b) sobbing
4 a) your general well-being. In some contexts it might also be used with reference to someone's financial interests.
5 a) suffering
6 b) unpleasant

54.2 I've been offered a job that all my friends and family think I should take. The problem is that in my heart of **hearts** I really don't want it. It's always been my heart's **desire** to leave this city and work abroad, but I don't **have** the heart to tell my family this, as I know they'll be upset. I know you will tell me to **take** heart and be strong, but I really don't want to hurt them. After all, I know they have my best interests **at** heart. What should I do?

54.3 1 Don't expect so much of him – he's only four! **Have a heart!**
2 You'll only get hurt if you **wear your heart on your sleeve**.
3 **His heart was in his boots** as he thought about the difficult week ahead.
4 You know your parents **have your best interests at heart**.
5 He showed her round the city, but she could tell that **his heart was not in it**.

54.4

```
       ¹T  ²A
   ³B  O   O   ⁴T        ⁵D
               L          E
           ⁶B  L   E  E  D  S
               E         ⁷I  N
           ⁸T  V         R
       ⁹H  A   R   D  E  N  E  D
           K
      ¹⁰W  E   N   T
```

Unit 55

55.1
1 Mum finally said I could go to the party – she'd do anything for a quiet life.
2 When he retired, Steve got a new lease of life.
3 The children had the time of their lives at the party.
4 That film scared the life out of me!
5 Firefighters risk life and limb every day to help others.
6 Melanie is always the life and soul of the party.
7 He threatened to make her life a misery if she spoke to the police.
8 Diana got the shock of her life when she saw the snake.

55.2
1 We were within **an inch** of our lives when the lightning struck the tree beside us.
2 I don't like cycling to work. I feel like I'm risking life and **limb** in all that traffic.
3 The operation has given my grandmother a new **lease** of life.
4 Taking your final exams won't be easy, but I'm sure you'll live to tell the **tale**.
5 Clare **got** the shock of her life when she saw the police officer at her door.
6 Some people find living out of **a suitcase** away from home very stressful.
7 The company chairman is living on **borrowed** time after the latest fall in profits.
8 Lewis is really shy and isn't usually the life and **soul** of the party.

55.3
1 **You'll be living a lie** if you don't tell him you were once in prison.
2 In this life we have to **live and let live**.
3 Not many people have lived such **a charmed life** as Ed has.
4 We had **the time of our lives** in California last year.
5 Travelling is the best way to **see life**.
6 The explorers faced many challenges in the Arctic but **lived to tell the tale**.
7 The sudden scream **scared the life out of me**.
8 Jenny thinks she'll have a career as a model, but **she's living in a dream world** in my opinion.
9 The naughty child **made his teacher's life a misery**.
10 The full service has **given our old car a new lease of life**.

55.4
1 on   3 of   5 of
2 within 4 out   6 for

Unit 56

56.1
1 **There is a lot of dead wood** in my office. They should sack some people.
2 Putting Bernard in charge was **the kiss of death to the project.**
3 His idea of building a plane and flying round the world **is as dead as a dodo**.
4 The old family quarrel **is now dead and buried,** and they live in harmony.
5 The planning committee's decision was **a death blow to** the proposal to build the new airport. (You can also say **dealt a death blow to.**)

English Idioms in Use Advanced 157

56.2
1 a dead duck
2 kiss of death
3 in the dead of night
4 dead to the world
5 dead in the water
6 at death's door

56.3
1 in the dead of night
2 kiss of death
3 dead to the world
4 dead in the water
5 a dead duck
6 at death's door

56.4
1 You should only call an ambulance if it is **a matter of life and death** (or **a matter of life or death**).
2 The thieves stole the painting in the **dead** of night.
3 I am sick to **death** of people complaining all the time. It's not my fault!
4 That old car is so dangerous; it's **a death** trap.
5 Having to sit next to my boring uncle at the restaurant was **a fate worse than death**.
6 Many people suffered a **living death** in prison camps during the civil war.
7 The council are planning to demolish my house to build a motorway. **Over** my dead body!
8 **There is too much dead wood** on the school committee. They never do anything useful.

Unit 57

57.1
1 Nobody in their **right** mind would lend him money again. He never pays it back.
2 Correct.
3 He's always talking about cars. I've never met anyone with such a one-**track** mind.
4 Correct.
5 What can we do to take Marco's mind **off** his problems?
6 Now, I'd like you all to **cast** your mind back to your very first day at school.

57.2
1 Bye. **Mind how you go!**
2 **Mind your own business!**
3 I'm **bored out of my mind**.
4 You must be **out of your mind!**
5 No, it's **been (preying) on my mind** all day.
6 Please **cast your mind back** and tell us exactly what happened on the night in question.

57.3
1 He needs to **mind his back**.
2 I can **read her mind**.
3 Come on – **mind over matter!**
4 That singer **blows my mind!**

57.4
1 **Mind your step** on the ice – it's very slippery.
2 The actor's performance **blew my mind!**
3 It goes without saying that you should always **mind your Ps and Qs** at an interview.
4 People who drink and drive must be **out of their mind**.
5 My twin brother can **read my mind**.
6 I'm always **bored out of my mind** in physics lessons!
7 Their argument **preyed on Fiona's mind** for a long time.
8 You'll find it quite easy to learn the guitar **if you put your mind to it**.

Unit 58

58.1
1 I hate it when people try to give you the hard **sell** over the phone.
2 Her grandfather's illness has really **hit** her very hard.
3 I'm so glad we're friends again. No hard **feelings**, OK?
4 Walking home in the heavy snow was really hard **going**.
5 I find his constant criticism of me very hard to **swallow**.
6 Learning how to skate turned out to be much harder than Nina had bargained **for**.

58.2
1 True.
2 False. She will find it difficult to meet her deadline.
3 True.
4 False. It is not an enjoyable way to learn this lesson.

58.3
1 fall
2 nut
3 swallow
4 drive
5 fast
6 way
7 make
8 done

58.4
1 The truth is unpleasant, and I'm worried you'll find it **hard to swallow**.
2 Although Jack's grandfather used to be rich, he **fell on hard times** and the family lived in poverty.
3 There are no **hard and fast rules** as to how you should behave in circumstances like these.
4 I'm sure Suzi will **feel hard done by** when she discovers that her uncle has bought her twin sister a new sports car.
5 Children eventually **learn the hard way** that life is not always fair.
6 I have no idea how we're going to solve this problem. It's going to be **a hard nut to crack**, I'm sure.
7 Ruby always complains and seems to **make hard work of** any little problem.
8 You want me to reduce the price by £200? You certainly **drive a hard bargain**.

Follow-up
Some other idioms that you might find are:
be caught between a rock and a hard place: Whatever I decide to do there will be problems. *I'm caught between a rock and a hard place.*
be a hard act to follow: Colin was such a good manager that he is going to be *a hard act to follow*. I wouldn't want to take on his job when he leaves.
be too much like hard work: I certainly don't want to help my dad plant some rose bushes. It sounds *too much like hard work* to me.

Unit 59

59.1
1 through, floor
2 deaf ears
3 apart at the
4 the wrong hands

59.2
1 It seems that the prime minister's special adviser, Anne Sparks, **has fallen from grace**, and she is expected to resign soon.
2 Everyone had to **fall into line** and work longer hours for the same pay.
3 The deal **fell foul of** the export regulations and had to be cancelled at the last minute.
4 The report **falls short of** an outright condemnation of the government's actions, but it does contain strong criticism.

59.3
1 I didn't realise she was deceiving me, and I fell for it hook, **line and sinker**.
2 It looks as if the whole system is falling apart **at the seams**.
3 I didn't really have to do anything to get the job. It just fell **into my lap**.
4 Sally may not like the new rules, but she'll just have to **fall into line**.

59.4
1 If you fall for a thing (e.g. a trick or a lie) hook, line and sinker, you believe it completely. If you fall for a person hook, line and sinker, you fall madly in love with them.
2 Pride comes before a fall.
3 False. If someone falls over themselves to do something, it means they are very keen and eager to do it.
4 The bigger they are / come, the harder they fall.

Unit 60

60.1 I like Tina. She's her own **person**. In fact, she's very much a woman after my own **heart**. But I'm not keen on her boyfriend, Karl. He's always blowing his own **trumpet**, and when they come to my flat, he behaves as if he owns the **place**. I think it's time they went their own **ways**. In fact, I really think she'd **come** into her own if they did.

60.2
1 I must think of a way of **getting my own back** on Matt for playing that trick on me.
2 He told the police who had really planned the burglary, in order to **save his own skin**.
3 Tim was smaller than the other judo players, but he **held his own**.
4 You're **digging your own grave** by putting your boss in such a difficult position.
5 If women want to succeed in politics, they have to **play men at their own game**.

60.3

		¹P				
	²F	E	A	T	³H	E	R
		R			A	
		⁴S	K	I	N	
		O			D	
⁵D	⁶I	G	G	⁷I	N	⁸G	S
	A			F		⁹O	F
¹⁰T	I	M	E			A	
	E			¹¹H	O	L	D

Phonemic symbols

Vowel sounds

Symbol	Examples		
/iː/	sleep	me	
/i/	happy	recipe	
/ɪ/	pin	dinner	
/ʊ/	foot	could	pull
/uː/	do	shoe	through
/e/	red	head	said
/ə/	arrive	father	colour
/ɜː/	turn	bird	work
/ɔː/	sort	thought	walk
/æ/	cat	black	
/ʌ/	sun	enough	wonder
/ɒ/	got	watch	sock
/ɑː/	part	heart	laugh
/eɪ/	name	late	aim
/aɪ/	my	idea	time
/ɔɪ/	boy	noise	
/eə/	pair	where	bear
/ɪə/	hear	beer	
/əʊ/	go	home	show
/aʊ/	out	cow	
/ʊə/	pure	poor	

Consonant sounds

Symbol	Examples		
/p/	put		
/b/	book		
/t/	take		
/d/	dog		
/k/	car	kick	
/g/	go	guarantee	
/tʃ/	catch	church	
/dʒ/	age	lounge	
/f/	for	cough	
/v/	love	vehicle	
/θ/	thick	path	
/ð/	this	mother	
/s/	since	rice	
/z/	zoo	houses	
/ʃ/	shop	sugar	machine
/ʒ/	pleasure	usual	vision
/h/	hear	hotel	
/m/	make		
/n/	name	now	
/ŋ/	bring		
/l/	look	while	
/r/	road		
/j/	young		
/w/	wear		

Index

The numbers in the Index are **Unit** numbers not page numbers.

be taken aback 15
about
   out and ~ 10
   Tell me ~ it! 45
   That's ~ the size of it! 45
be head and shoulders above sb 19
be a chapter of accidents 38
a fait accompli 14
play your ace/trump card 20
Achilles heel 21
across the board 31
get your act together 6
ad
   ~ hoc 14
   ~ infinitum 14
spirit of adventure 5
after
   ~ your own heart 60
   It's easy to be wise ~ the event. 13
   time ~ time 10
the dice are loaded against sb 20
hammer out an agreement 39
ahead
   ~ of its time 40
   ~ of the game 46
castles in the air 23
rolling in the aisles 25
an Aladdin's cave 23
an albatross around your neck 23
all
   ~ in ~ 51
   ~ in good time 51
   ~ or nothing 51
   ~'s fair in love and war. 11
   ~-singing, ~-dancing 51
   ~ told 51
   an ~-time high/low 51
   at ~ hours 51
   be ~ in the mind 51
   be ~ over sb like a rash 9
   be ~ smiles 51
   be ~ things to ~ men 51
   for ~ sb cares 51
   get the ~-clear 51
   hold ~ the cards 20
   in ~ but name 51
   it will ~ end in tears 44

it's ~ systems go 51
laugh ~ the way to the bank 33
push ~ the right buttons 24
that's ~ we need 44
that's sb ~ over 51
tick ~ the boxes 32
to cap it ~ 51
when ~'s said and done 43
worship at the altar/shrine/temple of 31
in the altogether 12
amid mounting calls 39
in the final/last analysis 41
answer
   ~ the call of nature 12
   not take no for an ~ 52
do anything for a quiet life 55
be falling apart at the seams 59
upset the applecart 42
no-go area 52
arm
   give your right ~ for 19
   the long ~ of the law 29
armchair critic/traveller/gardener 25
call to arms 16
an albatross around your neck 23
You may well ask! 44
no strings attached 52
a last-ditch attempt 39
be au fait with 14
do sth on autopilot 17
away
   be blown ~ by sth 6
   be light years ~ from sth 24
back
   ~ on track 17
   be ~ to square one 6
   behind sb's ~ 3
   cast your mind ~ 57
   get your own ~ 60
   go ~ a long way 26
   mind/watch your ~ 57
   that's sb over the ~ 7
get off your backside 3
bring home the bacon 33
have a bad hair day 35
not be your bag 37
on balance 41

162   English Idioms in Use Advanced

ball
　　a whole new ~ game 20
　　drop the ~ 7
　　take your eye off the ~ 38
go down like a lead balloon 46
a ballpark figure 31
bank
　　laugh all the way to the ~ 33
　　not break the ~ 33
baptism of fire 16
bare-faced lies 47
bargain
　　drive a hard ~ 58
　　into the ~ 43
harder than you'd bargained for 58
be barking up the wrong tree 45
touch base 32
on a weekly basis 32
right off the bat 7
batten down the hatches 15
be batting a thousand 7
battle
　　~ of wills 16
　　be half the ~ 49
There are plenty more pebbles on the beach. 13
like a bear with a sore head 5
beat
　　~ a retreat 16
　　~ sb/sth hands down 40
　　If you can't ~ 'em, join 'em! 45
Beauty is in the eye of the beholder. 28
as red as a beetroot 9
beg
　　~ the question 41
　　I ~ to differ. 45
behind
　　~ your back 3
　　at/~ the wheel 17
　　the power ~ the throne 34
Beauty is in the eye of the beholder. 28
I'll believe it when I see it. 13
go belly up 30
below the belt 20
fringe benefits 6
give sb/sth a wide berth 15
have your best interests at heart 54
bête noire 14
better
　　~ safe than sorry. 11
　　two heads are ~ than one 50
between
　　~ a rock and a hard place 32
　　~ you and me 43

beyond
　　~ your wildest dreams 40
　　be ~ the pale 3
big
　　~ Brother 23
　　~ fish in a small pond 31
　　~ time 8
　　give sb a ~ hand 53
　　if and it's a ~ if 39
　　Mr ~ 34
　　the ~ C 12
the bigger they are/come, the harder they fall 59
eat like a bird 35
in your birthday suit 12
take the biscuit/cake 7
a bit on the side 12
bite
　　~ off more than one can chew 42
　　~ the bullet 42
　　~ the hand that feeds you 53
　　hold/~ your tongue 19
black
　　~ and blue 10
　　~ and white 10
　　a ~ mark 4
a wet blanket 27
my heart bleeds 54
effing and blinding 12
be on the blink 24
Ignorance is bliss. 13
block
　　a chip off the old ~ 26
　　new kid on the ~ 34
blood
　　~, sweat and tears 10
　　burst a ~ vessel 37
　　have ~ on your hands 39
　　make your ~ boil 37
　　your own flesh and ~ 26
bloody confrontations 39
blow
　　~ your mind 36, 57
　　~ your own trumpet 60
　　a death ~ 56
be blown away by sth 6
blue
　　~-sky thinking 32
　　be a bolt from the ~ 43
　　black and ~ 10
　　the boys in ~ 29
bluff your way 4

board
   across the ~ 31
   go by the ~ 15
tread the boards 25
boat
   it doesn't float my ~ 8
   Whatever floats your ~! 8
not be short of a bob or two 50
over my dead body 56
make your blood boil 37
be a bolt from the blue 43
drop a bombshell 16
bone
   ~ dry 47
   as dry as a ~ 9
book
   bring to ~ 29
   throw the ~ at 29
that's a turn-up for the books 43
your heart is in your boots 54
bored out of your mind 57
live on borrowed time 55
cut both/two ways 50
all hot and bothered 37
bottom
   rock ~ 47
   the ~ drops/falls out of the market 31
know no bounds 3
have plenty of strings to your bow 27
box
   Pandora's ~ 21
   think outside the ~ 32
tick all the boxes 32
the boys in blue 29
the brainchild of sb 24
put the brakes on 17
be the breadwinner 33
break
   a comfort ~ 12
   Give me a ~ !13, 44
   not ~ the bank 33
eat sb for breakfast 27
breathe your last 12
cross that bridge when you come to it 42
bright
   as ~ as a button 9
   Look on the ~ side. 13
bring
   ~ home the bacon 33
   ~ sb down a peg or two 50
   ~ the house down 25
   ~ to book 29
   ~ to the table 32

in broad daylight 47
If it ain't broke, don't fix it! 24
Big Brother 23
cry/weep buckets 7
built
   be ~ on sand 46
   Rome wasn't ~ in a day. 11
bite the bullet 42
bumper to bumper 10
have a bun in the oven 12
be a bundle of nerves 37
dead and buried 56
burn
   ~ the midnight oil 35
   money to ~ 33
have sth burning a hole in your pocket 6
fiddle while Rome burns 21
burst a blood vessel 37
bury your head in the sand 19
mind your own business 57
go bust 30
hustle and bustle 10
no ifs and buts 52
butter wouldn't melt in sb's mouth 28
as bright as a button 9
push the right buttons 24
the big C 12
rattle sb's cage 37
cake
   take the biscuit/~ 7
   the frosting/icing on the ~ 7
call
   ~ a spade a spade 23
   ~ to arms 16
   answer the ~ of nature 12
amid mounting calls 39
launch a campaign 4
like the cat that ate the canary 7
eye candy 28
a loose cannon 27
to cap it all 51
card
   get the red ~ 20
   play your ace/trump ~ 20
cards
   hold all the ~ 20
   keep/play your ~ close to your chest 20
for all sb cares 51
sweep sth under the carpet 38
a case in point 41
cash
   cold/hard ~ 7
   be strapped for ~ 33

cast your mind back 57
castles in the air 23
be a casualty of 4
cat
    fight like ~ and dog 7, 9
    like the ~ that ate the canary 7
    like the ~ that got the cream 7
    not have a ~ in hell's chance 18
    play ~ and mouse 48
    the ~'s whiskers 18
catch
    a ~-22 situation 23
    ~ some z's 7
like a deer/rabbit caught in the headlights 3
an Aladdin's cave 23
a glass ceiling 30
be/take centre stage 4, 25
nearly fall off your chair 43
chalk and cheese 10
chance
    a fighting ~ 16
    fat ~ 44
    given half a ~ 49
    not have a cat in hell's ~ 18
change
    a leopard can't ~ its spots 18
    plus ça ~ 14
ring the changes 42
plunge into chaos 39
a chapter of accidents 38
live a charmed life 55
Prince Charming 23
a wild-goose chase 22
the chattering classes 34
cheap and cheerful 33
take a rain check 20
turn the other cheek 21
cheap and cheerful 33
chalk and cheese 10
keep/play your cards close to your chest 20
bite off more than you can chew 42
be no spring chicken 52
a chip off the old block 26
as poor as a church mouse 9
a second-class citizen 34
drop a clanger 43
the chattering classes 34
clean
    come ~ 40
    squeaky- ~ 47
take sb to the cleaner's 33
clear
    as ~ as crystal 9

as ~ as mud 9
crystal ~ 47
too clever by half 49
clip sb's wings 5
keep/play your cards close to your chest 20
a wolf in sheep's clothing 18
cloud
    a ~ on the horizon 31
    Every ~ has a silver lining. 11
a cog in the machine 24
two sides of the same coin 50
cold
    ~ /hard cash 7
    in the ~ light of day 38
    stone ~ 47
be on a collision course 17
come
    ~ clean 40
    ~ into your own 60
    ~ out fighting 16
    ~ to a standstill 17
    ~ up trumps 46
    a dream ~ true 36
    cross that bridge when you ~ to it 42
    first ~, first served 11
    The bigger they are/~, the harder they fall. 59
    until the cows ~ home 18
comes
    Pride ~ before a fall. 59
    take each day as it ~ 35
a comfort break 12
creature comforts 35
coming
    not know whether you're ~ or going 35
    What is the world ~ to? 44
Two's company, three's a crowd. 50
compos mentis 14
bloody confrontations 39
a contradiction in terms 41
the conventional wisdom 41
cool
    be ~ with 8
    play it ~ 48
corner
    ~ the market 30
    in a tight ~ 38
can count sth on the fingers of one hand 53
under the counter 29
war-torn country 39
course
    as a matter of ~ 41
    be on a collision ~ 17
    run its ~ 2

the ~ of true love never did run smooth 22
under cover of darkness 39
until the cows come home 18
a hard nut to crack 58
from the cradle to the grave 5
nook and cranny 10
like the cat that got the cream 7
creature comforts 35
it's not cricket 20
an armchair critic 25
shed crocodile tears 18
cross that bridge when you come to it 42
be at a crossroads 4
crowd
    a ~-puller 25
    stand out from the ~ 40
    Two's company, three's a ~. 50
cry
    ~ /weep buckets 7
    ~ wolf 18
    ~ your heart out 54
crystal clear 47
crème de la crème 14
curl
    ~ your lip 3
    make sb's toes ~ 19
throw sb a curveball 7
a cushy number 30
cut
    ~ and run 15
    ~ both/two ways 50
    can't ~ the mustard 46
at the cutting edge 24, 32
C'est la vie. 14
as fresh as a daisy 9
the sword of Damocles 21
all-singing, all-dancing 51
under cover of darkness 39
day
    have a bad hair ~ 35
    in the cold light of ~ 38
    not give sb the time of ~ 26
    Rome wasn't built in a ~. 11
    take each ~ as it comes 35
in broad daylight 47
days
    sb's/sth's ~ are numbered 5
    the good old ~ 5
    the halcyon ~ 21
de facto 14
dead
    ~ and buried 56
    ~ in the water 56
    ~ to the world 56
    ~ wood 56
    a ~ duck 56
    as ~ as a dodo 56
    drop-~ gorgeous 28
    flog a ~ horse 18
    in the ~ of night 56
    over my ~ body 56
fall on deaf ears 59
be dealt a lousy hand 53
nearest and dearest 26
death
    a ~ blow 56
    a ~ trap 56
    a fate worse than ~ 56
    a living ~ 56
    a matter of life and / or ~ 56
    be at ~'s door 56
    dice with ~ 20
    sick to ~ of sth 56
    the kiss of ~ 56
debt of honour 2
all hands on deck 15
like a deer/rabbit caught in the headlights 3
be sb's heart's desire 54
dice
    ~ with death 20
    the ~ are loaded against 20
every Tom, Dick and Harry 5
I beg to differ. 45
difference
    a world of ~ 40, 45
    same ~ 44
dig your own grave 60
not be worth a dime 7
dressed up like a dog's dinner 28
play dirty 48
a recipe for disaster 46
note of discord 45
a last-ditch attempt 39
as dead as a dodo 56
dog
    ~ eat ~ 32
    ~ in the manger 18
    a ~'s life 18
    be like a ~ with two tails 50
    dressed up like a ~'s dinner 28
    fight like cat and ~ 7, 9
    work like a ~ 9
domino effect 2
donkey/grunt work 7
door
    be at death's ~ 56

get a foot in the ~ 30
open the ~ to 2, 41
double whammy 46
down
~ in the dumps 37
~ the line 17
~-at-heel 28
beat sb/sth hands ~ 40
bring sb ~ a peg or two 50
bring the house ~ 25
go ~ a storm 46
go ~ a treat 36
go ~ like a lead balloon 46
send shivers ~ your spine 25
shoot sb ~ in flames 16
throw money ~ the drain 33
win hands ~ 53
in dribs and drabs 10
throw money down the drain 33
dream
a ~ come true 36
be/live in a ~ world 55
beyond your wildest dreams 40
dressed
~ to kill 28
~ up like a dog's dinner 28
~ up to the nines 28
mutton ~ as lamb 28
in dribs and drabs 10
You can lead a horse to water (but you can't make him drink). 13
drive
~ a hard bargain 58
~ like a maniac 9
a back-seat driver 17
in the driving seat 17
drop
~ a bombshell 16
~ a clanger 43
~ in on 2
~ the ball 7
~-dead gorgeous 28
~/fall into your lap 59
the penny drops 43
the bottom drops/falls out of the market 31
punch-drunk 20
dry
as ~ as a bone 9
as ~ as dust 9
bone ~ 47
leave sb high and ~ 15
a dead duck 56
down in the dumps 37

as dry as dust 9
ear
have the ~ of sb 26
listen with half an ~ 49
make a pig's ~ of sth 38
ears
fall on deaf ~ 59
prick your ~ up 2
easy
~ on the eye 28
It's ~ to be wise after the event. 13
Take it ~. 13
eat
~ like a bird 35
~ like a horse 35
~ like a pig 35
~ sb for breakfast 27
~ sb out of house and home 22
dog ~ dog 32
eating
be ~ for two 12
have sb ~ out of the palm of your hand 53
be economical with the truth 12
edge
at the cutting ~ 24, 32
keep sb on the ~ of their seat 25
domino effect 2
effing and blinding 12
rig an election 34
the elephant in the room 18
eleventh-hour 39
end
~ of (story)! 8
help sb no ~ 52
it will all ~ in tears 44
make your hair stand on ~ 22
no ~ of 52
make ends meet 33
public enemy number one 34
engulfed in flames 39

enough
~ is as good as a feast. 13
fair ~ 44
enter into the spirit of sth 36
push the envelope 32
epic proportions 21
Don't even go there! 8
It's easy to be wise after the event. 13
every
~ cloud has a silver lining. 11
~ Tom, Dick and Harry 5
here, there and everywhere 10

English Idioms in Use Advanced 167

it does exactly what it says on the tin 8
no expense spared 33
go the extra mile 8
eye
   ~ candy 28
   a twinkle in your father's ~ 26
   be in the public ~ 34
   be one in the ~ for sb 19
   Beauty is in the ~ of the beholder. 28
   easy on the ~ 28
   in the twinkling of an ~ 22
   see ~ to ~ 1, 6
   take your ~ off the ball 38
   there's more to sth than meets the ~ 19
   watch with half an ~ 49
the green-eyed monster 22
eyes
   have stars in your ~ 36
   pull the wool over sb's ~ 29
face
   ~-saving 19
   a ~ like thunder 9
   a slap in the ~ 38
   not be just a pretty ~ 28
   lose ~ 19
   sb's ~ doesn't fit 19
faced
   bare-~ lies 47
   poker-~ 20
the fact of the matter is 32
de facto 14
fair
   ~ enough. 44
   ~'s ~ 13
   a ~-weather friend 26
   All's ~ in love and war. 11
fait
   a ~ accompli 14
   be au ~ with 14
fall
   ~ foul of 59
   ~ from grace 59
   ~ into line 31, 59
   ~ into the trap of 59
   ~ into your lap 59
   ~ into the wrong hands 59
   ~ off the radar 8
   ~ on deaf ears 59
   ~ on hard times 58, 59
   ~ on your sword 21
   ~ over yourself to do sth 59
   ~ short of 59
   ~ through the floor 59

   ~ for sb/sth hook, line and sinker 59
   nearly ~ off your chair 43
   Pride comes before a ~. 59
   The bigger they are/come, the harder they ~. 59
be falling apart at the seams 59
the bottom drops/falls out of the market 31
run in the family 26
the shit hits the fan 3
footloose and fancy-free 26
far
   I wouldn't trust sb as ~ as I could throw them. 44
   So ~, so good. 13
fast
   hard and ~ rules 58
   life in the ~ lane 17
fat
   ~ chance 44
   It's not over until the ~ lady sings. 13
fate
   a ~ worse than death 56
   tempt ~ 42
a twinkle in your father's eye 26
do me a favour 44
Enough is as good as a feast. 13
feather your own nest 3, 60
bite the hand that feeds you 53
feel hard done by 58
have a sinking feeling 37
no hard feelings 58
feet
   have two left ~ 50
   pull the rug from under your ~ 38
at one fell swoop 22
sit on the fence 6
fiddle
   ~ while Rome burns 21
   be on the ~ 29
   play second ~ 48
play the field 12
fight
   ~ for your life 39
   ~ like cat and dog 7, 9
fighting
   ~ fit 47
   a ~ chance 16
   come out ~ 16
a ballpark figure 31
filthy rich 47
in the final/last analysis 41
finger
   keep your ~ on the pulse 19
   point the ~ at 19

fingers
    ~ and thumbs 10
    can count sth on the ~ of one hand 53
    put/stick two ~ up at sth 50
fire
    baptism of ~ 16
    friendly ~ 12
    hang ~ 16
first
    ~ and foremost 41
    ~ come, ~ served 11
    at ~ glance 43
    the ~ lady of sth 8
fish
    big ~ in a small pond 31
    There are plenty more ~ in the sea. 13
fit
    ~ like a glove 9
    fighting ~ 47
    sb's face doesn't ~ 19
If it ain't broke, don't fix it. 24
get/take the flak 4
an old flame 26
flames
    engulfed in ~ 39
    shoot sb down in ~ 16
flash
    a ~ in the pan 1, 16
    as quick as a ~ 9
flesh
    your own ~ and blood 26
    pound of ~ 22
it doesn't float my boat 8
Whatever floats your boat! 8
flog a dead horse 18
fall through the floor 59
fly
    ~ by the seat of your pants 17
    ~ the nest 26
be flying high 17
fool
    be no/nobody's ~ 52
    play sb for a ~ 48
    act/play the ~ 27
foot
    be six ~ under 12
    get a ~ in the door 30
    put your ~ in it 1
    shoot yourself in the ~ 16
footloose and fancy-free 26
join forces with 4
first and foremost 41
a small fortune 47

fall foul of 59
four-letter words 12
free
    footloose and fancy- ~ 26
    There's no such thing as a ~ lunch. 52
pardon my French 12
fresh
    as ~ as a daisy 9
    be ~ out of sth 7
Girl / Man / Person Friday 23
friend
    Any ~ of yours is a ~ of mine. 13
    a fair-weather ~ 26
friendly fire 12
have friends in high places 26
fringe benefits 6
the frosting/icing on the cake 7
full
    ~ of the joys of spring 36
    ~ stop 47
    live life to the ~ 40
no pain no gain 11
Nothing ventured, nothing gained. 11
play to the gallery 25
game
    a ~ plan 48
    a whole new ball ~ 20
    ahead of the ~ 46
    play a/the waiting ~ 48
    play sb at their own ~ 60
    play the ~ 48
    raise your ~ 48
    the ~'s up 48
    the name of the ~ 48
    two can play at that ~ 50
poacher turned gamekeeper 29
play games 48
gardening leave 31
gas guzzler 24
run the gauntlet 16
go/move/step up a gear 17
get off your backside 3
be getting/going nowhere 4
give
    ~ me a break! 13, 44
    ~ your right arm for 19
    ~ and/or take 10
    ~ sb a big hand 53
    ~ sb/sth a wide berth 15
    ~ sb the hard sell 58
    ~ sth a miss 35
    ~/get the green light 17
    not ~ sb the time of day 26

wouldn't ~ sth house room 37
given
   ~ half a chance 49
   be ~ / get your marching orders 4
   be ~ the go-ahead 39
   be ~ the sack 3
your glad rags 28
at first glance 43
a glass ceiling 30
fit like a glove 9
the gloves are off 32
a glutton for punishment 27
go
   ~ back a long way 26
   ~ belly up 30
   ~ bust 30
   ~ by the board 15
   ~ down a storm 46
   ~ down a treat 36
   ~ down like a lead balloon 46
   ~ haywire 24
   ~ off the rails 17
   ~ out like a light 35
   ~ out on the town 35
   ~ spare 3
   ~ the extra mile 8
   ~ the whole hog 23
   ~ their own ways 60
   ~ to your head 19
   ~ to the wall 30
   ~ up in the world 2
   ~ with a swing 36
   ~ /move/step up a gear 17
   be given the ~-ahead 39
   Don't even ~ there! 8
   from the word ~ 43
   get-up and ~ 27
   happy-~-lucky 36
   it's all systems ~ 51
   Mind how you ~. 57
   no- ~ area 52
an own goal 60
move the goalposts 20
get your goat 37
sort (out) the sheep from the goats 18
play God 48
your heart goes out to sb 54
going
   be ~ great guns 30
   be getting/~ nowhere 4
   be heavy-~ 25
   hard ~ 58
   not know whether you're coming or ~ 35

a heart of gold 54
golden
   ~ handshake 30
   ~ hello 30
good
   ~ riddance (to bad rubbish)! 13, 44
   all in ~ time 51
   do sb the world of ~ 40
   Enough is as ~ as a feast. 13
   for ~ reason 43
   have a ~ head for sth 19
   have a ~ mind to 49
   make ~ headway 15
   no news is ~ news 52
   So far, so ~. 13
   the ~ old days 5
a wild-goose chase 22
play gooseberry 48
drop-dead gorgeous 28
You've got me there. 44
fall from grace 59
would sell your own grandmother 33
grass roots 34
grave
   as silent as the ~ 9
   dig your own ~ 60
   from the cradle to the ~ 5
gravy train 34
be going great guns 30
green
   give/get the ~ light 17
   the ~-eyed monster 22
grey
   ~ vote 34
   men in ~ suits 34
donkey/grunt work 7
no prizes for guessing sth 52
be going great guns 30
slog your guts out 30
gas-guzzler 24
hair
   have a bad ~ day 35
   make your ~ stand on end 22
split hairs 45
the halcyon days 21
half
   ~-measures 49
   a ~-baked scheme 49
   a sth and a ~ 49
   be ~ the battle 49
   be not ~ 49
   given ~ a chance 49
   have ~ a mind to 49

listen with ~ an ear 49
not ~ 49
not know the ~ of it 49
too clever by ~ 49
watch with ~ an eye 49
meet sb halfway 49
hammer out an agreement 39
hand
~ over the reins 53
~ sth to sb on a plate 53
be an old ~ at sth 53
be dealt a lousy ~ 53
bite the ~ that feeds you 53
can count sth on the fingers of one ~ 53
give sb a big ~ 53
have your ~ in the till 29
have sb eating out of / in the palm of your ~ 53
have the upper ~ 53
lay a ~ on 53
on the one ~ , on the other ~ 41
out of ~ 53
put your ~ on your heart 53
show your ~ 53
you have to ~ it to sb 53
hands
all ~ on deck 15
beat sb/sth ~ down 40
can't lay your ~ on sth 53
fall into the wrong ~ 59
have blood on your ~ 39
off your ~ 53
play into sb's ~ 53
sit on your ~ 53
sb's ~ are tied 53
take matters into your own ~ 60
win ~ down 53
golden handshake 30
hang fire 16
happy
~-go-lucky 36
as ~ as Larry 36
hard
~ and fast rules 58
~ going 58
~ to swallow 58
~ up 58
a ~ nut to crack 58
be ~ pressed to 58
be ~ put to 58
between a rock and a ~ place 32
cold/~ cash 7
drive a ~ bargain 58
fall on ~ times 58, 59

feel ~ done by 58
give sb the ~ sell 58
hit sb ~ 58
learn the ~ way 58
make ~ work of 58
no ~ feelings 58
rock ~ 47
play hardball 20
harden your heart 54
harder
~ than you'd bargained for 58
The bigger they are/come, the ~ they fall. 59
every Tom, Dick and Harry 5
batten down the hatches 15
do a hatchet job on 25
go haywire 24
head
be ~ and shoulders above sb 19
be in over your ~ 38
bury your ~ in the sand 19
get your mind/~ round 57
go to your ~ 19
have a good ~ for sth 19
like a bear with a sore ~ 5
like a deer/rabbit caught in the headlights 3
heads
~ will roll 31
put our ~ together 19
two ~ are better than one 50
make good headway 15
heart
a ~ of gold 54
a ~ of stone 54
after your own ~ 60
be your ~'s desire 54
cry your ~ out 54
harden your ~ 54
have a ~ 54
have your best interests at ~ 54
in your ~ of hearts 54
my ~ bleeds 54
not have the ~ to 54
your ~ goes out sb 54
your ~ is in your boots 54
your ~ isn't in sth 54
put your hand on your ~ 53
strike at the ~ of 54
take ~ 54
wear your ~ on your sleeve 54
in your heart of hearts 54
be heavy going 25

heel
  Achilles ~ 21
  down-at-~ 28
hell
  not have a cat in ~'s chance 18
  the sb/sth from ~ 8
golden hello 30
help sb no end 52
here, there and everywhere 10
high
  an all-time ~/low 51
  be flying ~ 17
  be on a ~ 36
  have friends in ~ places 26
  leave sb ~ and dry 15
  ride ~ 46
  shoot sky-~ 31
highly strung 27
Hindsight is a wonderful thing. 13
hit
  ~ and miss 10
  ~ sb hard 58
  ~ the jackpot 36
  ~ the mark 40
  ~ the right note 36
  ~ the spot 36
the shit hits the fan 3
ad hoc 14
go the whole hog 23
be hoist with your own petard 22
hold
  ~ all the cards 20
  ~ your own 60
  ~/bite your tongue 19
have sth burning a hole in your pocket 6
pick holes in 25
home
  bring ~ the bacon 33
  eat sb out of house and ~ 22
  until the cows come ~ 18
debt of honour 2
on the hoof 35
fall for sb/sth hook, line and sinker 59
hopping mad 3
cloud on the horizon 31
horse
  a Trojan ~ 21
  eat like a ~ 35
  flog a dead ~ 18
  straight from the ~'s mouth 18
  You can lead a ~ to water (but you can't make him drink). 13
wild horses couldn't make me 37

hot
  ~ off the press 24
  all ~ and bothered 37
  piping ~ 47
eleventh-hour 39
at all hours 51
house
  bring the ~ down 25
  eat sb out of ~ and home 22
  on the ~ 35
  wouldn't give sth ~ room 37
mind how you go 57
huff and puff 10
might as well be hung for a sheep as a lamb 18
hustle and bustle 10
sing from the same hymn sheet 45
be (skating) on thin ice 42
the tip of the iceberg 5
the frosting/icing on the cake 7
no ifs and buts 52
Ignorance is bliss. 13
be under no illusions 31
the spitting image 26, 28
within an inch of your life 55
ad infinitum 14
information
  a mine of ~ 27
  too much ~ 8
inside
  an ~ job 29
  know sth ~ out 3
have your best interests at heart 54
Necessity is the mother of invention. 11
an ivory tower 23
hit the jackpot 36
like nailing jelly to a wall 8
job
  an inside ~ 29
  do a hatchet ~ on 25
join
  ~ forces with 4
  ~ the ranks of 16
  If you can't beat 'em, ~ 'em! 45
joined-up thinking 32
put sb's nose out of joint 38
joke
  be no ~ 52
  see the ~ 4
full of the joys of spring 36
more by luck than judgement 43
not be just a pretty face 28
as keen as mustard 9

keep
- ~ your finger on the pulse 19
- ~/play your cards close to your chest 20
- ~ sb on the edge of their seat 25

kick yourself 37

kid
- a whizz ~ 27
- new ~ on the block 34

dressed to kill 28
kith and kin 3
be two of a kind 50
the kiss of death 56
kith and kin 3

knock
- ~ into shape 2
- ~ sb for six 20, 37

tie the knot 5

know
- ~ no bounds 3
- ~ your place 3
- ~ sth inside out 3
- not ~ the half of it 49
- not ~ whether you're coming or going 35

at the top of the ladder 30

lady
- It's not over until the fat ~ sings. 13
- the first ~ of sth 8

laissez-faire 14

lamb
- might as well be hung for a sheep as a ~ 18
- mutton dressed as ~ 28

win by a landslide 34

lane
- life in the fast ~ 17
- life in the slow ~ 17

drop/fall into your lap 59
by and large 41
as happy as Larry 36

last
- a ~ditch attempt 39
- breathe your ~ 12
- in the final/~ analysis 41
- ~ but not least 41

laugh all the way to the bank 33
launch a campaign 4
rest on your laurels 21
the long arm of the law 29

lay
- ~ a hand on 53
- ~ it on with a trowel 22
- can't ~ your hands on sth 53

lead
- go down like a ~ balloon 46

You can ~ a horse to water (but you can't make him drink). 13
a leading light 25
turn over a new leaf 42
learn the hard way 58
get a new lease of life 55

least
- last but not ~ 41
- to say the ~ 43

leave
- ~ no stone unturned 21
- ~ sb high and dry 15
- gardening ~ 31

have two left feet 50
a leopard can't change its spots 18
live and let live 55
four-letter words 12
take to the next level 31
live a lie 55
bare-faced lies 47

life
- ~ in the fast lane 17
- ~ in the slow lane 17
- a dog's ~ 18
- a matter of ~ and/or death 56
- do anything for a quiet ~ 55
- fight for your ~ 39
- get a ~ 44
- get a new lease of ~ 55
- get the shock of your ~ 55
- have the time of your ~ 55
- live a charmed ~ 55
- live ~ to the full 40
- make sb's ~ a misery 55
- risk ~ and limb 55
- scare the ~ out of 55
- see ~ 55
- the ~ and soul of the party 55
- Variety is the spice of ~. 11
- within an inch of your ~ 55

throw a lifeline 31

light
- a leading ~ 25
- be ~ years away from sth 24
- be out like a ~ 35
- give/get the green ~ 17
- go out like a ~ 35
- in the cold ~ of day 38
- see the ~ 4

have your name in lights 25
risk life and limb 55

line
- ~ your own pockets 29

English Idioms in Use Advanced 173

down the ~ 17
fall for sb/sth hook, ~ and sinker 59
fall into ~ 31, 59
every cloud has a silver lining 11
curl your lip 3
listen with half an ear 49
little by little 10
live
~ a charmed life 55
~ a lie 55
~ and let ~ 55
~ in each other's pockets 26
~ life to the full 40
~ in a dream world 55
~ on a shoestring 33
~ on borrowed time 55
~ out of a suitcase 55
~ to tell the tale 55
a living death 56
the dice are loaded against 20
a lone voice 45
long
go back a ~ way 26
not ~ for this world 12
the ~ arm of the law 29
look
~ on the bright side 13
~ out for number one 27
~ the part 28
be not much to ~ at 28
a loose cannon 27
lose
~ your touch 38
~ face 19
~ the plot 38
not ~ sleep over sth 35
at a loss for words 5
there's a lot to be said for 43
be dealt a lousy hand 53
love
a ~ -rat 27
All's fair in ~ and war. 11
The course of true ~ never did run smooth. 22
star-crossed lovers 22
an all-time high/low 51
more by luck than judgement 43
happy-go-lucky 36
like it or lump it 3
There's no such thing as a free lunch. 52
a cog in the machine 24
hopping mad 3
self-made man 34
in the main 41

silent majority 34
make
~ a mountain out of a molehill 5
~ a name for 3
~ a pig's ear of 38
~ ends meet 33
~ good headway 15
~ hard work of 58
~ sb's toes curl 19
~ sb's life a misery 55
~ the supreme/ultimate sacrifice 12
~ your blood boil 37
~ your hair stand on end 22
wild horses couldn't ~ me 37
that makes two of us 50
of your own making 60
man
a ~/woman of many parts 27
Girl / ~ / Person Friday 23
self-made ~ 34
dog in the manger 18
drive like a maniac 9
a man/woman of many parts 27
marathon talks 39
steal a march on sb 16
be given / get your marching orders 4
mark
a black ~ 4
hit the ~ 40
market
corner the ~ 30
the bottom drops/falls out of the ~ 31
take matters into your own hands 60
matter
a ~ of life and death 56
as a ~ of course 41
mind over ~ 57
the fact of the ~ is 32
You may well ask! 44
a square meal 35
half-measures 49
meet
~ sb halfway 49
make ends ~ 33
there's more to sth than meets the eye 19
butter wouldn't melt in sb's mouth 28
men
~ in grey suits 34
be all things to all ~ 51
compos mentis 14
a mere pittance 47
on message 45
the Midas touch 21

a middle-age spread 28
burn the midnight oil 35
might as well be hung for a sheep as a lamb 18
to put it mildly 43
go the extra mile 8
mind
   ~ how you go 57
   ~ your back 57
   ~ your own business 57
   ~ your Ps and Qs 57
   ~ your step 57
   ~ over matter 57
   be all in the ~ 51
   blow your ~ 36, 57
   bored out of your ~ 57
   cast your ~ back 57
   get your ~/head round 57
   have a good ~ to 49
   have a one-track ~ 57
   have half a ~ to 49
   if you put your ~ to it 57
   nobody in their right ~ 57
   of like ~ 45
   of the same ~ 45
   out of your ~ 57
   prey on your ~ 57
   read sb's ~ 57
   take your ~ off it 57
be in two minds 45
mine
   a ~ of information 27
   Any friend of yours is a friend of ~. 13
be a minefield 4
up-to-the-minute 5
make sb's life a misery 55
miss
   give sth a ~ 35
   hit and ~ 10
make a mountain out of a molehill 5
at this moment in time 32
money
   ~ for old rope 33
   ~ to burn 33
   monopoly ~ 20
   put your ~ where your mouth is 42
   throw ~ down the drain 33
monopoly money 20
the green-eyed monster 22
tuned to the moon 7
more
   ~ by luck than judgement 43
   bite off ~ than one can chew 42
   There are plenty ~ fish in the sea. 13

There are plenty ~ pebbles on the beach. 13
there's ~ to sth than meets the eye 19
Necessity is the mother of invention. 11
motion
   set in ~ 41
   set the wheels in ~ 24
make a mountain out of a molehill 5
amid mounting calls 39
mouse
   as poor as a church ~ 9
   as quiet as a ~ 1
   play cat and ~ 48
mouth
   butter wouldn't melt in sb's ~ 28
   put your money where your ~ is 42
   straight from the horse's ~ 18
   take the words right out of my ~ 45
move
   ~ the goalposts 20
   a smart ~ 40
   go/~/step up a gear 17
movers and shakers 34
Mr Big 34
as clear as mud 9
as stubborn as a mule 9
Mum's the word. 13
mustard
   as keen as ~ 9
   can't cut the ~ 46
mutton dressed as lamb 28
shrouded in mystery 39
like nailing jelly to a wall 8
stark naked 47
name
   have your ~ in lights 25
   in all but ~ 51
   make a ~ for 3
   the ~ of the game 48
on the straight and narrow 29
answer the call of nature 12
nearest and dearest 26
nearly fall off your chair 43
neat and tidy 10
Necessity is the mother of invention. 11
neck
   ~ and ~ 10
   an albatross around sb's ~ 23
   stick your ~ out 42
that's all we need 44
be a bundle of nerves 37
nest
   feather your own ~ 3, 60
   fly the ~ 26

never
It ~ rains but it pours. 11
The course of true love ~ did run smooth. 22
new
~ kid on the block 34
a whole ~ ball game 20
get a ~ lease of life 55
turn over a ~ leaf 42
no news is good news 52
next
in ~ to no time 52
take to the ~ level 31
nice work if you can get it 44
night
all right on the ~ 25
be like ships that pass in the ~ 23
in the dead of ~ 56
be a nightmare 38
nines
done up to the ~ 28
dressed up to the ~ 28
no
~ end of 52
~ expense spared 33
~ -go area 52
~ ifs and buts 52
~ news is good news 52
~ pain ~ gain 11
~ prizes for guessing sth 52
~ strings attached 52
~ time like the present 52
be ~ joke 52
be ~/nobody's fool 52
be ~ oil painting 52
be ~ picnic 52
be ~ spring chicken 52
be under ~ illusions 31
help sb ~ end 52
in next to ~ time 52
in ~ uncertain terms 52
know ~ bounds 3
leave ~ stone unturned 21
like there's ~ tomorrow 52
There's ~ such thing as a free lunch. 52
There's ~ time like the present. 40, 44
not take ~ for an answer 52
nobody
~ in their right mind 57
be no/~'s fool 52
bête noire 14
non sequitur 14
nook and cranny 10

nose
powder your ~ 12
put sb's ~ out of joint 38
take a nosedive 17, 31
note
~ of discord 45
hit the right ~ 36
nothing
~ ventured, ~ gained. 11
all or ~ 51
to say ~ of 43
be getting/going nowhere 4
number
a cushy ~ 30
look out for ~ one 27
public enemy ~ one 34
sb's ~ is up 12
sb's/sth's days are numbered 5
a hard nut to crack 58
odds
be at ~ with 45
pay over the ~ 33
in the offing 15
oil
~ the wheels 24
be no ~ painting 52
burn the midnight ~ 35
pour ~ on troubled waters 45
old
a chip off the ~ block 26
an ~ flame 26
be an ~ hand at sth 53
money for ~ rope 33
the good ~ days 5
one
at ~ fell swoop 22
be back to square ~ 6
be ~ in the eye for sb 19
can count sth on the fingers of ~ hand 53
have a ~-track mind 57
look out for number ~ 27
on the ~ hand, on the other hand 41
public enemy number ~ 34
two heads are better than ~ 50
open the door to 2, 41
be given / get your marching orders 4
other
on the one hand, on the ~ hand 41
turn the ~ cheek 21
think outside the box 32
outstay your welcome 35
have a bun in the oven 12

176   English Idioms in Use Advanced

over
- ~ my dead body 56
- be all ~ sb like a rash 9
- be in ~ your head 38
- fall ~ yourself to do sth 59
- hand ~ the reins 53
- It's not ~ until the fat lady sings. 13
- mind ~ matter 57
- not lose sleep ~ sth 35
- pay ~ the odds 33
- pull the wool ~ sb's eyes 29
- that's sb all ~ 51
- that's sb ~ the back 7
- turn ~ a new leaf 42

own
- after your ~ heart 60
- an ~ goal 60
- be hoist with your ~ petard 22
- blow your ~ trumpet 60
- come into your ~ 60
- dig your ~ grave 60
- feather your ~ nest 3, 60
- get your ~ back 60
- go their ~ ways 60
- hold your ~ 60
- in your ~ time 60
- line your ~ pockets 29
- mind your ~ business 57
- of your ~ making 60
- your ~ flesh and blood 26
- be your ~ person 60
- out of your ~ pocket 5
- play sb at their ~ game 60
- save your ~ skin 60
- take matters into your ~ hands 60
- would sell your ~ grandmother 33

as if (he) owned the place 60
pack a punch 40
send sb packing 22
a page-turner 25
no pain no gain 11
be no oil painting 52
be beyond the pale 3
have sb eating out of / in the palm of your hand 53
a flash in the pan 1, 16
Pandora's box 21
fly by the seat of your pants 17
a paper tiger 46
part and parcel 6
pardon my French 12
as sick as a parrot 18

part
- ~ and parcel 6
- look the ~ 28

parting shot 21
silent/sleeping partner 30
a man/woman of many parts 27
the life and soul of the party 55
be like ships that pass in the night 23
run out of patience 37
pay over the odds 33
uneasy peace 39
be like two peas in a pod 50
There are plenty more pebbles on the beach. 13
bring sb down a peg or two 50
not have two pennies to rub together 50

penny
- ~-pinching 33
- be two a ~ 50
- spend a ~ 12
- the ~ drops 43

be your own person 60
be hoist with your own petard 22
pick holes in 25
be no picnic 52
not the whole picture 41

pig
- eat like a ~ 35
- make a ~'s ear of 38

penny-pinching 33
piping hot 47
a mere pittance 47

place
- as if (he) owned the ~ 60
- between a rock and a hard ~ 32
- know your ~ 3

have friends in high places 26
a game plan 48
as thick as two short planks 9
hand sth to sb on a plate 53

play
- ~ cat and mouse 48
- ~ dirty 48
- ~ for time 48
- ~ games 38
- ~ God 48
- ~ gooseberry 48
- ~ hardball 20
- ~ into sb's hands 53
- ~ it cool 48
- ~ it safe 48
- ~ your ace/trump card 20
- ~ sb at their own game 60
- ~ sb for a fool 48
- ~ second fiddle 48
- ~ the field 12

~ the fool 27
~ the game 48
~ to the gallery 25
~ your cards close to your chest 20
two can ~ at that game 50
plenty
have ~ of strings to your bow 27
There are ~ more fish in the sea. 13
There are ~ more pebbles on the beach. 13
plot
lose the ~ 38
the ~ thickens 44
plunge into chaos 39
plus ça change 14
poacher turned gamekeeper 29
pocket
have sth burning a hole in your ~ 6
out of your own ~ 5
pockets
line your own ~ 29
live in each other's ~ 26
be like two peas in a pod 50
point
~ the finger at 19
~ the way to 41
a case in ~ 41
see the ~ 4
poker-faced 20
big fish in a small pond 31
as poor as a church mouse 9
any port in a storm 15
pound of flesh 22
pour oil on troubled waters 45
It never rains but it pours. 11
powder your nose 12
the power behind the throne 34
There's no time like the present. 40, 44, 52
hot off the press 24
be hard pressed to 58
not be just a pretty face 28
prey on your mind 57
prick your ears up 2
Pride comes before a fall. 59
Prince Charming 23
no prizes for guessing sth 52
epic proportions 21
mind your Ps and Qs 57
public
~ enemy number one 34
be in the ~ eye 34
huff and puff 10
pull
~ rank 4

~ the rug from under your feet 38
~ the strings 34
~ the wool over sb's eyes 29
not ~ any punches 20
a crowd-puller 25
keep your finger on the pulse 19
punch
~ -drunk 20
pack a ~ 40
not pull any punches 20
a glutton for punishment 27
push
~ the envelope 32
~ the right buttons 24
put
~ our heads together 19
~ your foot in it 1
~ your hand on your heart 53
~ your money where your mouth is 42
~ your shoulder to the wheel 42
~ sb's nose out of joint 38
~ the brakes on 17
~ to sleep 12
~ two fingers up at sth 50
be hard ~ to 58
if you ~ your mind to it 57
to ~ it mildly 43
a Pyrrhic victory 21
mind your Ps and Qs 57
beg the question 41
as quick as a flash 9
be quids in 33
quiet
as ~ as a mouse 1
do anything for a ~ life 55
status quo 14
like a deer/rabbit caught in the headlights 3
the rat race 30
fall off the radar 8
rags
~ to riches 33
your glad ~ 28
go off the rails 17
take a rain check 20
It never rains but it pours. 11
raise your game 48
as thin as a rake 9
as stiff/straight as a ramrod 2
pull rank 4
join the ranks of 16
be all over sb like a rash 9
rat
a love- ~ 27

the ~ race 30
rattle sb's cage 37
razor-sharp 47
reach for the stars 42
read sb's mind 57
reason
   for good ~ 43
   see ~ 4
receive a windfall 31
a recipe for disaster 46
track record 30
red
   as ~ as a beetroot 9
   get the ~ card 20
   see ~ 4, 37
reduce to tears 37
rein in spending 31
hand over the reins 53
reinvent the wheel 24
rest on your laurels 21
beat a retreat 16
filthy rich 47
rags to riches 33
riddance
   Good ~ (to bad rubbish)! 13, 44
ride
   ~ high 46
   take sb for a ~ 29
rig an election 34
right
   ~ off the bat 7
   all ~ on the night 25
   give your ~ arm for 19
   hit the ~ note 36
   nobody in their ~ mind 57
   push the ~ buttons 24
   take the words ~ out of my mouth 45
ring the changes 42
risk life and limb 55
do a roaring trade 30
rock
   ~ bottom 47
   ~ hard 47
   between a ~ and a hard place 32
it's not rocket science 24
on the rocks 15
roll
   heads will ~ 31
   on a ~ 46
rolling
   ~ in the aisles 25
   be ~ in it 33

Rome
   ~ wasn't built in a day. 11
   fiddle while ~ burns 21
room
   the elephant in the ~ 18
   wouldn't give sth house ~ 37
grass roots 34
money for old rope 33
round
   get your mind/head ~ 57
   get your tongue ~ sth 19
rub
   ~ shoulders with sb 26
   not have two pennies to ~ together 50
Good riddance (to bad rubbish)! 13, 44
pull the rug from under your feet 38
hard and fast rules 58
run
   ~ a tight ship 3, 15
   ~ in the family 26
   ~ its course 2
   ~ like the wind 9
   ~ out of patience 37
   ~ out of steam 17
   ~ the gauntlet 16
   cut and ~ 15
   The course of true love never did ~ smooth. 22
do a runner 29
be given the sack 3
make the supreme/ultimate sacrifice 12
saddled with debt 31
safe
   ~ and sound 1
   better ~ than sorry 11
   play it ~ 48
said
   there's a lot to be ~ for 43
   when all's ~ and done 43
sails
   take the wind out of sb's ~ 15
   trim your ~ 42
same
   ~ difference 44
   be on the ~ wavelength 6
   of the ~ mind 45
   sing from the ~ hymn sheet 45
   two sides of the ~ coin 50
sand
   be built on ~ 46
   bury your head in the ~ 19
save
   ~ your own skin 60
   scrimp and ~ 33

face-saving 19
say
   to ~ nothing of 43
   to ~ the least 43
it does exactly what it says on the tin 8
scare the life out of 55
set the scene/stage 41
a half-baked scheme 49
it's not rocket science 24
settle a score 38
scrimp and save 33
There are plenty more fish in the sea. 13
be falling apart at the seams 59
seat
   a back-~ driver 17
   fly by the ~ of your pants 17
   in the driving ~ 17
   keep sb on the edge of their ~ 25
second
   for a split ~ 43
   play ~ fiddle 48
a second-class citizen 34
see
   ~ eye to eye 1, 6
   ~ life 55
   ~ reason 4
   ~ red 4, 37
   ~ sense 4
   ~ the joke 4
   ~ the light 4
   ~ the point 4
   ~ the writing on the wall 21
   can't ~ the wood for the trees 38
   I'll believe it when I ~ it. 13
   suck it and ~ 32
self-made man 34
sell
   give sb the hard ~ 58
   would ~ your own grandmother 33
send
   ~ sb packing 22
   ~ shivers down your spine 25
see sense 4
non sequitur 14
first come, first served 11
set
   ~ in motion 41
   ~ the scene/stage 41
   ~ the wheels in motion 24
settle a score 38
at sixes and sevens 10
movers and shakers 34
knock into shape 2

sharp
   a short ~ shock 29
   razor-~ 47
shed crocodile tears 18
sheep
   a wolf in ~'s clothing 18
   might as well be hung for a ~ as a lamb 18
   sort (out) the ~ from the goats 18
shell-shocked 16
take a shine to sb 1
run a tight ship 3, 15
be like ships that pass in the night 23
the shit hits the fan 3
send shivers down your spine 25
shock
   a short sharp ~ 29
   get the ~ of your life 55
shell-shocked 16
live on a shoestring 33
shoot
   ~ yourself in the foot 166
   ~ sb down in flames 16
   ~ sky-high 31
shut up shop 30
short
   a ~ sharp shock 29
   as thick as two ~ planks 9
   fall ~ of 59
   not be ~ of a bob or two 50
parting shot 21
put your shoulder to the wheel 42
shoulders
   be head and ~ above sb 19
   rub ~ with sb 26
show
   ~ your hand 53
   steal the ~ 25
worship at the altar/shrine/temple of 31
shrouded in mystery 39
shut up shop 30
sick
   ~ and tired 5
   ~ to death of sth 56
   as ~ as a parrot 18
side
   a bit on the ~ 12
   Look on the bright ~. 13
two sides of the same coin 50
silent
   ~ majority 34
   ~ partner 30
   as ~ as the grave 9
as smooth as silk 9

every cloud has a silver lining 11
sing from the same hymn sheet 45
all-singing, all-dancing 51
It's not over till the fat lady sings. 13
sink like a stone 2
fall for sb/sth hook, line and sinker 59
have a sinking feeling 37
sit
   ~ on the fence 6
   ~ on your hands 53
a Catch-22 situation 23
six
   be ~ foot under 12
   knock sb for ~ 20, 37
at sixes and sevens 10
That's about the size of it! 45
get your skates on 13
be (skating) on thin ice 42
save your own skin 60
sky
   blue-~ thinking 32
   shoot ~-high 31
a slap in the face 38
sleep
   ~ on it 35
   not lose ~ over sth 35
   put to ~ 12
sleeping partner 30
sleeve
   have sth up your ~ 4
   wear your heart on your ~ 54
slog your guts out 30
life in the slow lane 17
small
   a ~ fortune 47
   big fish in a ~ pond 31
a smart move 40
be all smiles 51
smooth
   as ~ as silk 9
   The course of true love never did run ~. 22
So far, so good. 13
for a song 33
like a bear with a sore head 5
Better safe than sorry. 11
sort (out) the sheep from the goats 18
the life and soul of the party 55
safe and sound 1
call a spade a spade 23
spick and span 10
throw a spanner in the works 24
go spare 3
no expense spared 33

spend a penny 12
rein in spending 31
Variety is the spice of life. 11
spick and span 10
send shivers down your spine 25
spirit
   ~ of adventure 5
   enter into the ~ of sth 36
the spitting image 26, 28
split
   ~ hairs 45
   for a ~ second 43
throw in the sponge 20
hit the spot 36
a leopard can't change its spots 18
a middle-age spread 28
spring
   be no ~ chicken 52
   full of the joys of ~ 36
win your spurs 46
square
   a ~ meal 35
   be back to ~ one 6
squeaky -clean 47
stage
   be/take centre-~ 4
   set the scene/~ 41
at stake 43
stand
   ~ out from the crowd 40
   make your hair ~ on end 22
come to a standstill 17
star-crossed lovers 22
stark naked 47
stars
   have ~ in your eyes 36
   reach for the ~ 42
status quo 14
steal
   ~ a march on sb 16
   ~ the show 25
run out of steam 17
step
   ~ on it 17
   mind your ~ 57
   go/move/~ up a gear 17
stick
   ~ two fingers up at sth 50
   ~ your neck out 42
   stirred with a ~ 7
as stiff as a ramrod 2
stirred with a stick 7

stone
  ~ cold 47
  a heart of ~ 54
  leave no ~ unturned 21
  sink like a ~ 2
full stop 47
storm
  a ~ in a teacup 23
  any port in a ~ 15
  go down a ~ 46
  weather the ~ 15
end of (story) 8
straight
  ~ from the horse's mouth 18
  as ~ as a ramrod 2
  on the ~ and narrow 29
be strapped for cash 33
be a tower of strength 26
do a stretch 29
strike at the heart of 54
strings
  have plenty of ~ to your bow 27
  no ~ attached 52
  pull the ~ 34
highly strung 27
as stubborn as a mule 9
There's no such thing as a free lunch. 52
suck it and see 32
in your birthday suit 12
live out of a suitcase 55
men in grey suits 34
make the supreme/ultimate sacrifice 12
hard to swallow 58
blood, sweat and tears 10
sweep sth under the carpet 38
go with a swing 36
at one fell swoop 22
sword
  fall on your ~ 21
  the ~ of Damocles 21
it's all systems go 51
bring to the table 32
be like a dog with two tails 50
take
  ~ centre stage 4, 25
  ~ a nosedive 17, 31
  ~ a rain check 20
  ~ a shine to sb 1
  ~ each day as it comes 35
  ~ heart 54
  ~ it easy 13
  ~ matters into your own hands 60
  ~ your eye off the ball 38
  ~ your mind off it 57
  ~ sb for a ride 29
  ~ sb to the cleaner's 33
  ~ the biscuit/cake 7
  ~ the flak 4
  ~ the wind out of sb's sails 15
  ~ the words right out of my mouth 45
  ~ to the next level 31
  ~ years off sb 40
  ~ centre stage 4, 25
  give or ~ 10
  not ~ no for an answer 52
be taken aback 15
It takes two to tango. 11, 50
live to tell the tale 55
marathon talks 39
It takes two to tango. 11, 50
a storm in a teacup 23
wear and tear 10
tears
  blood, sweat and ~ 10
  it will all end in ~ 44
  reduce to ~ 37
  shed crocodile ~ 18
get your teeth into sth 19
teething troubles 19
tell
  ~ me about it 45
  live to ~ the tale 55
  time will ~ 44
worship at the altar/shrine/temple of 31
tempt fate 42
terms
  a contradiction in ~ 41
  in no uncertain ~ 52
uncharted territory/waters 4
thick
  as ~ as thieves 9
  as ~ as two short planks 9
  through ~ and thin 26
the plot thickens 44
as thick as thieves 9
thin
  as ~ as a rake 9
  be (skating) on ~ ice 42
  through thick and ~ 26
thing
  Hindsight is a wonderful ~. 13
  There's no such ~ as a free lunch. 52
be all things to all men 51
think
  ~ outside the box 32
  ~ twice 42

thinking
   blue-sky ~ 32
   joined-up ~ 32
I thought as much. 44
be batting a thousand 7
Two's company, three's a crowd. 50
the power behind the throne 34
throw
   ~ a lifeline 31
   ~ a spanner in the works 24
   ~ in the sponge 20
   ~ money down the drain 33
   ~ sb a curveball 7
   ~ the book at 29
   I wouldn't trust sb as far as I could ~ them 44
fingers and thumbs 10
a face like thunder 9
tick all the boxes 32
neat and tidy 10
tie the knot 5
sb's hands are tied 53
a paper tiger 46
tight
   in a ~ corner 38
   run a ~ ship 3, 15
have your hand in the till 29
time
   ~ after ~ 10
   ~ will tell 44
   ahead of its ~ 40
   all in good ~ 51
   an all-~ high/low 51
   at this moment in ~ 32
   big ~ 8
   do ~ 29
   have the ~ of your life 55
   in next to no ~ 52
   in your own ~ 60
   live on borrowed ~ 55
   no ~ like the present 52
   not give sb the ~ of day 26
   play for ~ 48
   There's no ~ like the present. 40, 44
fall on hard times 58, 59
it does exactly what it says on the tin 8
the tip of the iceberg 5
sick and tired 5
toes
   make sb's ~ curl 19
   tread on sb's ~ 19
together
   get your act ~ 6
   not have two pennies to rub ~ 50

   put our heads ~ 19
all told 51
every Tom, Dick and Harry 5
like there's no tomorrow 52
tongue
   get your ~ round sth 19
   hold/bite your ~ 19
too
   ~ clever by half 49
   ~ much information! 8
at the top of the ladder 30
torn
   be ~ 45
   war-~ country 39
touch
   ~ base 32
   lose your ~ 38
   the Midas ~ 21
tough it out 42
tower
   an ivory ~ 23
   be a ~ of strength 26
go out on the town 35
track
   ~ record 30
   back on ~ 17
   have a one-~ mind 57
do a roaring trade 30
gravy train 34
trap
   a death ~ 56
   fall into the ~ of 59
tread
   ~ on sb's toes 19
   ~ the boards 25
go down a treat 36
be barking up the wrong tree 45
can't see the wood for the trees 38
trim your sails 42
a Trojan horse 21
pour oil on troubled waters 45
teething troubles 19
lay it on with a trowel 22
true
   a dream come ~ 36
   The course of ~ love never did run smooth. 22
play your ace/trump card 20
blow your own trumpet 60
come up trumps 46
I wouldn't trust sb as far as I could throw them 44
truth
   ~ will out 13
   be economical with the ~ 12

tuned to the moon 7
turn
    ~ over a new leaf 42
    ~ the other cheek 21
    do a U-~ 17
    done to a ~ 35
poacher turned gamekeeper 29
a page-turner 25
that's a turn-up for the books 43
think twice 42
a twinkle in your father's eye 26
in the twinkling of an eye 22
two
    ~ can play at that game 50
    ~ heads are better than one 50
    ~ sides of the same coin 50
    ~'s company, three's a crowd. 50
    as thick as ~ short planks 9
    bring sb down a peg or ~ 50
    be eating for ~ 12
    be in ~ minds 45
    be like a dog with ~ tails 50
    be like ~ peas in a pod 50
    be ~ a penny 50
    be ~ of a kind 50
    cut both/~ ways 50
    have ~ left feet 50
    It takes ~ to tango. 11, 50
    not be short of a bob or ~ 50
    not have ~ pennies to rub together 50
    put/stick ~ fingers up at sth 50
    that makes ~ of us 50
do a U-turn 17
make the supreme/ultimate sacrifice 12
in no uncertain terms 52
uncharted territory/waters 4
uneasy peace 39
leave no stone unturned 21
have the upper hand 53
upset the applecart 42
that makes two of us 50
Variety is the spice of life. 11
Nothing ventured, nothing gained. 11
burst a blood vessel 37
a Pyrrhic victory 21
C'est la vie. 14
a lone voice 45
grey vote 34
wade through 25
wait in the wings 25
play a/the waiting game 48
wake
    in sb's/sth's ~ 15

in the ~ of sb/sth 15
wall
    go to the ~ 30
    like nailing jelly to a ~ 8
    see the writing on the ~ 21
wax and wane 10
war
    ~-torn country 39
    All's fair in love and ~. 11
be on the warpath 16
watch
    ~ with half an eye 49
    mind/~ your back 57
water
    dead in the ~ 56
    You can lead a horse to ~ (but you can't make him drink). 13
waters
    pour oil on troubled ~ 45
    uncharted territory/~ 4
be on the same wavelength 6
wax and wane 10
way
    bluff your ~ 4
    go back a long ~ 26
    laugh all the ~ to the bank 33
    learn the hard ~ 58
    point the ~ to 41
    Where there's a will there's a ~. 11
ways
    cut both/two ~ 50
    go their own ~ 60
wear
    ~ and tear 10
    ~ your heart on your sleeve 54
weather
    ~ the storm 15
    a fair-~ friend 26
on a weekly basis 32
cry/weep buckets 7
outstay your welcome 35
You may well ask! 44
a wet blanket 27
double whammy 46
what
    ~ is the world coming to? 44
    it does exactly ~ it says on the tin 8
Whatever floats your boat! 8
wheel
    at/behind the ~ 17
    put your shoulder to the ~ 42
    reinvent the ~ 24

wheels
   oil the ~ 24
   set the ~ in motion 24
when
   ~ all's said and done 43
   cross that bridge ~ you come to it 42
   I'll believe it ~ I see it. 13
where
   ~ there's a will there's a way. 11
   put your money ~ your mouth is 42
not know **whether** you're coming or going 35
the cat's **whiskers** 18
black and **white** 10
a **whizz** kid 27
whole
   a ~ new ball game 20
   go the ~ hog 23
   not the ~ picture 41
give sb/sth a **wide** berth 15
wild
   ~ horses couldn't make me 37
   a ~ -goose chase 22
beyond your **wildest** dreams 40
battle of **wills** 16
win
   ~ by a landslide 34
   ~ hands down 53
   ~ your spurs 46
wind
   run like the ~ 9
   take the ~ out of sb's sails 15
receive a **windfall** 31
have a **window** 32
wings
   clip sb's ~ 5
   wait in the ~ 25
the conventional **wisdom** 41
It's easy to be **wise** after the event. 13
within an inch of your life 55
wolf
   a ~ in sheep's clothing 18
   cry ~ 18
a man/**woman** of many parts 27
Hindsight is a **wonderful** thing. 13
wood
   can't see the ~ for the trees 38
   dead ~ 56
pull the **wool** over sb's eyes 29
word
   from the ~ go 43
   Mum's the ~. 13
words
   at a loss for ~ 5
   four-letter ~ 12
   take the ~ right out of my mouth 45
work
   ~ like a dog 9
   donkey/grunt ~ 7
   make hard ~ of 58
   Nice ~ if you can get it! 44
throw a spanner in the **works** 24
world
   a ~ of difference 40, 45
   dead to the ~ 56
   go up in the ~ 2
   be/live in a dream ~ 55
   do yourself the ~ of good 40
   not long for this ~ 12
   What is the ~ coming to? 44
a fate **worse** than death 56
worship at the altar/shrine/temple of 31
not be **worth** a dime 7
lick your **wounds** 2
see the **writing** on the wall 21
wrong
   be barking up the ~ tree 45
   don't get me ~ 44
   fall into the ~ hands 59
   You're not ~! 45
years
   be light ~ away from sth 24
   take ~ off sb 40
catch some **z**'s 7